Cowboys, Yogis,
and One-Legged
Ski Bums

COWBOYS, YOGIS, AND ONE-LEGGED SKI BUMS

The Extraordinary Lives of
Ordinary Coloradans

Don Morreale

Library of Congress Control Number:		2014909381
ISBN:	Hardcover	978-1-4990-2401-2
	Softcover	978-1-4990-2402-9
	eBook	978-1-4990-2400-5

Cover Illustration by
Hunter James
www.focusinstudios.com
Denver, Colorado

Rev. date: 07/01/2014

To order additional copies of this book, contact:
Xlibris LLC
1-888-795-4274
www.Xlibris.com
Orders@Xlibris.com
543611

CONTENTS

ALSO BY DON MORREALE

Books

Buddhist America; Centers, Retreats, Practices (John Muir, 1988)

Complete Guide to Buddhist America (Shambhala, 1998)

Essays

"Pipi La Pushe" in *Let them Eat Crepes*, Edited by Melissa Doffing and Susan Koefod (Lulu, 2010)

"China My Heart" in *Azuria*, (Geelong Writers Inc., Summer 2013)

"Bookends" in *The Miraculous 16th Karmapa*, Edited by Norma Levine (Shan Shung Publications, 2013)

DEDICATION

For Nancy, my shipmate for life

IN MEMORIAM

Sam Morreale
Paul Briggs
Charles Nash

"Every man's memory is his private literature."
                                        —Aldous Huxley

"I speak in a poem of the ancient food of heroes: humiliation, unhappiness, discord. Those things are given to us to transform, so that we may make from the miserable circumstances of our lives things that are eternal, or aspire to be so."
                                        —Jorge Luis Borges

ACKNOWLEDGMENTS

By the fall of 2009, I was at loose ends. I'd completed the course work for a certificate in creative writing at Denver University College, and I wanted some real-world experience in writing and publishing before deciding whether to go on for a master's degree. Enter Kevin Huhn a.k.a. the Moose, whom I met in a water aerobics class at Wash Park Rec Center. Moose had lost his job as manager of the sports page when the *Rocky Mountain News* finally bit the dust. He told me that a lot of the Rocky's writers were now publishing in an online newspaper called *Examiner.com*. He suggested I start there. I followed his advice and am very glad that I did. So first of all, thanks, Kevin. Great advice.

While I'm on the subject, a special thanks to the folks at *Examiner.com*, who've been publishing my stories consistently since September 2009. It's been an education.

I also want to give a shout out to Laura Keeney, who was for some time the editor of the *Denver Post-YourHub*. Laura made it a point to get in touch with me and to meet me for coffee and conversation concerning my articles, the newspaper business, and the future of publishing. Thanks, Laura, for your encouragement and advice. Thanks also to the rest of the gang at *Denver Post-YourHub* for publishing me pretty much every week since August 11, 2011.

In case you're wondering, I did ultimately go back to DU for the master's. For my capstone project, I chose to write a collection of stories much like the ones you see in this book. At that time, I was still thinking in terms of "life-changing experiences," and my capstone advisor, Henry Rasof, did not make it easy for me. He wanted to know exactly *how* people's lives were changed. He also urged me to write more extemporaneously, which turned out to be good advice. So thanks, Henry, for not making it easy and for helping me to define this project more clearly.

Then there are the Jets, a group of guys I've been hanging with for at least a dozen years. We meet for coffee a couple of times a week, and not infrequently, they'll comment on one of my stories. Among the group is my good friend and fellow author, Andy Rooney, who has, on more than one occasion, read my rough drafts and given me constructive advice.

Finally, I want to give some props to the people whose stories you see in this book. It's no easy thing to unbosom yourself in front of the world, so thank you all for your courage and candor and for letting me publish your stories.

Don Morreale
Denver, Colorado
April 2014

INTRODUCTION

Colorado is colorful in more ways than one. Right from the start, the region attracted its fair share of gold panners, gunslingers, oddballs, and seekers. It's the kind of place you go to reinvent yourself. Where did the Beats go to discover themselves in the late '40s, early '50s? Dude . . . Colorado. And where did the gurus and yogis of the alternative consciousness movement come to establish their headquarters in the '60s? "Square State," baby.

Maybe it's the mountains. Or maybe it's the 250 days a year of sunshine we get here. I mean, where else do you see people walking around in shorts and T-shirts in the dead of winter? It beats freezing your nads off in Nebraska.

There's also a fairly liberal and open-minded citizenry here. Colorado was the first state in the Union to legalize recreational marijuana. (Okay, we're tied for first with Washington, but after the shellacking they gave us in the Super Bowl, I'm not inclined to give them any credit).

All of that having been said, I did not set out to write about the state's odd balls, at least not in the beginning. In fact, my original idea was to write about otherwise ordinary people who happened to find themselves in circumstances that ultimately led to a transformation in their lives: the convicted drug dealer who gets a presidential pardon, the Vietnam vet who survives a bullet to the heart, the artist and entrepreneur who gets impaled on a metal spike and comes out of the ordeal with a newfound passion for helping women launch their own businesses.

As I went about interviewing people and writing their stories, I underwent something of a life changer myself. I was finding it more and more difficult to find people able, or willing, to interpret their experience through the prism of "personal transformation." They might have had a traumatic event in their lives, but they had come to see it not as a line of demarcation, but as part of the ebb and flow of their day-to-day existence.

I remember one conversation in particular that brought this home to me. I contacted the PR department at the National Western Stock Show and asked to be put in touch with a rodeo cowboy, preferably a bull rider, who might have had a "life-changing experience."

"Honey," said the rep on the other end of the line, "cowboys don't *have* life-changing experiences."

"Sure they do," I argued. "You get thrown off a bull. That right there's a life-changing experience."

"No, bubba," she drawled, barely able to contain her exasperation with the greenhorn on the other end of the line. "Cowboy gets bucked off. He turns right around and gets back up on the danged thing."

Okay, maybe it was time to rethink the concept. So instead of asking people to tell me about their "epiphanic" moments, I decided to ask them how it was that they came to do what they do, be who they are, think what they think. That turned out to be much easier for people to grok. And it opened up a whole new world of stories for me to write about.

Each of the thumbnail bios contained in this book first saw the light of day on *Examiner.com*, an online news source with local editions in most major markets in the US and Canada (Google "Denver Examiner Don Morreale" for a complete archive of my stories, along with photos and slide shows). But I'm old school enough to believe that you haven't really published something until it appears in print in a real-time newspaper or magazine.

Which is how it happened that in August 2011, I started sending my stories off to *YourHub*, a neighborhood supplement that appears in the *Denver Post* every Thursday morning. Much of the *Hub*'s content is supplied by freelancers like me, and as such, it represents an important source of local news and information. It's also a dandy place for fledgling authors to get their work out in front of the public. Say what you will about the World Wide Web, there's nothing quite like getting your stuff published in your hometown newspaper on a weekly basis. People see it and respond to it, and pretty soon you're having a face-to-face conversation with your readers that you could never have as a content provider on the Web. I'm constantly running into people who tell me, "Hey, I saw your piece in the *Hub* this week. Great story.

Where do you find these people?" That, my friends, is music to the ears of a freelance writer.

I hope you enjoy reading these stories as much as I've enjoyed writing them. I'm glad you've decided to join me for the ride.

Don Morreale
Denver, Colorado
April 2014

PART 1

Accidents, Epiphanies, and Life-Changing Experiences

Keli Rae survives impalement, lives to help others

One sunny August afternoon in 2003, Denver artist Keli Rae was standing on the tailgate of her pickup truck when she felt what she describes as a "mysterious force" pushing on her chest.

"Suddenly, I just flew off the truck and landed hard on a two-foot-long spike that was sticking up out of a tire about four feet away."

The spike entered her right buttock, tore through her uterus, punctured her bladder, fractured her pelvis, grazed her spine, intestines, kidney, liver, and heart, and came to rest just behind her left scapula.

"It was like everything was happening in slow motion," she said. "I could hear myself screaming. But inside my head, my mind was talking to me very calmly and rationally, telling me, 'Don't worry, it's missing all of your vital organs. You're going to be okay.'"

When she hit bottom, her first impulse was to stand and get herself up off that spike. "It was pretty gruesome," she said. "There was blood and gore all over it."

She walked into the house and told her friend what had happened. He dialed 911, and within minutes, an ambulance was there.

"But then the EMTs couldn't get the gurney through the front door," she said. "So I told them, 'Just forget it. I'll walk.'"

Bleeding only moderately, she was able to get herself out the door and onto the gurney. But then settled in the ambulance, she went into deep shock; and by the time she arrived at the emergency room, she was lying in a pool of blood.

It took a team of five surgeons the better part of five hours to stitch her back together again. "They had to clean each of my vital organs in turn and sew up my uterus and bladder," Rae said.

Horrific as it was, the accident was something of a medical miracle. Her surgeon, Dr. James Smith, told her that had he attempted to put the spike through her intentionally, he could not have missed all of her vital organs. "It bypassed virtually everything that could kill me, paralyze me, or make me poop in a bag," she said.

Which is not to say that Rae emerged from her ordeal physically— or psychologically—unscathed. "Even today, no matter what position I take—walking, sitting, standing still—I can't get comfortable. I can't rest. I'm in constant pain. I think of myself as broken."

One day, Rae's daughter said, "You know, Mom, Frida Kahlo thought of herself as broken too."

It was an apt comparison. Like Rae, the Mexican artist had been impaled by a metal pole in a bus accident in Mexico City in 1925. She was eighteen years old. She referred to the incident forever after as "my deflowering."

"I've come to feel a strong spiritual kinship with Frida," Rae said. "I identify with her suffering. And both of us found our salvation through art." Unlike Kahlo, who started painting to pass the time while still in hospital, it took Rae three years before she felt well enough to make a piece of art.

"I lived through this," Rae said. "There's a reason I survived, a purpose for my survival, and I mean to fulfill it."

Last winter, she opened the Coffee Nook at the Workshops in Glendale as a prototype for a chain of stores to be staffed by single moms.

"I want to help them become financially self-sufficient," she said. "I want to help them fulfill their dreams. Frida Kahlo's passions were her art and her politics. Mine are my art and my desire to help others. That's the whole purpose of life as far as I'm concerned, to help others."

Tim Rains, rescued at sea

On a Thursday morning in July of 1980, Denver photographer Tim Rains got blown off the deck of an aircraft carrier in the Mediterranean. He spent the next sixteen hours treading water and praying for a miracle.

His assignment on that day was to photograph basic ops on the flight deck of the USS *Forrestal*.

"Most of the time, it's boring stuff," he said, "if a plane taking off from an aircraft carrier deck at two hundred miles per hour can be called boring. But still, it's routine."

He saw a shot he wanted to take of an A-7 attack bomber in mid-turn and signaled the traffic control guy to get it to stop. Dropping down on one knee and aiming his camera, he felt hot exhaust coming his way and realized the plane was still in motion. Before he could fall flat, it caught him and blew him over the side. He fell sixty feet and entered the water headfirst.

"All I could think going down," he said, "was 'Oh crap, I just dropped the navy's $1,500 Canon F-1, and they're gonna take it out of my paycheck.'"

Popping up just in time to see his ship steaming over the horizon, he checked his watch: 10:00 a.m. He pulled a cord and inflated his life vest. Then he kicked off his boots, adjusted his helmet, pulled down his goggles, opened a dye pack, and turned on the strobe light attached to his vest.

"I wasn't afraid," he said, "but I was angry that no one saw me go over and frustrated that there was nothing more I could do."

The water was in the high sixties, not frigid but cold enough that he'd have to keep moving to avoid hypothermia. When the sun set and no one had arrived to save him, he started thinking about swimming.

"I felt like I had to contact my parents before the navy reported me lost at sea. I didn't want to put them through that grief, and I sure as hell did not want to die out there."

Meanwhile, back on the Forrestal, nobody had any idea that he was even missing. It wasn't until he failed to report for evening muster that they finally sent his crewmates out to look for him. For the next hour, his name was called every five minutes over the loudspeaker system in the off chance that he might be sacked out in one of the carrier's 2,200 watertight compartments. It was after 9:00 p.m. before the captain finally called a man-overboard drill. But by now they were 160 miles away, and the sky was growing dark. Dark enough, as it happened, for Rains to identify the North Star.

"I knew we were somewhere southeast of Spain," he said. "I was able to coordinate with the North Star and get a fix on which direction I needed to swim."

Weak, hungry, and tired, but buoyed by the sense that he was at least making progress, he kept swimming. And then around 2:00 a.m., he heard the sound of a helicopter. He waved. The chopper came closer and dropped a two-man dive team. They hooked him up and hauled him aboard. He was only seven miles from the coast of Spain when they fished him out.

"I could have made it," he said.

Interestingly, the helicopter was not from the *Forrestal*. It was from the *Nimitz*, another ship that just happened to be cruising in the area.

"It was a total accident they found me," Rains said. "They saw the strobe light on my shoulder and dropped down to investigate." Lucky, lucky, lucky.

Long-term effects?

"I was a lot more careful in how I did things after that," he said. "It was a horrible ordeal, but I learned that there's not a whole lot I can't accomplish if I just calm down. It taught me how to work through adversity, and I came out of it knowing that I can overcome any difficulty."

Kiki Wetherbee: beautiful on the inside

If Kiki Wetherbee has a positive outlook, much of the credit is due to the way her mother, Janet, treated her as a child. She was born with a host of physical problems, most noticeable of which were a bilateral cleft palate and a clubfoot. To make matters worse, her eyes were set so far apart that "my left eye couldn't see past my nose to the right and vice versa. I'd stand in front of a blackboard," she said, "and could only write to the center. Then I'd have to switch the chalk and finish the sentence with the other hand."

Her infantile facial disfigurement was so disturbing to her grandmother that she tried to cover her face with a blanket as they were leaving the hospital. Kiki's mom promptly removed the blanket.

"This child," she declared, "will not be hidden. I'm going to show her off wherever I go." And show her off she did.

"When I was six weeks old, she took me to one of those mall photographers who was taking baby pictures. Some lady with a perfect baby said, 'How dare you bring that child out in public?' and my mom said, 'My kid's just as beautiful as yours.' She saw having a special-needs child as a privilege."

Even so, childhood was no trip to the candy store for Kiki Wetherbee.

"I knew I was different," she said. "One time, a bunch of kids followed me home, chanting, 'Monster, monster.' Mom said I should tell them 'I may not be beautiful on the outside. But I am on the inside. You may not like me now, but someday you will.'"

(Flash forward to the eighth grade when a boy came up to her and said, "You don't remember me, but I was one of the kids who followed you home that day. I still remember what you told us, and you were right.")

Wetherbee spent much of her childhood in surgery; twenty-four operations in all. When she turned five, Dr. Ted Huang, a renowned plastic surgeon at University of Texas, Galveston, performed an operation to bring her eyes closer together. It involved the removal of her forehead bone. He narrowed it and wired it back in place.

"Finally, I could see straight," Wetherbee said.

Today she is sufficiently comfortable with her looks to work as a cashier at Wal-Mart, at least for the time being.

"I don't see myself working there for the rest of my life," she said. "I want to go to art school and become a professional animator."

She's been drawing since she was a little girl. "Making art helps me to keep my imagination going. I have this passion to create something and to see how I improve with practice. I put all my heart and soul into it."

In addition, Wetherbee writes fantasy fiction. She's created a character named Drago, whom she thinks of as an alter ego.

"Drago is a picture of what I'd like to be. He's a guardian. Like an angel. He's fearless, the embodiment of love and compassion. His best friend is a dragon."

What have the years of social ostracism and painful surgery taught her?

"My looks have made me appreciate what people are like on the inside rather than how they look on the outside," she said. "A couple of years ago, I was waiting for a bus in front of the capitol building. This woman walked by, pushing a stroller with a baby in it who had a bilateral cleft palate. I said, 'I think your baby is beautiful.'

"She ignored me and just kept walking. Then she stopped, turned around, and looked at me. She said, 'You had it too, didn't you?'

"I said, 'Yeah. I did.' And she said, 'I think you're beautiful too.'"

James D. Chapman: "The Buttonman Can"

Life could not have been better for entrepreneur James D. Chapman. His company, Infinity Pro Painting, had won the bid to paint INVESCO Field, and he had jobs going on all over town. He was supporting a wife and five kids and making payments on a six-bedroom house in Northeast Denver.

But that was another life in another century, before a needless tragedy put him in a wheelchair and destroyed everything he'd spent a lifetime trying to build.

On a Friday night in January 2001, Chapman drove to the Shepherd Motel on East Colfax to pick up his wife. He parked his car, walked across the lot, and was accosted by some gangbangers who wanted to sell him drugs.

"Do I look like a user?" he said. Words were exchanged. Somebody pulled a knife.

"We tussled, and I got it out of his hands," Chapman remembered. "But then I got pushed down a flight of stairs and hit a wall." His wife found him sprawling on the concrete, unable to move. "My back is burning," he told her. "Call an ambulance."

He woke up two days later at Denver General.

"The doctor told me I had a T-7 spinal cord injury and that I would probably never walk again," he said. "They sent me home as soon as I could sit up in a wheelchair."

Determined to carry on despite the paralysis, Chapman had one of his foremen strap him into an ATV so he could drive around Mile High supervising the job. Big mistake. He ended up with an ulcerated tailbone that landed him in a nursing home.

"This was the lowest point of my life," he said. "The painting business went away. My employees took my equipment when they left."

He got behind on his mortgage and lost the house. His wife, unable to cope with so much bad news, walked out on him, taking her two sons from a previous marriage with her.

But Chapman is a fighter, and he fought back. He went to Craig Hospital as an outpatient and learned to drive a specially adapted car. He started drawing a social security check for $670 a month and managed to get a small two-bedroom apartment for himself and his kids through the state's housing voucher program.

With time on his hands, he began thinking of creative ways to make a living. One day, he came across an old button machine he'd stashed in a storage closet and volunteered to make some buttons for a friend's kid's birthday party. He and his children were sitting around the kitchen table, cranking them out, when his daughter chirped, "Hey, Dad, you should be the *buttonman*."

A light went on in Chapman's entrepreneurial brain. He went to Mile High United Way and got a grant that enabled him to buy a second button machine plus an inventory of 10,000 2 ¼ inch button blanks. The 2008 Democratic National Convention was months away, and Chapman started turning out Hillary and Obama buttons as fast as he could.

"Whenever they were in town, I'd be there selling buttons at a buck a pop," he said. "During the convention, I sold close to five thousand of them."

He plowed the money back into the business, bought computer programs and printer ink, and created a sideline of custom-printed T-shirts. Today he's the proprietor of the Buttonman Gift Shop, where he sells buttons, T-shirts, caps, earrings, watches, and handbags. His slogan? "The Buttonman Can!"

"If I was able to walk tomorrow," Chapman said, "I would never walk away from the experiences that God and this wheelchair have led me to. Before the wheelchair, I was 10 percent community. Now I'm 90 percent community. I'm for prosperity and success for all members of my community, especially the black community. And especially the kids."

Star Ray Blake: jail time fosters a new 'tude

The thing with the tats started when Star Ray Blake was fifteen. He did them on himself in the traditional way, using a sewing needle with thread wrapped around it to hold the ink. He began with his forearms and then moved to his hands, chest, stomach, legs, and finally his face. Tribal art.

"I was trying to make a statement," he said.

Which was?

"'I don't give a damn!' I was totally antisocial in those days. The tats were a way of weeding people out."

But the bad attitude and the psycho-killer looks mask a whole other side to Star Ray Blake. He comes from a talented, well-traveled family. His mother, a graduate of the School of Visual Arts in New York, owned a string of art galleries across the country; and for much of his childhood, he traveled with her internationally on buying trips.

"I was homeschooled until I was thirteen," he said. "By fifth grade, I was already reading at college level."

Then they moved to Longmont, and things started going to hell.

"Longmont felt like a prison," he said. "I didn't fit in. I got picked on because of my name and because my parents were artists. I dropped out when I was thirteen and started drinking, smoking pot, and listening to heavy metal."

Three years later, he joined the Job Corps, earned a GED, learned the welding trade, and met a girl named Stephanie. When she got pregnant, they quit the Job Corps and moved to Greeley, where the course of true love did not, unfortunately, run smooth. They argued a lot, especially over Blake's tattoos and his burgeoning drug habit. He'd done his face by then and had started using crystal meth.

"I knew I'd need a serious stress enhancer to get off the meth," he said. "Rehab wasn't going to cut it. I know it's weird, but I decided the best place for me was prison. I thought if I could make it through jail, I could make it through anything."

Which is why on New Year's Eve 2005, he walked into a Greeley gas station, wielding a knife, and proceeded to hold the place up.

"Are you sure you wanna do this?" asked the clerk.

"Just give me the money," Blake said. "I wasn't wearing a mask. I was trying to get caught. I even stood outside for a while smoking a cigarette. But the cops never came."

He went home and told Stephanie, figuring she'd probably turn him in. She did.

"The marshals showed up next day with shotguns," he said. "Way bigger reaction than I expected."

He copped a plea and was sent to Huerfano County Correctional near Walsenburg with a six-year sentence and a three-year "tail," which is jailhouse for "parole."

At 6'1" and 315 pounds and covered with some very scary-looking tattoos, nobody in the joint messed with the "Animal." It was quiet in there, and he kept to himself, thinking things through.

"After that first year," he said, "I'd pulled my head out of my ass. I could see the error of my ways, and I finally let go of my don't-care attitude. I became more self-aware. Started doing yoga, breathing, and stretching."

He began teaching it to his fellow inmates.

"It was worth my time to help just one person," he said. "My whole focus shifted to helping others."

Blake earned enough good time to be released after three years, three months, and eleven days. Today he's working as a welder in the town of La Salle, fabricating pressure vessels for oil fields. He's got a new girlfriend, Valerie, whom he plans to marry. He's also back in school, studying painting in the fine arts program at Aims Community College.

As for the tats . . .

"If I could afford it," he said, "I'd have every last one of them removed. It'd be the end of a really long day."

Brandy Moore: serving a sentence of a different sort

Brandy Moore's story is not a pretty one. It's not a tale of redemption, nor does it have a happy ending. Although it took place nearly fifteen years ago, Moore is still trying to put the pieces of her life back together again, so far without much success.

Late on the evening of October 1, 1995, Moore and her high school friend Jeff were sitting in Jeff's car, passing notes to each other because Jeff was deaf and Moore didn't know any sign language.

Out of nowhere, two guys materialized on either side of the car. The guy on Jeff's side, a recent Polish immigrant named Robert Kurzynowski, pointed a gun at him and said, "Get in the fucking trunk, both of you."

Within minutes, they found themselves rocketing east on I-70 in the direction of Bennett. It was around 2:00 a.m. when the car finally rolled to a stop and the trunk opened. The hapless pair stepped out onto a dark country road with farm fields all around.

"Oh, you're a chick!" said Jay Johnson, the second kidnapper, realizing for the first time that Moore was female. "Get in the backseat!"

Jeff took advantage of the momentary distraction to flee in the direction of a nearby farmhouse. Kurzynowski raised his pistol and fired at him. But Jeff could not hear the gunshots and just kept running.

"Then we're going down the road," Moore said, "and I'm crying and begging them not to kill me, and they offer me beer and cigarettes like this is some kind of party or something."

Kurzynowski stopped the car, and Johnson climbed into the backseat and raped Moore, who was only sixteen at the time. The two men traded places, Kurzynowski covering his face with a shirt to prevent her from identifying him Johnson, behind the wheel, high on booze and coke, screaming down the road at a hundred miles an hour. He managed to run the car straight into a telephone pole.

"When I woke up," Moore said, "the car was upside down, and I was lying in the road with one shoe missing and my face covered in blood."

Neither of her captors was injured. They told her to get up and start walking.

"I saw myself getting shot execution style in the middle of a field," she remembered. "I was sure I'd never see my family again."

Just then, a car pulled up. The driver rolled down the window and said, "Are you Brandy?"

It was Jeff's dad. "Get in the car," he said. "I'll get you some help."

"You're not going anywhere," Kurzynowski said, pointing the gun at him. They forced him out of the car, pushed Moore into the backseat, and drove off with her. Soon they were back on I-70 heading west toward Aurora.

By now it was 6:00 a.m. They dropped her off at 6th and I-225, and she hobbled to a nearby convenience store.

"I saw my mutilated face in the store window," she said. "The left side was torn and bleeding. So was my left shoulder."

X-rays later revealed that her back had been fractured in eight places.

Johnson and Kurzynowski pled guilty to charges of kidnapping and rape and are now serving forty-year sentences. But Moore has been serving a sentence of a different sort, imprisoned by her memories of that horrific night. She has chronic back pain that led her, she said, to a serious Oxycontin addiction.

"I also had a $200-a-day heroin habit," she added, "but I finally got clean last year."

She spent ten years in counseling, has had two DUIs, and was forced to relinquish custody of her two children.

"I can't sleep because of the pain and anxiety," she said. "I still have nightmares. I've been running from this my whole life."

Is there a way out for Brandy Moore?

"I don't know," she said. "I'm still not at a point where I can forgive those guys. I'm full of so much hatred for what they did to me. If I *could* forgive them, maybe I could move on."

Pete Ninemire gets a presidential pardon

Pete Ninemire got his get-out-of-jail card on the last day of Bill Clinton's presidency, January 20, 2001.

"The commutations were issued fifteen minutes before he left office," said Ninemire, one of twenty-one prisoners nationwide to receive a presidential pardon that day. "I heard my name over the loudspeaker, ordering me to go to the unit manager's office."

The prison MD was waiting for him when he got there, and Ninemire, whose mother had died four months earlier, figured it was another death in the family.

"Sit down, Ninemire," he said.

"He looked me straight in the eye and said, 'Ninemire, you're free!'

"I looked back at him and said, 'Fuck you!'

"'No, really,' he said. 'The president commuted your sentence. Go back to your cell and pack your stuff. You're outta here.'"

Pete Ninemire served ten years out of a twenty-seven-year sentence for cultivation of a controlled substance. He doesn't deny the charges.

"Back in my dealing days, they used to call me '12 by 12' 'cause I used to smoke a dozen joints every day by twelve o'clock noon."

He'd already been busted twice by the State of Kansas, so this time around, the feds were ready to lock him up and fling the key as far as Tierra del Fuego. Ninemire fled. He was picked up the following year in Miami. The twenty-seven-year term he received was based on federal minimum mandatory sentencing guidelines. As a three-strikes offender, he would not be eligible for parole.

He spent the next six months in solitary confinement at Fort Leavenworth, Kansas.

"It's a 24-7 lockdown out there," he said. "Hundred and ten degrees and no air-conditioning."

It was at Leavenworth that he first heard about Families Against Minimum Mandatory Sentencing (FAMM), an organization working to change the harsh federal sentencing guidelines that denied parole to habitual offenders like him.

"It was a ray of hope," he said, "in a very bleak and difficult situation."

Transferred to Englewood Federal Correctional in southwest suburban Denver, Ninemire went to work with a vengeance. He petitioned the prison administration and won permission to start a FAMM Chapter at the facility.

"We started writing letters to our congress people, trying to get them to change the sentencing laws for future generations," he said. "Everybody got involved—whites, blacks, Hispanics—which is unusual in a prison setting."

Ninemire discovered that he had a talent for political organizing and for bringing people together. His fellow prisoners started calling him "the President," and he soon found himself in the role of negotiator whenever disputes arose between inmates and staff.

Buoyed by his success with the FAMM campaign, Ninemire became "the busiest man in captivity," establishing a prison Toastmasters Club, a smoking cessation program, and an eight-week counseling and mentoring curriculum for at-risk kids called Jericho Road.

"We wanted to help them see where their rebelliousness and defiance were leading them. Working with those kids changed my life."

The day after his release, Ninemire and his brother, a Catholic priest, went for a month-long "freedom tour" around Kansas, visiting old friends and relatives.

"We stopped in to see my aunt Tuckey," he remembered, "and she said, 'To whom much is given, much is expected. Now you go make your mother proud.'"

Today he's the addiction treatment supervisor for the Adult Felony Drug Court in Wichita, working in collaboration with judges, prosecutors, and probation officers to help addicts get off drugs and stay out of prison.

"I'm living the dream I used to be afraid to dream," he said. "Every day I remind myself I could have been spending this day in jail. Since Bill Clinton pardoned me, I've never had a bad day."

Matt Kailey mans up

Before Matt Kailey was Matt Kailey, he was Jennifer Kailey, a twice-married, very feminine female who knew in her heart of hearts that something was not right with her.

"From the age of ten," he said, "I suspected that I was a male, but there were not a lot of resources to help me figure it out. So I just lived with it."

But after her second divorce, Jennifer Kailey sought the help of a therapist who was able to identify her issues as gender related. She was, the therapist explained, "gender misaligned," in other words, a male trapped in a female body. The diagnosis came as a relief.

"I realized there was a name for my condition and that others had the same issues and that there were options."

Over the next eight months in therapy, Kailey pondered her alternatives.

"Many transgender people are suicidal," he said, "so just living with it was not a viable option."

A more radical alternative would be to transition completely by means of gender reassignment surgery, a prohibitively expensive procedure. Genital surgery costs $65,000; a double mastectomy another $6,500. And since such procedures are considered optional, they are not covered by insurance.

"Most of us don't have a spare sixty-five grand lying around," Kailey said, "so the compromise is to look externally as one feels internally."

In Kailey's case, that meant breast removal surgery and twice-a-month testosterone shots that he will have to take for the rest of his life. He began receiving hormone injections in January 1998. Over the ensuing ten months, his voice deepened, and he started growing body and facial hair.

But looking the part was only half the battle. "I was a very feminine female," he said. "I had been socialized to be female. I had to learn new behaviors and get a new outlook."

He taught himself to stand with both feet square and to sit like a man with his legs spread wide. "Men take up a lot of space," Kailey said. "Women are more contained and closed in."

He was also treated differently after he became a man. "I had to learn to change my own tires," he said. "And as a woman, I'd go into a hardware store, and they'd assume I needed help and offer it. Not so as a male."

Women wait for him to open doors for them. Cops tend to see him as a threat, as do other men, not to mention mothers with kids. "I don't smile and make casual conversation in say, a public restroom," Kailey said, "and I don't approach women with kids and tell them how cute the kids are."

It's in the realm of sexual preference that the story becomes a little harder to understand because gender reassignment does not necessarily signify a change in one's sexual orientation. As a woman, Kailey was attracted to men; and now as a man, that fact has not changed. He's still attracted to men and now identifies as a gay man.

"Before the transition, I knew nothing about the gay community," he said. "It was not even on my radar. After the transition, the gay community became *my* community." (Kailey is the managing editor of Denver's *Out Front Magazine*, the third oldest LGBT publication in the country.)

Any advantages to being male?

"I'm less afraid to go out and walk alone at night," he said. "I'll go anywhere, which is something I wouldn't do as a woman. I'm no longer afraid of being raped."

Is he happier having made the transition?

"I get asked that a lot," he said. "I'm certainly more comfortable in my own skin. Most transsexuals think that gender reassignment will solve all their problems, but really, what you get is a whole new set of problems."

John Hoistion finds refuge in "a church full of misfits"

If you're a registered sex offender in the State of Colorado, there are two things you can't be without: the first is a job, the second is a place to live.

"It's kind of a Catch-22," said John Hoistion, who served nine years in the Colorado State Penitentiary for a sex crime he freely admits to having committed. "It's illegal to be homeless if you're a sex offender, but if you put it on a rental application, you don't get the apartment."

It's also, according to Hoistion, not uncommon for a sex offender's probation officer to call an employer to inform him or her of a client's criminal past.

"I've lost a dozen jobs and been thrown out of at least three places of residence because of it," he said.

No money, no job, and no place to live: that was precisely the position he found himself in when, in the spring of 2008, he started going to the Sunday morning homeless breakfasts at St. Paul's Church in Denver's North Capitol Hill. On one such morning, there was a call for volunteers to help with some painting. Hoistion raised his hand.

"I could see that the church needed a lot of repairs," he said. "I was a carpenter, so I volunteered to be the church's repair guy."

Pretty soon he was coming in three times a week. "I made it clear that I was a registered sex offender," he said, "and nobody even batted an eye."

Within six months, Hoistion, who was homeless and therefore in danger of being sent back to prison, had begun singing in the choir. One day, a fellow choir member approached him and asked, "Is this something money can fix?"

"When you're on the streets, it's impossible to put together a nest egg to get tools, a truck, an apartment, a job," Hoistion said. "It's even harder if you have a criminal history. Even homeless shelters won't allow a violent felon in. So I told her, yeah, this was definitely something money could fix."

Without a second thought, she wrote out a check for $1,000 and handed it over. It was enough for a deposit on an apartment and to pay off some outstanding debts.

"It was an act of complete unselfish generosity," Hoistion said, "and it just blew me away. It took me a full year to accept that people could care about me as a person without judgment. And they cared without expecting anything in return."

Hoistion said he grew up a sensitive, intelligent kid who liked to read, despite the fact that his dad was a hard-assed ex-marine who thought reading was for sissies. At seventeen, Hoistion joined the marines mainly to prove to the old man that he "wasn't a sissy or a baby or a girl." Where his dad had "failed," the marines succeeded brilliantly. "They taught me how to control my environment with anger," Hoistion said.

Out of the corps, Hoistion went to work in sales for a corporation in Texas.

"But I had developed a split personality in the marines," he said. "By day, I was a suit dealing with clients and handling million-dollar accounts. By night I was a bar-brawling thug. I'd go out to clubs and pick fights and knock the beans out of people. I enjoyed hurting them. I was a complete Jekyll and Hyde."

In 1987, Hoistion moved to Denver, where his nighttime escapades continued. One night, he brought a woman home with him and, he said, "verbally intimidated her into having sex." The following day, she lodged a complaint.

"At first, the cops weren't buying it," he said. "But she kept at it for the next ten months, and finally they busted me. I pled guilty and got what I deserved."

What he got was fourteen years in the Colorado State Penitentiary. Hoistion said he went through every rehab program the prison had to offer: AA, NA, psychotherapy. He even managed to get an associate's degree in small business management.

Finally out of jail after nine years, Hoistion found his way to St. Paul's.

"It was the best thing that ever happened to me," he said. "It's a safe place for me. If I get into trouble with my thinking, I call someone at the church and bounce it off of them. Even when I screw up, they empathize. Their attitude is 'You're human. What can we do to help?'"

Garry Rudd: hit by lightning

On the day he was struck by lightning, Garry Rudd was working as a game warden for the Division of Wildlife. His assignment on August 18, 1999, was to irrigate a field of alfalfa in the Ouray State Wildlife Area.

"Where I was, it was a clear late summer day, though I could see lightning at Aspen Ridge, forty miles away," he recalled. "I was raised in the wilderness, so I had a healthy respect for the power of lightning."

He jammed a pitchfork into the ground and went to the truck to retrieve his two-way radio.

"Then I walked back to the pitchfork, and as soon as I reached for it, I went blank," he said. "I don't know how else to describe it, except to say that if you were killed instantly, that would be how it was. There one minute, not there the next."

He awoke flat on his back, dazed and confused, with a strange metallic taste in his mouth. It felt like all of his internal organs were on fire. He rolled into a nearby ditch and lay in the water, trying to cool himself off. Dizzy and unable to stand, he pulled himself out of the ditch and dragged himself to a nearby tree stump.

When he failed to come home that night, his wife Linda tried reaching him on his pager.

"But I'd lost 90 percent of my hearing," he said, "and I could barely hear my own voice, much less the beeper."

Frantic, Linda got in her car and drove to the wildlife area to look for him. Had it been daylight, she might have seen his truck parked three hundred yards up a two-track jeep trail. She went home and called his supervisor, who, in turn, phoned the sheriff's office. Together they formed a search party and found him eleven hours after the strike, leaning against the tree trunk, half covered with dirt.

"The dirt was self-insulation," Rudd said. "I pulled it up around me to protect myself from the elements. Like I say, I was raised in the wilderness."

A few minutes later, the paramedics showed up; and at first, they couldn't figure out what the deal was.

"They figured it was either an animal attack or a stroke," Rudd said.

When they cut his clothes off, they saw a laceration that ran the length of his right leg and burn marks that looked like dimples or teeth marks. There was also something sticking out of the palm of his right hand which they at first took to be a compound fracture but later determined was a large splinter from the exploded pitchfork.

Rudd was airlifted to St. Anthony's in Denver, which is action central for strike victims in Colorado. Based on his injuries, the doctors were able to piece together what had happened.

"The lightning hit the rivet on my jeans next to my back pocket," Rudd said. "That was the entry point. Then it travelled down my leg and exited my calf."

Later, his right femur had to be clamped and wired back together again.

"Something about the bone wasn't right," Rudd said. "The surgeons told me that it looked like a scarred tree trunk."

He began having petit mal seizures that were strong enough to break a couple of teeth, and a form of narcolepsy that he experiences as "lost time."

"Looking up at a plane crossing the sky," he said, "it goes, stops in midair, then goes again."

Twelve years later, he still suffers from memory loss, which makes it difficult for him to learn new things.

"Simple actions, like which direction to turn a screw to tighten it, I now have to think about," he said.

Spiritual repercussions?

"I was raised by the Good Book," Rudd said, "but now I'm a hard left agnostic. I've been playing the lottery since the strike. I figure if you can get hit by lightning, you can probably win the jackpot. As you can see, I still have my warped sense of humor."

Bob Haugen gets a message from the other side

The dominant paradigm emerging in business schools in the 1960s when finance guru Bob Haugen was a student, was something called the "Efficient Market Hypothesis (EMH)." Proponents of this theory, many of them centered in and around the University of Chicago, believed that left to its own devices, the market would accurately set the price of a stock based on information available simultaneously to all investors. Since everybody was working with the same data—so the theory went—it was impossible to beat the market either by expert stock picking or astute market timing. In fact, the only way to make a killing was by buying ever riskier investments. Early in his career, Haugen came to the conclusion that the EMH was—and I'm quoting here—"total crap."

As a PhD candidate at University of Illinois, Haugen and Professor Jim Heins ran the numbers and discovered that stocks with the greatest risk had the lowest returns, while those with the lowest risk had higher returns.

"This was the exact opposite of what they were teaching at the University of Chicago," he said. "They were practicing a religion that the market was perfect. But I knew different. I was a heretic right off the bang, and my career became a very difficult struggle."

In the late 1970s, Haugen began teaching finance at the University of Wisconsin, writing papers and books critical of the EMH and "getting increasingly vitriolic and angry because nobody was paying attention to me."

He married Tiffany Meyer, a feisty former law professor who encouraged his contrarian stance. In 2002, the couple dropped out of academic life altogether and retired to a home they owned in Durango. Tiffany had been diagnosed with lung cancer, and for the next four years, Haugen spent his every waking minute caring for her.

After she died, odd things started happening. Like at her funeral, where a hawk flew over the assembled mourners and a rainbow appeared in a clear blue sky and stayed there for the entire service. Or later, in the house, when lights kept turning on and off for no apparent reason.

And then there was that time when Tiffany appeared to him as a vision of her younger self, or that very weird occasion when Haugen, who was in the kitchen doing the dishes, heard a crash in the living room. When he went to investigate, he discovered the Wedgewood china frame around Tiffany's picture lying in fragments on the table.

"I was getting a lot of signals," he said. "I consulted a medium named Jennifer Farmer, who just lit up when I told her what was going on. She said, 'This is one of the biggest spirits I've ever seen.'" Tiffany, she told him, was trying to send him a message, and this is what it said: "Get off your ass and finish what you started."

"We were married twenty-one years, two months, eight days, and eleven hours," Haugen said. "When she died, I just sort of stopped."

He'd written fourteen books and innumerable papers, and now at sixty-four, he figured his career was pretty much over. But after he got his late wife's message, he sat down and wrote another book plus a new article called "Case Closed" in which he set out all of his arguments against the EMH.

And then something quite unexpected happened. He got an invitation to speak at one of the oldest investment firms in the world, Alfred Berg of Oslo, Norway. From there, invitations started pouring in from all over Europe and Asia. And everywhere he went, he was given rock-star treatment.

"Somehow they knew who I was," Haugen said. "The new markets have begun to respond to my ideas, and I'm getting cited in papers and receiving invitations to speak all over the world. Academics have not yet acknowledged that the EMH is crap, but real-world investors are beginning to do so. Real evidence is coming forward and destroying everything believed and taught in the business schools. Fifty years of academic teaching is about to teeter and fall."

Pamela Esquibel sees the *Light*

On August 25, 2010, Pamela Esquibel's car was rear-ended while sitting at a traffic light at Federal and Louisiana in Denver. The sudden jolt caused her head to snap forward violently and then to snap backward. Whiplash.

"It felt as if it was going to fall off my neck," she remembered. "My ears were ringing, and I just felt really, really tired."

She called her husband, who came and dealt with the police. The damage to the back bumper was not serious, and she was able to drive home. She put herself to bed. Three hours later, she awoke, feeling nauseous and confused.

That evening, her temperature spiked, and her husband took her to the ER at Swedish Hospital. One of the intake nurses asked if she had a made out a will.

"Why?" she asked, beginning to panic. "Is everything okay?"

"This," said the nurse, "may be your last night."

Hearing those words, Esquibel had an instantaneous whole life review.

"I thought of all the time I'd wasted worrying," she said, "and of all the things I hadn't done in my life."

Needless to say, she didn't die that night. Her tests and X-rays all came back negative, and with no medical reason to keep her there, the docs put a brace on her neck, wished her well, and sent her home. Later, as she was drifting off to sleep, she had a vision of an aunt who had passed away several years before.

"It was as if we were looking at each other in a waking state," Esquibel remembered. "It was a tangible presence."

On the second night, she had another face-to-face encounter, this time, with a grandfather who'd been dead for six years.

"He gave me a warm welcoming smile," she said, "and blew me a kiss."

She was at once delighted to see him and terrified at what this vision might portend.

"I was afraid I was going to die in my sleep," she said. "I kept thinking, 'I can't go now. I have a daughter to raise.'"

On the third night, she received another visitation, this time, from her maternal grandparents.

"I asked them, 'Am I going to die?'"

"They pointed to a bed and said, 'No, you're okay. Go to sleep and rest. We're here to protect you.'"

Something like redemption finally came on the fourth night. That's when Esquibel saw "the light." It was bright and white, enormous and embracing.

"I remember feeling so small compared to this huge magnificent light," she said. "It was the best feeling, warm and cozy, such a contrast to the normal pain of living. It was like having someone hug you. I was completely content, like I'd never have to eat or drink again."

Then a voice came out of the light, a man's voice, ancient and admonishing. "Why do you want to live?" it asked. "You haven't been treating your life as a gift. If we let you live, from now on, you will work for us."

"I'm still trying to figure that one out," Esquibel said. "I feel like they want me to give a message, but I don't yet know what it is."

Her near-death experience pulled her out of a depression that had been with her since she'd witnessed the death of her seventy-five-year-old grandmother four years before.

"It shocked me to see her last dying breath," she said. "How you can just stop breathing and be gone? That's when it dawned on me that I was going to die. So why bother? Why get up and go to work if I'm just going to die? It was a totally existential depression. Nobody wanted to be around me because of it. But since the *Light*, I've started reaching out to old friends and reconnecting with life. I don't know yet what my mission is, but every day I feel like I'm getting closer to it. The phrase, 'Only love is real,' keeps popping into my head. I think there's bigger healing I need to do."

There's a pickup truck in Marilyn Wells's living room

You're going along, minding your own business, and the next thing you know your house is a wreck, and your life has taken a totally unexpected turn. That's exactly what happened to Denver artist Marilyn Wells. Three days after she and her daughter walked into the bank to make the last of twenty-five years of mortgage payments, she was startled awake at three in the morning by what she thought at first were earthquake tremors.

"Then I heard this huge cracking sound," she said. "I waited, listened a minute, got up, and stepped out into the hallway."

What she saw made her hair stand up on end. There in the middle of her living room sat a huge pickup truck, a young man behind the wheel revving the motor and trying to get it into reverse, two young women in the seat beside him, crying hysterically. "Where's my cell phone?" one of them wailed. "I can't find my cell phone!"

"I didn't know what was going on," Wells said. "I tried calling 911 on my landline, but the line was dead. So I slipped out the back door and ran over to my neighbor Buster's house."

He'd heard the crash and had already summoned the police.

Wells watched as the three kids abandoned the vehicle and ran off down the street. Then the driver stopped, turned, and walked slowly back.

"He was obviously shaken," Wells said, "an eighteen—or nineteen-year-old kid."

"Sorry about your house," he said as they stood side by side, surveying the damage. Within minutes, the cops and fire department were on the scene, along with a reporter from Channel 7. The fire chief stepped in to retrieve her purse, laptop, and cell phone, and Wells called her daughter. By 4:00 a.m., a crew of workmen had arrived and was boarding the place up.

"I was oddly composed that night," Wells remembered. "My daughter came and got me, and the next morning, I woke up and went back over to the house. It was a shambles. The whole front was in rubble, and there were dishes everywhere."

The rest of the story reads like a good-news/bad-news joke. First, the bad news: asbestos was discovered, and the abatement team did almost as much damage as the truck, tearing out ceilings and kitchen cabinets and wrecking china and tchotchkes in the process. The good news? The house got a much-needed work over.

"While I wouldn't wish this on anyone, it all turned out okay," Wells said. "We had to do $100,000 worth of repairs. Everything had to be brought up to code. We negotiated with the insurance company and redid the bathroom, flooring, kitchen, and bedroom. They even put me up in an apartment while the repairs were in process."

As for the kid, he pretty much got off scot-free, although he did have to spend one uncomfortable night in jail before being remanded to the custody of his father. Wells never saw him again.

Nearly two years since the accident, she said she still feels tension and anxiety whenever she talks about it. She credits her Christian contemplative practice for helping her get through the ordeal.

"I'm finally feeling that my house and my self are all put together again. I have a lot more empathy now for people who lose their homes to flood and fire. I came away from this with a huge appreciation for the beauty of life."

The fall—and rise—of stuntman Mark Dissette

Act 1

Every once in a while in the life of a professional stuntman, something goes horribly amiss. July 1, 1988, was such a day for veteran Denver stuntman Mark Dissette. He'd been getting thrown out of cars, being lit on fire, and diving through windows since he was eighteen. So far he'd had an excellent safety record.

On this particular shoot, Dissette's assignment was to don a harness, step over a balcony, and lower himself five floors to an air bag waiting on the street below. But just as he began his descent, the cable snapped. This would not have been a big deal had the fall not been interrupted by a third-floor balcony twenty feet below. He hit the railing, broke his right femur, cracked five vertebrae, and plummeted the remaining three stories.

"When I hit the air bag," he said, "a voice deep inside said, 'This happened for a reason.'"

It took three operations and two-and-a-half years of rehab to stitch him back together again. During that time, his wife divorced him, and Shur-Escape, the company that had manufactured the failed harness and cable, declared bankruptcy. When the dust settled, Dissette walked—or rather hobbled—away with a piddling sixteen grand for his troubles. His career as a stuntman was over.

Act 2

"The pain was so intense I didn't have a full night's sleep for the next six years," he said. "Pain meds were useless. I'd lie awake and cry all night and fall asleep at dawn."

Here's the thing. Despite the pain, the exhaustion, and the desperate loneliness, the accident was probably the best thing that ever happened to him. At least in retrospect.

"I'd been on a self-destructive path," he said. "I wasn't happy with my life. In fact, I hated myself. I'd had a rough childhood with an alcoholic father and a couple of sibs who were mentally ill and prone to violence. I realized that I couldn't move forward with my rehabilitation if I maintained an attitude of self-hatred. I had to love myself enough to heal."

47

Somewhere in the middle of his dark night, all of his negativity just disappeared.

"It felt like a load had been taken off me. The accident gave me a chance to reset everything. It made me stop and appreciate who I was."

Act 3

In addition to his stunt work, Dissette had been directing plays and musicals off and on since high school. One day he got a call from a woman named Kathleen Traylor.

"Hey," she said, "we need your help. Our theatre group is doing *Guys and Dolls*, and it's a complete disaster."

What Traylor didn't tell him was that everyone in the cast was in some way physically disabled.

"Nobody would cast them because of their disabilities," Dissette said. "So they'd started their own troupe. This was their first show."

Before agreeing to take the project on, Dissette addressed them with deliberate forthrightness.

"Do you want to do a show that people will say, 'Nice job for a bunchy of cripples,'" he asked, "or do you want them to applaud you with an earned right to the applause?"

"We wanna earn the applause," they said, and Dissette stepped in as music director. With only two weeks 'til opening night, he worked them pretty hard.

"My injury helped me understand the psychology," he said. "It never occurred to me to pity them."

The show was, of course, a huge success, and the troupe went on to gain notoriety as Denver's Physically Handicapped Actors & Musical Artists League (PHAMALY).

"I felt a tremendous sense of accomplishment," he said. "A fire was lit in me. I knew I'd found my calling."

Mark Dissette has been part of the PHAMALY for the past twenty-two years.

"Heroism," he said, "is not about rushing into a burning building. It's about waking up with a crippled body, knowing you're gonna face pain and ostracism, and still you say, 'I'm gonna be a part of this. I'm gonna, by God, get up and go out and do it.'"

Gerald Garcia's dog predicts, prevents seizures

Gerald Garcia was out riding his motorcycle back in 1987 when, in his words, "some guy didn't pay attention to a stop sign, and I became road pizza."

His injuries included facial fractures around the left eye, which left him with double vision, and some scarring of the brain. Still, after some recuperation time, he was able to go back to his job as an RN, specializing in spinal cord injuries and long-term care.

Ten years went by, and everything seemed fine. But then one day, his arm started flopping around uncontrollably in what was later diagnosed as a partial complex seizure. "Probably due to the traumatic brain injury you sustained in the motorcycle accident," his doctor told him. To make matters worse, he also started having "focal seizures," in which he'd zone out and wake up later with no sense of what had happened to him. In one particularly horrific incident, he came to on the floor at work, having chewed off part of his tongue. Needless to say, his nursing career was over.

The future looked bleak, but then something unexpected happened. Garcia was staying with friends who owned a Dalmatian named Reebok. Reebok, he noticed, had this uncanny ability to sense whenever a focal seizure was about to happen.

"Some people have a sense or an aura that a seizure is coming on, which can range from tingling on the tongue or a smell or flashing lights," Garcia explained. "I get none of that. Reebok would get up and start nibbling at my hand to break the cycle of absence. Theoretically, any dog that has a bond with a human can sense when something isn't right. Research has shown that they can smell a shift in their owner's neurochemistry. They can also pick up on predictors such as lip smacking, fine tremors, or repetitive human gestures, that the person may be unaware of."

Recognizing the special bond between them, Reebok's owners gave her to Garcia as a gift.

"I was blessed to get her," he said, his eyes welling.

Unfortunately, the story did not end happily. In 2010, somebody stole Reebok while Garcia was in the hospital; and search as he might, he was never able to find her. But his experience had taught him how invaluable a dog can be when it comes to predicting seizures. His neurologist advised him to get another dog.

"I started looking for a young female because females tend to be more nurturing," Garcia said. "I also wanted a puppy so I'd have time to establish a stronger bond with her."

Last August, he finally found what he was looking for, a four-month-old shepherd/collie mix named Goldie.

"I got her from Four Paws Dog Rescue out of Aurora," he said. "She was such a bundle of cuteness that I had to have her. She's been very easy to train. When she's got her vest on, she's all business. When the vest is off, she's like any other dog, a full-fledged puppy who likes to push the envelope."

Looking back on the motorcycle accident, Garcia said, "At first I had a lot of issues. My life had been turned upside down. I was angry. I got suicidal more than a few times. But once Reebok entered my life, a lot of those behaviors changed. I had someone to look out for me and for me to take care of. Same with Goldie. You've got something in your life that's more important than the diagnosis. Oddly, I like myself better now, and I look at life differently. I see it as a gift rather than just an opportunity to get something accomplished. I've long since forgiven the guy who ran into me, and I've also forgiven myself for all the resentment I felt."

Bill Mahoney takes 12-steps

Like a lot of guys who've been through the 12-Step Program, Denver real estate developer Bill Mahoney is both self-deprecatingly funny and ruthlessly honest about his history of substance abuse.

"Booze is God's way of keeping the Irish from taking over the world," he quipped and then turned serious. "I have the Irish gene."

Mahoney started drinking when he was fifteen. Big time.

"I scored a fake ID and toured the local taverns. I'd go home shit faced every night and sleep it off." Home was a one-bedroom apartment in Brooklyn, which he shared with his parents and older brother. "The place was so cramped, I spent most of my time out in the streets," he said.

By the time he got to college, he was doing—and dealing—coke, pot, booze, hash, "just about anything to get twisted and stay that way. The end of that first semester, I got busted for stealing $2 Christmas trees."

The judge sentenced him to thirty days, during which time he missed all his exams and got kicked out of school. Minus a student deferment, it wasn't long before Uncle Sam caught up with him. He was sent to Vietnam, where he served as a radio teletype operator at a point camp at Pleiku.

"Everybody there was ripped," he said. "I mean, ripped all the time. No wonder we lost."

Out of the army and back in school, he appeared to be getting his life in order. He got straight A's, married "a nice Jewish girl," cut his hair short, wore a respectable-looking tweed jacket, smoked an academic-looking Meerschaum pipe, and resumed his decidedly unacademic habit of getting plastered every night.

"My wife kept me together for a while," he said. "But finally, she couldn't take it anymore and left."

It was around this time, 1972, that an old Irish drinking buddy named Bob O'Shaughnessy called him from Aspen and invited him to come out and be a ski bum.

"Hey, I'm from Brooklyn," Mahoney said. "I did not know from skiing. But there were chicks in Aspen and plenty of dope. Exactly where I wanted to be."

He hooked up with a wealthy older woman, and in 1981, they bought a bar in Glenwood Springs. It was at the Joker's Inn that the drinking and drugging started getting really out of hand. One night, Mahoney went berserk, beat up his girlfriend, stole her car, and wrapped it around a tree. She called the cops.

Mahoney called O'Shaughnessy, who urged him to check into rehab. What better place, O'Shaughnessy argued, than a dry-out center to hide from the cops? Mahoney took him up on it and checked in. Once inside, he was handed a book on the 12-Steps, which he pored over.

This is what he learned: If you want to get sober, the first thing you need to do is acknowledge that you have a problem and that the problem is out of your control. Next, you need to take a personal moral inventory and be willing to make amends for the harm you have caused others.

"Alcoholics Anonymous is a spiritual program," Mahoney said, "but a big stumbling block for me was the 'G-word.' I was a lapsed Catholic, and I did not believe in God. But what made the program work for me was that AA defines 'God' as the 'higher power of your understanding.' For me, that higher power was the group itself. That's where the energy was. For the next five years, I stayed sober by going to meetings every night of the week."

It's been nearly thirty years since Bill Mahoney took his last drink. He doesn't go to AA meetings anymore. He's become a Baha'i, and he's no longer afraid to say the "G-word."

Trish Rainbow's trip through Cancerland

Among the many things elementary school principal Trish Rainbow had on her plate that first day of classes in 2002 was an appointment for a routine mammogram. The test results were not good.

"You've got breast cancer," the surgeon told her later that week. "I'm recommending an aggressive course of treatment—surgery, chemo, radiation. It'll take four months. Then we'll see."

A replacement principal had to be hired, a "school accountability plan" written, staff trained, school children comforted. Rainbow spent the next thirty days scrambling to get her affairs in order.

"The first and last month of the school year are always the hardest," she said. "But the busyness kept me from thinking about why I would not be at school. I remember being very dismissive about it. Like, 'I'll get this over with and go right back to work.'"

But then during the long slow days of recuperation, the reality of her situation began to set in.

"Nights were especially hard," she remembered. "There was a lot of fear and anxiety, and I was alone much of the time. Except I had a friend in Italy, Lori DeMori. 2:00 a.m. in Denver is 9:00 a.m. there, so whenever I found myself freaking out in the middle of the night, I'd give her a call and have a trans-Atlantic meltdown. Lori was a godsend."

One night she had a dream that completely turned the situation around.

"I saw myself walking down a dry dusty road on a hot summer day. In the distance, I could see this dark fleshy blob, maybe three feet tall. I was curious about it. Not afraid, just curious. I wanted to know what it was and whether it would run away or turn on me. But it held its ground, and as I got closer, I realized that the blob was my cancer. Then out of its side, something started to grow: an appendage or an arm or something. I took its hand, and the two of us went for a walk together, and as we walked, it got smaller and smaller. What I felt coming from *it* was a feeling of relief. It was like this scared little kid, my cancer, as afraid of me as I was of it."

Her psyche, she realized, had given her a great gift.

"It turned the dial down on my anxiety and made it all okay somehow. Before that, I was fighting the disease and felt a lot of hostility toward it. But now I felt nothing but friendliness. I was just taking a trip through Cancerland, and I could relax."

Maybe we need to reconsider the way we think about disease in this country. We're so busy waging war on cancer, fighting off illness, aggressively treating disease, that we forget that it's our own bodies we're talking about here. Unwittingly, we turn ourselves against ourselves, turn our bodies into battlefields upon which titanic struggles are waged—life vs. death, health vs. sickness, me vs. my disease. Maybe that's what it means to *suffer* a disease.

For ex-*gangsta* Tony Crocker, boot camp prompts a course change

Tony Crocker is a very big guy. Like, twenty-inch-bicep-fifty-four-inch-chest big. He got that way by training five hours a day, six days a week at Denver's Wash Park and Eisenhower Rec Center gyms. He owes his self-discipline to a drill instructor named Sergeant Littles, whom he met at an army boot camp in 1984.

Crocker grew up in Atlanta, Georgia. When he was in middle school, he got caught up in a street gang called Down by Law. With over two thousand members, he said, "There wasn't a part of the city we didn't control."

To get some sense of how tough this bunch was, their initiation rites involved being cooked, literally, for forty-five minutes in a fifty-five gallon drum.

"They covered you with grease, stuck you in a barrel, and lit a fire under it," Crocker said. "If you survived, you was in. If you fainted or quit, you got beat up and sent home."

One night, the *gangstas* decided that a neighborhood drug dealer who was holding out on them needed to be taught a lesson.

"Me and three other guys went over to collect some money and rough him up," Crocker said. Because of his size (6'3"/280 lbs), Crocker acted as *doorman* ("first guy in the door, last guy out.")

"I kicked the door down, and in we went. Everybody was packin', and a gun went off."

When the smoke cleared, the dealer was dead. Though he was not the shooter, Crocker took the rap. But when it came time for sentencing, the judge presented him with an interesting choice. He could do ten to fifteen in the Georgia State pen or serve a stint in the US Army. Crocker chose the army.

He was in deep kimchi from the moment he stepped off the bus at Fort Bliss. A drill instructor got right up in his face and ordered him to spit out the gum he was chewing.

"Now, I'd been running with The Law since I was fourteen," Crocker said, "and no white man ever talked to me that way. I told him, 'Get outta my face or you'll be eatin' corn without no teeth.'"

That did it.

"They made lunch meat outta me," he said. "Put me on KP for four months straight, stuck dead birds on my head, hollered at me from morning till night."

The average soldier breaks down in less than a month. But Crocker didn't break down, nor did he give in. One day, his DI, the aforementioned Sergeant Littles, saw him pick up a 450-pound tank bar and carry it across the room, a job that would normally have taken four guys. The dumbfounded DI sat him down for a little heart-to-heart.

"Crocker," he said, "you have the makings of a rock soldier. You know what that is?"

"No, sir."

"That's a warrior who never, ever surrenders. You catch my drift here, troop?"

"Yes, sir."

"You got leadership potential, son. But you gotta listen to what we have to teach you. You apply yourself, and you could be promoted right out of basic."

It was a pivotal moment in Crocker's life.

"I made a decision to focus on who I was and what I could do with my life," he said. "Before boot camp, I just acted. But Sergeant Littles taught me to think about the consequences of my actions. I learned to control my temper and my emotions."

Crocker made buck sergeant and saw action in Panama and Operation Desert Storm.

"I came out a more compassionate person," he said. "These days I'm looking for people that's hurting. I want to go into nursing homes and reach out to the elderly and pray with them and help them. I want God to use me to give something back. I took so much away when I was running with The Law."

PART 2

Paddlers, Twirlers, and Phone Pole Flippers

Maurice "Mo' Betta" Wade: "Goin' down the road"

Maurice Wade's heroes have always been cowboys.

"I grew up in the '50s watching Roy Rogers, the Cisco Kid, and Gene Autry," he said. "My granddad was a farrier down in Greenwood, Mississippi, and I used to go out to his farm and ride his mules and pretend I was a cowboy. That's all I ever wanted to be."

After high school, Wade joined the army and served in Vietnam with the 101st Airborne Division.

"I was on a fire support team that shot the big guns for the infantry," he said. "We'd get mortared every night."

He came back shattered and angry.

"I used to go around and inspect my house every night as if I was checking the perimeter," he said. "And we didn't get no hero's welcome either. They called us baby killers."

After his discharge, he went to work full-time as a compliance monitor for the USDA in Denver, and part-time at Allen Stables in Aurora.

"The cowboys'd come in and drop off their horses," he said, "and they kept asking me if I knew a guy named Henry Lewis."

Henry Lewis, as it happened, was a legendary black cowboy who ran a small cattle operation on ten acres behind Aurora's Hinkley High School. One day, Wade's curiosity got the better of him, and he went over there and introduced himself.

"Henry was a loner," he remembered, "an old-time cowboy who stayed off to himself a lot. He was in his late sixties when I met him and in his nineties when he finally passed. He was tough as nails, Lewis. Talk about *True Grit*. That was Henry. He was roping and tying calves right up 'til the day he died."

Lewis had a small arena on his property where he used to practice calf roping in the afternoons. Wade started going there after work to lend a hand.

"That was how you learned from Lewis," he said. "You hung out and worked for him. He taught me some skills, and I got to where I could rope a calf pretty good. Next thing I know, I've got horses, a truck, and some ropes, and I'm goin' down the road, doin' two or three rodeos a weekend. Wherever there was a rodeo and some prize money, we'd go."

In 1985, his first year on the tour, Wade was named Bill Pickett Rookie of the Year. He was nicknamed "Mo' Betta" by his fellow cowboys, most of whom were at least twenty years his junior. Maurice "Mo' Betta" Wade is sixty-two years old, which would be over the hill in *any* sport, but especially so in professional rodeo.

Wade disagrees. "I still have a lot of spunk in me," he said. "I stay physically fit, work out, don't drink or smoke. Course, at my age, you're more cautious. You don't bail off the horse at flat full speed like the younger guys do. But then the younger guys don't have the experience I've got, so they make more mistakes. The key is being consistent. You wanna stay smooth and correct and make the best run on that cow as you can."

Like his mentor Henry Lewis, Wade practices calf roping two or three hours a day, and tours the small town rodeo circuit on weekends.

"Rodeo-ing, you ain't gonna get wealthy," he said. "If you win, you might take home $800 on a weekend, maybe ten to fifteen grand in a season. There's not a lot of money in it."

So why do it?

"'Cause I love it," he said simply. "I have a passion for it. It also keeps me from thinking about Vietnam and the friends I lost over there. I'm pretty much a loner these days. I was married once, but that didn't last. So I hang out with the guys I rodeo with. Cowboys are genuine, and we get along. It's a brotherly relationship. Cowboys look at you for the man that you are."

Paul Brekus: "The whole world smiles when you're on a *penny-farthing*"

Paul Brekus is a man of many parts. He's a collector of antiques, especially old phonograph players, which he's been restoring since he was a kid.

"My mother likes to tell people that I took apart my first phonograph machine when I was four," he said. "But what she always fails to add is that I put it back together again."

He runs a disc mastering studio out of his basement, where he cuts old-timey vinyl records for the likes of *Big Head Todd and the Monsters*. Oh, and he's also the technologies systems administrator for the Denver Civil Service Commission.

But what's more interesting even than what he does for a living is the fact that he gets himself to the office every morning on a penny-farthing bicycle, one of those Victorian jobs with the big wheel up front and the mini wheel out back.

The penny-farthing was invented in the 1870s by a guy named James Starley, who is today considered the father of the bicycle industry in Britain. In an age before gears were invented, Starley built bikes with big front wheels that enabled the rider to get more distance per revolution.

If the penny-farthing seems ungainly and, well, freaking dangerous, it's because it is. Big wheelers are prone to bone-busting accidents. Should the hapless rider hit a pothole or an unexpected rock, he might find himself flying headfirst over the handlebars or, in the parlance of the Victorian era, "taking a header."

To be sure, the aptly named Paul Brekus (it's pronounced "break us") has "come a cropper" on more than one occasion while out on his penny-farthing. His first major accident took place on I-80, just outside of Cheyenne, Wyoming, on June 6, 2000. He'd joined his friend Steve Stevens, who was on his way across the country on a penny-farthing from San Francisco to Boston.

"I crested a hill, and that was the last thing I remember," Brekus said. "Steve came upon me lying on the side of the road with a severe concussion, a couple of busted teeth, and blood coming out of my mouth. He revived me and called an ambulance."

A subsequent inspection revealed that the big front wheel had come loose from its forks, pitching Brekus arse over tea kettle onto the asphalt below.

"Since I had no memory of the accident, I decided to continue riding," Brekus said, "although because of the concussion I had to stay away from anything that might cause a head injury for at least six months."

His next penny-farthing was a Kennedy, which he was out riding exactly one year to the day of the Cheyenne accident when a woman ran into him at 32nd and Salisbury. The Kennedy was munched under the car's front tires while Brekus was busying himself sliding over the roof, bouncing off the trunk, and landing butt down on the pavement.

"She looked in her rearview mirror to see if I was alive," he said, "and then just kind of tootled away. I could still wiggle my fingers and toes—always a good sign—plus there was no damage to the helmet. I went home and repaired the bike and rode it for another four years."

By now you may be asking yourself, "What the hell?"

"Actually, I ask myself that a lot," Brekus said, "especially when I'm riding home in the snow. I guess one reason is that it's a natural merge with my love for antiques, but the real reason is . . . I'm nuts."

Then again, it's a great way to stay in shape. Brekus estimates that he's done over thirty-six thousand miles in the ten years he's been riding a penny-farthing. That's almost one and a half times the circumference of the planet.

"It also makes me more socially interactive," Brekus said. "I'm normally soft-spoken and shy, but when people see me coming, they smile and wave and shout out all kinds of things. One day, I was riding through downtown, and this Rasta in dreads called out, 'Thank you for messing with my fragile sense of reality.'"

As his biking buddy Steve Stevens likes to say, "The whole world smiles when you're on a penny-farthing bicycle."

Paralympic gold medalist Jason Regier: "Murder ball saved my life"

Driving back to Oregon State University to begin his senior year, Jason Regier reached down to change the station on his car radio. In that split second, his right front tire caught on the edge of the pavement, and his jeep flipped over and rolled three times.

"All the windows blew out," he said. "It was the most violent thing I'd ever been in." He kept telling himself as he lay there, waiting for an ambulance, that this had to be a nightmare and that soon he'd wake up. "But I didn't wake up," he said. "I couldn't move. Couldn't breathe. And I had this killing pain in my neck."

X-rays later in Salt Lake City revealed that he'd sustained a dislocation fracture in his neck. "C-6 and C-7 had separated," he explained. "The bump in your neck is C-7. C-6 is the one just above it."

While he hadn't actually severed the spinal cord, he had bruised it seriously enough that all communication with the rest of his body was disrupted. He was wheeled into surgery at two in the morning, and two plates were attached to the vertebrae in his neck: one in front, one in back.

"It's like this big steel claw holding my neck together," he said.

When he woke up the following morning, he was surrounded by friends and family.

"Tell them to unstrap me," he said to his mother.

"You're not strapped in," she replied. "That's the sheet holding you down."

That's when it struck him that he was paralyzed, at least for the time being.

"I couldn't even scratch my nose," he said. "The hardest thing was not knowing the extent of the damage or how much function I would retain after I recovered. I lay there looking at the ceiling, remembering all the hiking and camping I'd done, the sports I'd played, the plans I'd made. That life was gone."

During the long hours of his recuperation, he found himself asking the big questions: "What is the purpose of life? How can I find meaning? How am I supposed to live?"

Regier was transferred to Craig Hospital in Denver, where he spent the next three and a half months rebuilding his life.

"I had to relearn balance and muscle memory. I had to re-teach myself all the basics of daily living—dressing, going to the bathroom, drinking a cup of tea."

After a month, he was able to sit up, and he'd regained the use of his arms. But for the rest of his life, he would be confined to a wheelchair.

Two years after the accident, he began playing a sport called quad rugby, a cross between basketball and football played by guys in wheelchairs on an indoor court.

"The object," said Regier, "is to kill the guy with the ball." A natural athlete (he'd lettered all four years in high school and played Division 1 Soccer in College), Regier threw himself into it. "It took me three years of hard work to be able to push my wheelchair a mile," he said. "After that, it took just a month and a half to go five miles, much of it uphill."

Regier trains up to four hours a day, six days a week with the Denver Harlequins. As a member of Team USA, he competed at the 2005 World Wheelchair Games in Rio, the 2006 World Quad Rugby Championships in New Zealand, and the 2008 World Paralympics in Beijing, where he won a gold medal.

"Rugby is the number 1 factor in my rehabilitation," he said. "When I play, I don't think about being disabled. Out on the court is where I feel most alive."

Looking back on the dark days of his recuperation, Regier takes heart from a motto that was pasted over his bed. "Faced with adversity," it read, "your true character shines through."

Jocelyn Gutierrez fights her way to self-respect

There's a rose tattoo on Jocelyn Gutierrez' left shoulder, but it's not there because she's fond of flowers. She had it done when she quit Las Traviesas Crew (LTC), an all-female street gang that claimed Southside Greeley as its turf.

"There used to be a 13 there," she explained. "Southside's number. Thirteen stands for the thirteenth letter of the alphabet, M, which means 'Mexican.' You gotta be Hispanic to get in."

The rose tattoo commemorates an important turning point in Jocelyn Gutierrez' young life: the moment when she decided, once and for all, to put the gang life behind her.

Although she did not officially get "jumped in" until she turned fifteen, Gutierrez started "representing" for LTC when she was ten years old.

"When I was growing up, everybody in Southside wanted to be in it," Gutierrez said. "It sounded really cool. The OG (Original Gangster) tagged me 'Baby Gangsta.'"

Despite the random shootings and the occasional windshield bashings, the gangs were not, Gutierrez said, necessarily criminal. "We were supposed to be there to protect one another and to fight other gangs," she said. "That's what gangs do. They fight other gangs."

About a year after she joined, she was at a party when some guys started picking a fight with her boyfriend. She, of course, went to his aid, expecting her sisters to join in. But this time, for whatever reason, they didn't.

"Me and him had bottles broken in our faces. He had to have his head stitched. I busted a tooth and opened a lip. My so-called sistas did not have my back. I mean, that's why I joined in the first place. I decided if they weren't gonna be there for me, there was no reason for me to stay in."

Jocelyn Gutierrez jumped out.

Still, there was something about the fighting that appealed to her. "Maybe it's the adrenaline rush," she said, "but I've always loved it. I used to watch MMA (mixed martial arts) on TV, but I thought girls were not allowed to compete."

Then her boyfriend found out about Top Notch, an MMA gym in Greeley, where girls were more than welcome.

"It's actually easier for girls to get ahead in this sport," said Mike Alirez, Top Notch founder and Gutierrez' personal trainer. "Mainly because there are so few of them that stay with it. The training is hard. *Seriously* hard. Your muscles ache. You feel pain all the time. And you're gonna get a black eye or a bloody nose. That's just the way it is. Most girls quit in a week."

But not Jocelyn Gutierrez, who's been at it since September 2009.

"I'm very determined," she said, "and I never quit. I know I'm gonna get hit, but I'm willing to take the risk because that's how much I love this sport."

In May 2010, Gutierrez fought her first public bout at Red and Jerry's Sports Bar on S. Santa Fe in Denver. Unlike her male counterparts, who tended to dance around, sizing each other up before getting down to business, Gutierrez came on swinging and did not let up until her opponent called it quits. The bout lasted something like a minute and a half, and the crowd was on its feet the whole time. It was, hands down, the most exciting fight of the evening.

"It's a fun sport," Gutierrez said. "It's also something not everybody can do. But *I* can do it, and I'm good at it. And the more I train, the better I get. Also, I get a lot of support and a lot of respect, which is not something I ever got in the gangs."

Marc Romero: one-legged ski bum

Colorado adaptive skier Marc Romero's tone is laconic as he describes how, at the age of seventeen, he lost his right leg. "I was out riding my motorcycle, and I got hit by a stoner on a street bike doing sixty miles an hour. I woke up two weeks later in ICU, and the leg was gone. That's all there was to it." It took a year for him to recover.

Prosthetic legs back in the late '70s were heavy, awkward, and uncomfortable. "You'd sweat in them," Romero said. "The stump would bleed. Your friends would be embarrassed and stop coming around. So you wound up falling back on your family."

The turnaround for Romero and others in his position came in 1980, the year a guy named Terry Fox ran across Canada on a prosthetic leg. "This just electrified me," Romero said. "I figured if he could do it, so could I."

At that time, he was living with his family on Long Island Sound, about two hundred feet from the water's edge. Every morning, young Marc would leave the artificial leg behind and hop down to the beach to go swimming.

"Once I was in the water," he said, "my disability no longer mattered. I was just another kid out for a swim."

The daily exercise led him to try waterskiing with somewhat mixed results until his grandfather bought a speedboat so he could have more practice time. It wasn't long before he'd taught himself to water-ski on one leg.

Six years later, Romero heard about a program being offered by the New England Handicapped Sports Association (NEHSA) to teach people with disabilities how to ski. He went to Mt. Sunapee, New Hampshire, to find out more.

"There were a lot of Viet vets up there," he said. "These were guys who were like twenty years older than me, and they were skiing on one leg with outriggers. And I mean they were skiing awesome. Just flying around and having a great time. I'm seeing this with my own eyes, and I'm saying, 'I can do this, and I can do it well.'"

He took up the sport with a vengeance, and as it happened, he *was* good at it. So good that he was invited by the coaches at the National Sports Center for the Disabled to come to Winter Park, Colorado, to try for the US Paralympic Ski Team. It took him four years of dedicated training, but he finally made the team in 1990.

Naturally, he started getting a lot of press, though he was not particularly happy with the tone of the articles.

"They were full of pity," he said. "Disabled people don't need the pity, and we don't need you to hold the doors open for us either."

Romero started writing articles about the sport from an insider's point of view. "I wanted to encourage other disabled people to try it," he said. In the process, he discovered that he liked promoting the sport almost as much as he liked doing it.

He got hold of a movie camera and began filming his fellow adaptive skiers. "I wanted to show the world that disabled skiers could complete with able-bodied skiers and do just fine, thank you very much. You look at the times, and we're really only split seconds behind them."

He eventually quit his job with Farmer's Insurance to work full-time on a documentary called *Heroes of the Slopes*, a compilation of stories about the very best adaptive skiers. The fifty-four-minute film aired on PBS during the 2007-2008 season.

"I'm driven by a passion for top-level adaptive skiing," he said. "I bond with those who want to be independent. I am a voice for the disabled community."

Mexican wrestler Joel Floriano gets back in the game

Professional wrestler Joel Floriano left home when he was thirteen. He got as far as Mexicali, on the Baja Peninsula, just south of the US border. Strolling through town one morning, he came upon an arena plastered with posters advertising *lucha libre*, Mexico's answer to big-time wrestling. He walked in and asked for a chance to show his stuff.

"Everybody laughed," he said. "They were all grown-ups, and here I was, this cocky little kid challenging them to a duel. They thought they would teach me a lesson, but I ended up showing them. Nobody could beat me. They hired me on the spot."

Floriano had learned to wrestle in grade school. Born into a family of nine children, he grew up dirt poor on a small farm in Aguascalientes.

"We lived in an adobe house with no electricity and no running water," he said. "We ate beans, tortillas, and *nopali* cactus. Scrambled eggs were a big deal."

When he was seven, the family moved to Guadalajara, where his mother promptly enrolled him in school. The city kids, however, did not cotton to this rube from the sticks who came to class shoeless and clad in the one shirt and pair of pants he had to his name.

"I got into a lot of fights," he said.

One of his teachers, seeking to channel his aggression, invited him to join the school's wrestling team. Although he became the best wrestler in his school, by the end of junior high, he'd had his fill of formal education. That's when he dropped out and headed north to Mexicali. A year later, he was a professional *luchadore* with the moniker "Sangre Frio" and a turquoise mask with a trademark splotch of crimson sewn around the mouth and eyes.

A lot of big names were coming to Mexicali in those days, and Floriano worked the shows as an opening act. Soon he was touring the country and making more money than he'd ever seen in his life.

"I became well known as the last guy ever to fight Santo, the most famous luchadore in Mexico."

The strenuous schedule—five shows a week—began taking a toll.

"People think we're faking it," he said, "but wrestlers really do get hurt in the ring. A lot of them get hooked on painkillers."

For his part, he medicated himself with booze and cocaine. One drunken night, he got into a fight with a couple of cops. He managed to dislocate one cop's shoulder and wrestle his gun away before the second cop bashed him over the head. He woke up in a cell, bruised and bloody from the beating he'd received from his jailers. He bailed himself out and went home where, a few days later, his father found him cowering in the dark.

"Don't turn the light on," Floriano said. "I don't want you to see me like this."

"How far down do you want to go, *mi hijo*?" replied his father.

"I was so ashamed," Floriano said, "that I resolved never to take another drink."

His wrestling career came to an abrupt halt in 1980 during a bout for the welterweight championship of Mexico's Pacific Coast Division.

"I jumped off the ropes, landed with my feet crooked and broke both ankles."

During the two years it took him to recuperate, Floriano went to jewelry making school in Los Angeles and eventually came to work as a jeweler in Denver.

"But in my mind," he said, "I never left the sport. I'm never truly happy unless I'm wrestling."

In December 2009, Floriano opened a gym in a warehouse in Commerce City, where he provides free training to anyone who wants to learn the sport.

"Lots of kids are angry and need an outlet for their aggression," he said. "I guarantee that *lucha libre* will help them conquer their anger."

Lacey Henderson: "I'm not disabled. I've just got one leg."

During the summer of 2010, Denver University cheerleader Lacey Henderson got a job as a dance instructor and counselor at a summer camp for kids aged ten to seventeen. Not an unusual occupation for a college student on summer break except for one thing: each of the one hundred kids at her camp had suffered the loss of a limb. Sponsored by the Amputee Coalition of America (ACA), the retreat was designed to help them come to terms with their loss. As a role model for kids with disabilities, there could be no one more suitable than Lacey Henderson.

When she was nine, Henderson went to her mother complaining of pain in her right leg.

"I was limping. I couldn't flatten my foot or put any weight on it," she said.

Her mother figured it was growing pains, but when Lacey showed her the two grape-sized lumps at the back of her knee, she made an appointment to see a pediatrician.

"Baker cysts," he said. "Go home, do some stretches, pop a couple of Advil."

Two weeks later, the pain had intensified, and the lump was as big as a lightbulb. An MRI at Denver's Presbyterian/Saint Luke's revealed a synovial sarcoma plus a spot on the lungs. The doctors there ordered an immediate amputation and chemotherapy. The Hendersons went to Children's Hospital for a second opinion.

At Children's, the oncologists offered experimental chemotherapy that was, in Henderson's opinion, almost worse than the disease.

"There were lots of complications, including kidney and liver damage," she said. "A couple of times they thought they'd lost me. But, hey, I'm a tough girl."

After three rounds of chemo, the Hendersons met with the surgeons. The news was not good. While the spot on her lung had disappeared, the tumor at the back of her knee had only shrunk by 1 percent. She was offered two options: amputate and have a fighting chance or do nothing and die.

"For me, it was a no-brainier," Henderson said. "I was like, 'cut it off.'"

They amputated the leg six inches above the knee, gave her one final round of chemo, and sent her home with this bit of advice for her parents: "Treat her like you would any normal kid."

"My dad took my crutches away and got me walking within two months," she said. "My mom said, 'You still have one leg, so hop your ass around that bed and make it.'"

Once she was able to walk, she began throwing herself into every sport imaginable: volleyball, rock climbing, skiing, snowboarding, soccer, even pole vaulting. In middle school, she did tumbling and gymnastics and made the cheerleading squad her freshman year.

Today she's majoring in Spanish (with a minor in French and international health) at Denver University. She's been invited to train for the US Paralympic Ski Team, works as a waitress at Abrusci's Italian Eatery in Cherry Creek, and has done fashion modeling for the likes of Quentin Tarantino.

But for all her accomplishments, her stint at last summer's ACA camp was perhaps the most rewarding.

"On the last night of camp, we were having our final cabin discussion," she remembered. "My kids were the older girls, and they were worried their disability would keep them from getting a boyfriend."

Henderson who, in case you're wondering, does have a boyfriend ("one of those boring two-legged people") told her charges, "You may be missing an arm or a leg, but you still have a heart. You're still a complete person."

Coming as it did from someone who'd lived through all the challenges and managed to emerge triumphant, the message came through loud and clear.

"I could see that I could influence and inspire people with similar disabilities," Henderson said. "Holy Moley, I can actually change how they think about themselves."

Her philosophy in a nutshell? "I'm not disabled. I've just got one leg."

Tricia Downing: "Redefining able"

It was while doing what she loved most—riding her bike—that Trish Downing lost the use of her legs. She and her cycling buddy Matt were on the homeward stretch of a Sunday training ride to Lookout Mountain back in September 2000, when a careless driver in Lakewood plowed into her.

"I was ejected off the bike, flipped in midair, and landed on my back on the windshield," she said. "When I hit the pavement, I couldn't feel my legs."

She'd cracked two ribs, fractured her scapula, broken a vertebra in her neck, and damaged her spinal cord. After three and a half weeks in intensive care, the prognosis was not good.

"Nobody told me I wouldn't walk again," she said. "There was no big sit-down or anything. I was in a lot of pain, and I wasn't thinking about the future. It didn't hit me 'til I left the ICU for rehab at Craig Memorial."

There had never been a time in Tricia Downing's life when sports were not the main focus of her attention. She had earned a master's in sports management and had served as press officer for the US Olympic Table Tennis Team at the 1996 Games in Atlanta. She'd also been communications coordinator for the US Olympic Swim Team. But it was as a competitive cyclist that she'd found her true passion.

After three months at Craig, there were still no signs of change.

"I did have some sensation in my legs," she said, "but basically no control of my muscles from T4 (midchest) down."

Tricia Downing was staring at the rest of her life confined to a wheelchair and the end of a promising career as a competitive cyclist. Or so she thought.

"At Craig, they teach you new ways to do all the things you did before," Downing said, "so you can get back to work, sports, family, and your social life. I learned to transfer in and out of my wheelchair and how to drive a car."

Best of all, Craig gave her the tools to relearn sports.

There were three in particular that appealed to her: hand cycling, wheelchair racing, and swimming. In the beginning, she concentrated on swimming. Nine months after the accident, she was able to do the backstroke using her upper-body strength to keep her legs afloat.

But Downing longed to get back into competition, and in 2002, she began looking into a triathlon—swimming, biking, and running— which, in her case, would mean pushing her wheelchair. She found out about a race in Fort Collins and gave the organizers a call. Would it be okay, she asked, for a disabled athlete to compete?

There was a long pause. "Okay," said the voice on the other end, "but bring a helper."

Five of Downing's friends volunteered immediately.

"I was the only disabled athlete in the race," she said, "but I finished ahead of seven able-bodied ones. I realized that I could compete again, and that inspired me to keep on going."

Downing trains six days a week, lifting weights and riding her handcycle as much as five hours a day. Not infrequently, she'll do eight—to ten-hour bike rides between the Cherry Creek and Chatfield reservoirs.

A couple of years ago, she quit her job as a high school counselor to devote herself full-time to motivational speaking, encouraging her audiences to set goals and overcome challenges. She also hosts a yearly get-together called Camp Discovery for Women in Wheelchairs.

"After a traumatic injury, people tend to look backward as if the past was all happy and the future dismal. My advice is don't look back. It's not about being disabled. It's about having a challenge and turning adversity into strength instead of a sobbing point. I've learned you can take a tough situation and use it to change your life in positive ways."

James Creasey: croquet's the way for people with dementia

Two weeks after James Creasey lost his job as VP at a Denver-based publishing firm, his dad was diagnosed with vascular dementia.

"At that point, I made a commitment to spend two out of every ten weeks with him," Creasey said, which was no mean feat since it required him to fly to England every couple of months. Creasey grew up twenty miles south of London, and though he's lived in the States for the past thirty-five years, he's lost neither his British accent nor his wry English wit.

On a visit home in June of '08, he found his father confused, isolated, and barely able to construct a coherent sentence. He decided to take his folks on a summer vacation to the southwest of England.

"We stayed in a little hotel on the cliffs of Cornwall," he said. "To my delight, I discovered it had the most perfectly kept croquet lawn."

Creasey had been introduced to croquet at his company's summer picnics in Denver. He loved the game and the camaraderie it afforded, so much so that he joined the Denver Croquet Club.

"I had two summers of experience by the time I saw my folks," he said. "I told my mum, 'You're off deck for the next two weeks. Go shopping. Get your hair done. I'm playing croquet with Dad.'"

So for the rest of the vacation, father and son could be seen out on the lawn every morning, quietly playing croquet together. Then something quite unexpected happened.

"A whole bunch of other guests from the hotel started playing with us," Creasey said. "Suddenly, my dad wasn't isolated anymore. People who couldn't carry on a conversation with him could at least play croquet with him. And even though his condition continued to deteriorate, over time and with a little guidance, he could still play a cracking game of croquet."

Creasey returned to Denver and immediately called Linda Mitchell, president of the Colorado Chapter of the Alzheimer's Association. He described to her what had happened with his dad and suggested that they collaborate on a croquet program for people and families living with dementia.

"Let's see if we can put a few more smiles on a few more faces," he told her. Mitchell was intrigued.

In February of 2009, Creasey founded Jiminy Wicket, a Colorado-based nonprofit, the goal of which is to introduce the game to long-term-care facilities and senior centers as a means of raising their quality of care for Alzheimer's patients.

"Sixty-four percent of Americans in long-term care get one visit per year," Creasey said. "They're tranquilized with antipsychotic drugs and parked in front of a TV set all day. We don't need to abandon these people. There is another way."

Creasey likes to enumerate the many reasons why croquet is the ideal sport for people suffering from dementia.

"For one thing," he said, "it's simple. Unlike golf, which utilizes identical white balls, each of the four balls in a croquet set is a different color. This makes them easier to identify. For another, leaning on the mallet helps with balance. For a third, the grass on a croquet lawn is absolutely flat, so the ball goes in a straight line. It's low cost, high benefit, and intergenerational."

Creasey's ideas are beginning to catch on. He's utilized his entrepreneurial expertise to forge alliances between the US Croquet Association and the US Alzheimer's Association and between the

World Croquet Federation and Alzheimer's Disease International. In recognition of his efforts, Governor Hickenlooper last fall issued a proclamation designating September 21 as Jiminy Wicket Day.

"People with Alzheimer's live entirely in the moment," Creasey said. "My feeling is, why not make it a pleasant moment?"

Kenny Rhoades takes the plunge

If you've been out to Casa Bonita lately, you've probably seen ultra-high diver Kenny Rhoades doing his thing. He's the guy dressed up as an outlaw, duking it out with the sheriff on the edge of a cliff. He takes a swipe, the sheriff steps aside, and Rhoades plunges into the roiling waters thirty feet below. It's all in a day's work for a guy who's been swimming and diving since he was a kid.

"I swam competitively with the Brighton Bullfrogs until puberty hit," he said. "Everyone else shot up. I stayed short (Rhoades is five feet five). Taller people have a natural advantage due to their extra reach. I couldn't compete on their level anymore, but fortunately, a diving team was forming in Brighton, and I was naturally good at it."

Good enough to win an athletic scholarship to Metro State, where he dove for two years and went all the way to Division 2 Nationals. A guy he met at Division 2 suggested he contact Mirage Entertainment about a job.

In the summer of 2008, Mirage hired him on as an ultrahigh diver and sent him to Holiday World in Santa Claus, Indiana.

"Normally, it's a three-month learning curve," Rhoades said. "But a week after I started there, I did my first high dive off a sixty-five-foot tower."

What's it like, the first time you're up there, looking down?

"You feel like you're diving into a Dixie Cup," he said. "Don't lean out. That's pretty much all you're thinking. You don't want to overshoot. You've done all the prep work, so you're confident. But there's still that voice in back of your head saying, 'WTF?'"

Rhoades said that, from a technical standpoint, an ultrahigh dive is no different than a dive from a lower elevation. He starts with a front one and a half and at fifty feet goes into a *barani*—a summersault with a half twist. This slows the dive and allows him to get his feet under him.

"The standard approach is to cup your crotch and go in feet first," he said. "You're gonna be hitting the water at fifty to fifty-five mile per hour, and at that speed, if you went in headfirst, you'd blow your shoulders out."

To hear Rhoades tell it, dropping sixty-five feet into a thirty-foot-diameter pool is almost a religious experience.

"You're only in the air for one and a half seconds," he said, "but you'd be surprised how much can go through your head in that brief period of time. The mind slows down. You come out of the one and a half and see the blue circle of the pool, which is your visual cue that said, 'Okay, I've finished my one and a half. Now it's time to go into the barani.' You're operating out of a calm, disciplined center that is the natural result of a dozen years of training."

Rhoades estimates that he's done maybe five hundred ultrahigh dives, including one particularly hairy eighty-foot drop off a cliff in Black Canyon, Colorado.

Despite his extensive training, Rhoades has taken his share of hits. Like the time he missed the Barani and went in on his side. "I had a wet suit on, so it didn't sting," he said. "But the impact was like having your best friend tackle you to the ground from a standing position."

He plans to do ultrahigh dive shows until he's saved enough to go to graduate school.

"Diving is a passion of mine," he said. "There's no feeling like it in the world. It's not the drop so much as the adrenaline rush you feel when you leave the perch. That and knowing you've got to do this right, or it's really, really, really gonna hurt."

Wayne Staggs flips phone poles to stay fit

To stay in shape, most guys in their sixties might go, like, twenty minutes on the elliptical or take a water aerobics class or something. Wayne Staggs, on the other hand, gets *his* fitness jollies by hoisting a 70- to 115-pound telephone pole, leaning it against his right shoulder, running forward with it, and somehow tossing it up and getting it to flip end-over-end so that it lands in a straight line directly in front of him. It's called caber tossing, and it's the preeminent event in Scottish athletics.

Staggs—who, in real life, designs industrial electrical systems—excels at it. So much so that in 2009, he won the Masters World Championships in Inverness, Scotland, for his age category, in a competition that included not only caber, but also the hammer toss and the stone put (think shot put with a rock the size of your head).

Other events involved flinging cannon balls attached to chains and picking up twenty-pound sheaves of wheat with a pitchfork and lobbing them over a high bar.

The origins of the sport are shrouded in Highland mist. Some historians think it may have been introduced to Scotland by the Vikings. Others believe it began as a quick way to build bridges over wide streams. Still, others will tell you that cabers with rudimentary steps notched into them were used in battle to storm fortress walls. A lone warrior would charge in and flip it so that it landed leaning against the palisades, at which point the rest of the lads would charge in, scramble up the pole, and vault over the top.

Whatever the case, Staggs got into it after a 1995 trip to the "Auld Sod" with his ex-wife, who was born there but raised here. In Scotland, he discovered that he too had Scottish blood coursing through his veins, "which would explain," he said, "the red hair and freckles."

Back in Denver, the couple joined the St. Andrews Society, a local 501(c)(3) that promotes all things Scottish. It was at St. Andrews that Staggs met professional highlands athlete Mike Ganzel, who introduced him to the ancient sport of phone pole flipping.

"Three evenings a week, I'd go out to an open field near my home at 67th and Indiana with a sixteen-foot-long, seventy-pound caber," Staggs remembered. "I'd stand it up and throw it until I couldn't do it anymore. I was forty-six at the time and very determined. After a couple of weeks, I got to where I could flip it two or three times in a practice."

Caber tossing, he discovered, is not just a matter of getting the pole to flip. It's also a matter of accuracy. In order for a flip to count, the pole has to fall between nine o'clock and three o'clock. A perfect throw means that it lands at high noon; that is, in a straight line with the tosser.

"It's also not just about brute strength," he said. "It requires agility and explosion. A highland athlete turns slow-twitch muscles into fast-twitch muscles. That's where the explosion comes from."

Despite the intensive training, accidents can and do happen, and we're not just talking the occasional pulled muscle here. "At the Longs Peak Games at Estes Park in 1998," he recalled, "both feet went straight out from under me. I sat flat on my butt with a one-hundred-pound caber just barely missing my particulars."

Which brings us to the ultimate question, which is: "What exactly do Scottish guys wear under their kilts?"

"Other than your girlfriend's lipstick," Staggs said without missing a beat, "nothing is *worn* under the kilt. Everything is in perfect working order."

What's in it for Wayne Staggs?

"Highland games competitors are like family," he said. "There's camaraderie, openness, and a willingness to help one another even at one's own competitive expense. That plus it's the most fun I've ever had competing at anything."

Jon Gates: "grandfather of off-string yo-yo"

Denver resident Jon Gates is the reigning Sport Ladder Champion of the United States. Sport Ladder, in case you didn't know, is a yo-yo competition in which contestants demonstrate mastery of thirty increasingly complicated tricks.

Gates threw his first yo-yo when he was five, but it wasn't until high school that the bug really stung him. "I was eighteen years old," he remembered. "I saw Tommy Smothers do this bit on TV called the Yo-Yo Man. After that, I really dove in. There were no videos in 1989, and books were static. But I'd see a picture of a trick, and I could figure out for myself how to make it work."

Gates describes himself as "a little weird" and something of an outsider. That realization came early. At age four, still as bald as a billiard ball, it dawned on him that his hair would probably never grow. He was right. He's as bald now as he was then.

He was also borderline ADD, which, for a yo-yo vampire, is not necessarily a bad thing. "I was always looking for something to do with my hands," he said, "something to focus my nervous energy on. Through yo-yo, I could direct it to something that was fun and cool. There've been studies that show that kids who do yo-yo get better grades because they're able to create focus and discipline. I made the best grades of my life the year I started playing yo-yo."

Once the class clown, he became his high school's yo-yo Yoda, attracting a small coterie of kids eager to learn the, um, ins and outs of the sport. To make extra walking-around money, Gates dealt high-end yo-yos to his young disciples. Buying them wholesale in such large quantities, he soon came to the attention of one Donald Duncan Jr., son of the eponymous Donald Duncan Sr., a Cleveland entrepreneur who, in 1932, trademarked the name Yo-Yo and eventually became the world's largest manufacturer of the popular toy. Impressed with Gates's energy and enthusiasm, Duncan Jr. invited him to Arizona to work for the company as a professional demonstrator.

There he met the legendary Dale Oliver, a yo-yo thrower who'd been at it since the early '50s. "Dale was the best there was," Gates said. "He kept trying to stump me, but everything he showed me I either already knew how to do or could figure out on my own."

Dale Oliver, however, had one last trick up his sleeve. He disconnected the string, wound it around the axel, and threw it. When it flew off, he caught it on the string and made it do a little summersault.

"He told me to go practice and figure it out for myself," Gates said. "So being the ADD compulsive guy that I am, I became obsessed and figured it out. Then I started making up other tricks to keep it entertaining. It took me a day, but I worked out a way to get the disconnected yo-yo to come back, which was a variation Dale hadn't thought of."

It was the birth of "off-string yo-yo," a radically different approach to the sport and a unique division in the World Yo-yo Competition. It also earned Gates a place in the history books as the grandfather of off-string yo-yo.

These days, he teaches the physics of yo-yo ("lever friction, inertia, gyroscopic stability, distribution of mass") to kids in the public schools.

"A big part of what I do is about empowering them to believe in their own abilities," he said. "Especially special needs kids. Becoming a teacher means more to me than the competitions and international travel. I love to hear a kid say, 'Hey, I did it!' I get emotional just thinking about it. I can't see a world where on some level I'm not pushing it forward every day. If I lost all my fingers, I'd be doing it on my toes. It definitely defines me."

Coby Crowley: dragon boating "paddle-ista"

The martial arts have always been a big part of Coby Crowley's life. In her thirties, she earned a black belt in tae kwon do and studied Ninpo Taijitsu. Rock climbing was also a major fitness passion. But that all changed when the arthritis in her hands made it too painful to keep on going. She started looking around for an activity that would allow her to stay fit and keep active despite her physical limitations.

Fortunately, she didn't have to look far. The company she works for, CH2MHill, had a dragon-boating team that competed once a year at the Colorado Dragon Boating Festival. In 2008, Crowley signed on and discovered a whole new reason to get out of bed in the morning.

"Dragon boating just fit the bill," she said. "It offered exercise, competition, and camaraderie, and it was something I could do. It was kind of like an addiction. 'Hi, I'm Coby, and I'm addicted to paddling.'"

Dragon boating may be the new kid on the block in terms of sporting events in the West, but it's been a big deal in Asia for more than two and a half thousand years. The competition forms part of the annual Duanwu Festival, which in South Central China commemorates the summer solstice and the planting of rice. Dragons in China are venerated as benevolent spirits of water in all its forms—rivers, lakes, seas, ice, mist, and rain.

Modern dragon boating comes in two flavors: Taiwanese and Hong Kong. Taiwanese boats weigh in at 1,200 pounds and have a big dragon's head on the prow. They hold a crew of 18 paddlers, a drummer, a steersman, and a flag catcher, whose job it is to hurl himself onto the head of the dragon at the finish line, and pull a flag out of a buoy to stop the clock.

Hong Kong-style boats—"canoes on steroids"—are narrower, lighter, and longer than their Taiwanese counterparts. These bad boys hold anywhere from twenty to fifty paddlers plus a steersman and a drummer who keeps time with the lead paddlers, calling out encouragement and commands during the five-hundred-meter sprint.

Dragon boating offered a totally new kind of workout for the 5-foot-1-inch, 110-pound former ninja.

"Paddlers don't bend their arms," she said. "It's all about the rotation of the body. Paddling promotes agility, strong core, and wind. It's definitely a cardiovascular workout."

It took her two months of hard practice to get comfortable with the cardio side of it, but once she got there, she was hooked. So much so that she wanted more than just to compete once a year with her corporate team. She wanted to paddle the entire season, May through September, and to travel to races all over the country.

So it was fortuitous that she found the Flying Dragons, a Denver-based race team consisting of both Asians and round eyes.

"This was the team I'd been looking for," she said. "We've all aspired to be on it, so it's a real honor. It feels like I'm part of a family."

The Dragons practice twice a week on Wednesday evenings and Sunday afternoons.

"Our average time for the five-hundred-meter race is 2:17," Crowley said. "We're striving to hit two minutes."

During the off-season, the self-described *paddle-ista* stays in shape by running and working out at a gym five days a week and "pool paddling" indoors on Saturday mornings.

"Dragon boating has given me a lot of self-confidence and self-understanding," she said. "Age really *is* just a number. Never give up, never stop. There's always something out there you can do. I found dragon boating when I thought I had run out of options. Dragon boating was my destiny, and I didn't even know it."

Melissa Thomas: fighting dancer

Capoeira. Is it a fight that looks like a dance, or a dance that looks like a fight? Hard to say, but however you look at it, it's rapidly becoming one of Brazil's most popular cultural exports, right up there with the Bossa Nova and Carman Miranda's banana-bedizened hat.

Capoeirista Melissa Thomas first encountered it at a Brazilian carnival in Boulder.

"When I saw people doing handstands and cartwheels and kicking the crap out of one another, all the while doing it as a dance, it was awesome," she said. "Awesome meets beautiful equals power. I needed something powerful in my life. I'd had twelve years of gymnastics, and I missed the discipline and sense of purpose. I wanted people to sweat with again."

So she began training at Denver's Canto Do Galo Capoeira School. Nine years later, she's become a *mestre* (teacher) in her own right.

Although its origins are shrouded in the proverbial mists, capoeira is believed to have begun in Angola as a competition for brides among the young warriors. When in the sixteenth century Portugal laid claim to Brazil, it began importing slaves, many of them from Angola, to work the sugarcane plantations. Although they far outnumbered their masters, the slaves lacked weapons to mount an effective revolt, much less to defend themselves against armed agents sent to hunt them down when they tried to escape. Ergo, capoeira, a martial art masquerading as dance, which could be practiced right under the unsuspecting noses of the overlords.

When slavery was officially abolished in 1888, former slaves continued the tradition on the streets of Recife, Rio, and Salvador.

With their superior fighting skills, capoeiristas found work as mercenaries, hit men, and bodyguards. This in turn led the Brazilian government to ban the sport altogether.

"People playing it on the streets had a special rhythm on the *berimbau* (a stringed percussion instrument) to warn when the cops were coming," Thomas explained. "It was called the *cavalaria*, or cavalry charge, because it sounded like horses hooves: dong shiki dong shiki dong dong dong. Everybody'd take off when they heard it and come back later when the cops were gone."

The ban was finally lifted in 1940, and today capoeira schools can be found not only in Brazil, but also in cities across the globe.

Capoeira matches are decided in small circles called *rodas* or wheels. There's an orchestra at one end of the roda made up of berimbaus, tambourines, bells, and conga drums. Participants gather round, singing and clapping. At a signal from the mestre, the combatants enter the roda and shake hands.

"But it's a guarded shake," Thomas explained, "with one hand up to protect your face. Capoeira can be tricky. You can't assume a person's going to be nice . . . *or* mean."

There's no scoring in capoeira, but there is always a winner, based in part on who dominates the game, whose kicks make the most sense in terms of throwing an opponent off balance or surprising them, or maybe even making contact, although it's not necessarily a contact sport.

Nor is it not. Contact can and does happen, and when it does, it can be devastating. Thomas herself has sustained four black eyes, a broken thumb, and a cracked rib. On one occasion, she got knocked cold with a spinning kick to the head. All of which she seems to have taken in stride.

"Injuries are your biggest teachers," she said. "What I learned from getting knocked out was that I was trying to be bigger than I actually am. I'm only 115 pounds. So I've learned to play with the skills I have as a smaller person to get in and under my opponent. I've come to see adversity as an opportunity. In the larger dimension, capoeira is about how you live your life. It teaches you that you don't have to be a victim of circumstance and that you can own your actions and their consequences."

Ashley Dolan: born to twirl

Ashley Dolan was born to twirl.

At the tender age of two and a half, somebody stuck a baton in her hand, and she's been doing it ever since. You might even say it's in her blood. Her mom, Ann Osborn Dolan, twirled for the Denver Broncos back in the age of Elway. She's also past president of the Colorado Baton Council. Dolan's grandmother, Sheryl Osborn, also a lifelong twirler, now teaches it at Westminster Parks and Rec.

"Most people think of twirling as the majorette in the tasseled boots leading the band," Momma Dolan said. "We're proud of our past, but that's an image from the 1950s. Twirling has evolved. It's become much more athletic and artistic. Twirlers at the highest level train as hard as any other athlete."

"I put it in the same category as figure skating and gymnastics," echoed daughter Ashley, a graduate of Cherry Creek High School and now a junior at the University of Texas, where she's the featured twirler for the school's football team. "You need stamina and upper-body strength. There's a lot of leaping and jumping."

Twirlers at Dolan's level practice three to five hours a week, in addition to lots of cardio and strength training. Dolan runs as many as six miles a day, five days a week, and lifts weights at least three times a week, "mainly for injury prevention," she said.

"Baton twirling is a contact sport," her mom explained. "We don't wear pads or helmets. If the baton hits you, it hurts. There are lots of bumps and bruises, bloody noses, and broken nails."

Every spring, Dolan spends one weekend a month training with her baton twirling team—KOS (which stands for Karen Ogden Studios)—in Sulphur, Louisiana, a tiny town three hours east of Houston. KOS recruited her after seeing her perform at the 2011 Internationals in Jacksonville, Florida. This August, the team goes to the internationals in Almere, Netherlands, and Dolan is going with them.

She's pretty good at it too. She can do five spins under a toss. She can do a hands-free cartwheel and come out of it in time to catch the baton before it hits the floor. She's also perfected a little wonder known as the One Spin Double Illusion, a trick that involves throwing the baton thirty feet into the air, spinning once, leaning over to rest her trunk on her extended left leg while simultaneously pivoting the right one two times in a clockwise direction, all before straightening up to catch the baton. The whole maneuver unfolds in under five seconds, almost quicker than the eye can see.

"A lot of physics goes into it," Dolan said. "I've been working on it since I was a kid."

In addition to the "aerials," a one-and-a-half—to three-minute routine has to incorporate "rolls" (rolling the baton over the arms, neck, elbows, etc.) and "contact materials," which consist of "flips, whips, swings, wraps, and finger twirls, all in close contact with the body. These are the small moves that connect the big tricks," Dolan explained. "You want the baton to spin quickly because it looks more exciting when it's moving fast."

As difficult as such tricks are to perform—and they are—the mental component of competition is by far the hardest to master.

"You have to get into your zone before you hit the floor," Dolan said. "I do lots of deep breathing. I visualize the routine and try not to stress about the outcome. I remind myself how much I love the sport and how much fun it is to perform. For me, twirling is a form of artistic expression, a way for me to convey my deepest thoughts and feelings to my audience. After I've performed, there's this huge sense of satisfaction. You're proud of your team and proud of yourself. You come off the floor so elated that you say, 'Right. This is why I do it.'"

Paul Arell: old man on the mountain

There are climbers whose goal is to summit all fifty-four of Colorado's fourteen-thousand-foot peaks in the least amount of time. Sixty-five-year-old environmental engineer Paul Arell is not one of them.

Back in August 1973, he was sitting in his office at the EPA when a co-worker said, "We're climbing Mt. Princeton this weekend. Wanna come?" He was twenty-five at the time and had done some climbing and backpacking in Alaska, but nothing like Mt. Princeton.

"It was a tremendous physical challenge," he said. "There's a big vertical gain. Looking down from the peak, you can see the Arkansas River seven thousand feet below. It was totally exhilarating."

Needless to say, he was hooked. He recruited some friends, and together they started doing day trips to the twenty-five relatively easy peaks within range of Denver. In the first five years, he did sixteen. By 1990, he was up to thirty-three. But in the ensuing nineteen years, his enthusiasm waned, and he only climbed an additional three.

"I had kids and a wife," he said. "Life took over, and it wasn't a big focus."

Flash forward to 2010. Newly retired, Arell decided that he really *did* want to complete the remaining 18. By then, however, none of his old climbing buddies were interested. So instead, he rounded up three new guys: Chris Wilson a retired educator; Bob La Greca, still working in telecommunications; and Glenn Crissman, a retired computer systems guy.

"We were all in our early sixties," Arell said, "four old guys with the most difficult and remote peaks still ahead of us. It took us four summers to complete them. The weather didn't always cooperate. Fortunately, our wives did."

It's a toss-up between Capitol and Little Bear as to which climb was the most difficult.

"Capitol has a knife edge that drops off to nowhere, 1,800 feet on both sides," Arell said. "For 150 feet, you're holding on to that knife edge with your boots on the rock going hand to hand sideways for maybe 20 minutes. Past that, there's another hour and a half to the summit. The whole climb took us 13 hours going and coming from Capitol Lake."

Little Bear, on the south end of the Sangres, was equally difficult. There's a narrow passage of smooth rock called the Hourglass that is, according to Arell, "slicker than snot on a doorknob" due to the algae-ridden meltwater from above. Below it, there's a sheer drop. Lose your footing and you're a dead man.

But there's another difficulty with the Hourglass. Climbers refer to it as "the Bowling Alley" because of the loose rock from above that tends to dislodge and zing down, bowling over anything in its path.

"This almost happened to us," Arell said. "We looked up and saw a good-sized chunk of rock coming our way. We all dropped flat, and it passed over our heads. We'd already done Mt. Blanca and Mt. Ellingwood on that trip, so we decided to call it quits and come back the following year with a better game plan."

Sadly, one of the group, Glenn Crissman, died at home in his easy chair in February of 2012 and never got to complete the list.

"He was the lead climber and the fastest of the bunch," Arell said. "He had four peaks left. We split his ashes into four parts and scattered them on Pyramid, Capitol, Mt. Wilson, and El Diente."

They finally completed number 54, Snowmass Mountain, in September 2013.

If you're thinking of trying it, here's some advice from the Old Man on the Mountain: "Don't wait until you're in your sixties. Had I known, I'd have done the harder ones earlier. Even so, it was a great feeling of accomplishment. You learn teamwork, persistence, and how to profit from your mistakes. I'd do it all over again."

Angela Cavaleri: half the woman she once was

Angela Cavaleri didn't think her weight was anything to worry about until one morning in May 2004, when, on the bus heading for work, she noticed that a guy had opted to stand rather than share a seat with her.

"It didn't make me mad or anything," she said. "But this was definitely a lightbulb moment. I realized that if I was too big to share a seat, it was time to do something."

The encounter also sparked some soul-searching about the potential health hazards of her obesity—diabetes, high blood pressure, joint and respiratory problems—not to mention the general lethargy that had been dragging at her since she was a kid.

"I never felt really great," she said. "I was always tired and run down. I'm the oldest of four kids, and I was the only fat person in my family. I was just born fat."

It didn't help that she wasn't getting any exercise. Gym class was not required at Edgewater's Jefferson High, where Cavaleri went to school in the mid-'90s. "I put on forty or fifty pounds in high school," she said. By the time she turned seventeen, she weighed in at a hefty 250 pounds.

It took her five months to stiffen her resolve and map out a plan of attack. If she was going to go to the trouble of losing all that weight, she reasoned, she would only do it once.

"I didn't want to be the type who loses it quickly and then gains it all back again," she said. "But I also knew that if I tried to change my whole lifestyle in one go, I'd probably fail."

So she devised a three-step program, the first phase of which would be to go cold turkey on the junk food: "no chips, no Big Mac, no soda, no Caramel Macchiato, no Cinna-monster."

Two months of no junk food and she was ready for step 2: eat a healthy diet—lean proteins, fresh fruits, and vegetables, no pasta, and only a modicum of processed foods. And watch those portions.

"One cookie doesn't make you fat," she said. "It's the box of cookies that's the problem. We live in an all-or-nothing society. We either gorge or starve. But those extremes are unrealistic. Moderation is key."

She chose February 2005 to launch step 3, a program of regular exercise. "I didn't start on New Year's Day because I didn't want to set myself up for failure," she said. "And also, between February and June, there are no big food holidays and not many weddings, so there are fewer opportunities to mess up."

For ten bucks, Cavaleri bought herself a stationary recumbent bike at a church auction and resolved to go for ten minutes on it every day. Ten minutes turned into twenty, twenty into thirty. In six months, she was cranking out two hours a day on it.

"I started getting bored," she said. "It was no longer a challenge, but by then, I'd lost thirty pounds."

She bought an elliptical trainer and started over, working up to two hours in the ensuing six months.

"I was losing clothing sizes faster than I could buy new clothes," she said, "and I was encouraged by how much better I was feeling emotionally and physically. I lost fifty pounds on the elliptical trainer."

She started a running program to lose the last twenty-five. Since then, she's been lifting weights, going twice weekly to ballroom dance classes, and walking four to six miles a day to keep herself at a trim and muscular 142 pounds.

"One night I was at an Avs game at the Pepsi Center, and there was lots of room around me in the seat. I felt tiny. I also felt kind of proud. I mean, I did this myself. But really, anyone can do what I did. My advice? Trying to do it all at once sets people up for failure. Go slow and do it in small increments."

Marathon runner Jason Romero: "Who needs sight when you have vision?"

When Denver attorney Jason Romero was fourteen years old, he was diagnosed with a degenerative eye disease called Retinitis Pigmentosa (RP). To explain the effect of RP on his vision, Romero invokes a donut.

"You can see through the donut hole, and you can see what's on the periphery of the donut. So to get the full picture of what's out there, you have to constantly scan back and forth between the two. It's not that the donut part is blurry. It simply doesn't exist."

As the disease progresses, the donut hole gets smaller while the donut gets bigger until, as Romero put it, "the lights go out."

"The eye doctor asked me what I wanted to be when I grew up," Romero remembered. "I said 'A doctor or a lawyer.'

"He said, 'Forget it, son. Do something blue collar. Something you can do with your hands because you'll be blind by the time you turn thirty.' He also said I'd never be able to drive a car. I gotta tell you, the guy's bedside manner was for crap."

His mother, who'd accompanied him to the appointment, burst into tears.

"That's when I knew it was serious," he said. "She was pretty tough, my mom. It was the first time I ever saw her cry."

A couple of years later, Romero had an experience that would enable him not only to cope with his encroaching blindness, but in a very real sense to triumph over it. His uncle Ted was doing a six-day endurance run in Boulder, and on day 6, young Jason went up to watch him run.

"Uncle Ted was into extreme sports," Romero said. "Anything *ultra*, like swimming around Manhattan or riding a bike coast to coast or running a hundred miles, and Ted would give it a shot. The weird part was that he was doing this endurance run on an eighth-mile indoor track. He'd run eight hours, sleep for an hour or two in a tent he'd set up on the gym floor, and then get up and do another eight hours. He couldn't talk. His feet were swollen to twice their normal size and were covered with blisters. His pace had slowed to a shuffle and the doctors were trying to get him to quit. But old Uncle Ted just kept on moving forward. I ran a few laps with him, and in that moment, I saw that there are no limits to what you can accomplish if you put your mind to it. Anything and everything is possible."

His senior year at Thomas Jefferson High School, Romero captained both the football and wrestling teams and graduated at the top of his class. After law school at CU, he took a job as in-house counsel for GE in Boulder and eventually moved up to head the company's operations in Puerto Rico.

Uncle Ted's example also inspired Romero to take up long-distance running.

"I just bought the shoes and started running," he said. "I'd have my mom drive me up to Boulder, and I'd run all the way back down to Denver."

He ran the first Denver International Marathon in 1993 while still in law school. Since then he's competed in more than thirty long-distance races, including the Boston Marathon.

"Running helps me live a more fulfilling life," he said. "When I run, I don't think about the past, and I don't worry about the future. I'm completely in the here and now, and I enter a zone of peace."

Jason's motto? "Who needs sight when you have vision?"

Double lung transplant lets triathlete Gavin Maitlin breathe, compete

Gavin Maitland came in dead last at Golden's Blasterblast Triathlon back in 2009, but he couldn't have been happier.

"Completion was my goal," he said. And a worthy goal it was considering that just thirteen months earlier, he was lying on an operating table getting his lungs replaced.

Maitland is himself a transplant. He moved here from Scotland in 2002 to be with his wife Julie, a Denver native. A natural athlete, he swam competitively in high school and college and has run the London and New York Marathons. So he wasn't too concerned at first when he developed a recurring cough. He became increasingly anxious, though, as his capacity for exercise began to diminish.

At National Jewish, the doctors were mystified.

"I didn't fit the profile," he said. "I was thirty-five and fit. I didn't smoke, and I had no family history of lung disease. All they could tell me was that my lung tissue was turning fibrous and that there was no known cure."

The Maitlands began exploring alternatives. "Homeopathy, Ayurvedic medicine, acupuncture, gluten-free diets," he said. "Nothing worked. By October of '07, I could hardly breathe."

After a particularly hellish bout of coughing, Julie bundled him into the car and drove him to CU Medical.

"They told me four things," Maitland said, ticking them off on his fingers, "one: your lungs are in bad shape, two: you've got six to nine months to live unless you get a double-lung transplant, three: the average wait time for a pair of lungs is twelve to eighteen months, and four: the procedure would be way too complex in your case, so we respectfully decline to operate."

Unwilling to accept such a dismal prognosis, Julie went online and found twenty-two hospitals in the US where they do double-lung transplants.

"We spent a weekend putting together information packets with CDs of my lung scans. Then we Fedex-ed them out."

Within a week, they'd received seventeen responses, all of them negative.

The folks at Duke University Hospital, however, were at least willing to consider his case, and they invited the Maitlands down to Raleigh-Durham. After a battery of tests, the Duke team said, "Yes, we can," and put him on a wait list.

"Lung transplantation differs from other organ donations," Maitland said. "The lungs not only have to come from a donor whose blood type matches yours, they also have to come from a donor who is roughly the same size as you. Lungs also have a very short shelf life, only about six hours, so you have to be ready to go."

They checked into a hotel and hoped for the best. "Which is a little strange when you think about it," Maitland said, "because what you're *really* hoping for is the death of a healthy person." Twenty-two days later, they got the call.

"When I woke up from the anesthesia, I was able to take a wonderful deep breath for the first time in years," he said. Urged by the staff to begin walking immediately, Maitland was circumambulating the hospital corridors within twenty-four hours.

"I wore running shoes to bed so I could get right up and start walking," he said. Within three months, he was jogging; and in six months, he was back at work.

"Exercise is a huge component in recovering from a lung transplant," Maitland said. "That's why I decided to train for the triathlon. I needed a goal to motivate myself."

How has the experience transformed his life?

"I can tell you my whole philosophy in four little words," he said. "Breathe and let go. I've learned to stop obsessing about stuff I have no control over. I try to focus on the things I *can* control and let the doctors worry about the rest."

Maitland now speaks at schools, senior centers, and service clubs, encouraging audiences to become donors. "Ninety percent support organ donation," he said, "but only twenty percent actually donate. I'm trying to bring some awareness to the process. That's my way of giving back."

David Westman: bulldoggin' drag queen

You know her as Nuclia Waste. But before *she* was Denver's favorite drag queen, *he* was steer ridin', calf ropin', bulldoggin' David Westman.

To cheer him up after a breakup with his boyfriend, a cowboy buddy named Woody took Westman to the *Zia Regionals* in Albuquerque. Woody was a competitor, so Westman got to watch from the chutes.

"I said to myself, *Hey, this looks like fun. I wanna try it.* So I jumped on a steer and off we went. I was a total city slicker. I had no training, and I hated country music."

Westman got bucked off and landed on his head (the first of many injuries that would include a dislocated shoulder, some cracked ribs, and the loss of his front teeth after a steer kicked him in the mouth). Even so, Westman was hooked. He started "chasing after the buckle," entering one rodeo after another and adding events as he went along.

"Gay rodeo has two sides to it," he said. "There's the normal straight rodeo stuff, like bull riding and calf roping. And then there's the camp events: goat dressing, steer decorating, and the wild drag race."

FYI, "goat dressing" means putting a pair of BVDs on a goat. "Steer decorating" means tying a ribbon to the animal's tail. And the "wild drag race" is where a cowboy and cowgirl help a third teammate mount a steer and ride it across the finish line in a wig and a dress.

"Since I knew how to ride," Westman said, "I was the one who got to wear the wig and dress."

Prizes were awarded for best costume, so Westman—who daylights as a freelance graphic designer—started creating more and more elaborate getups. A trademark strand of pearls around his hatband led to the nickname Pearlie May.

"The character started taking on a life of her own," he said. "People wanted to know, 'What's Pearlie May gonna be wearing today?'"

It wasn't long before Pearlie May came to the attention of the Denver Cycle Sluts, a troupe of comedy drag queens who satirize "glamour drag" by stuffing their bras with Nerf balls and making their beards, hairy backs, chests, legs, and armpits part of the ensemble. Taking on campy handles such as Holly Would, Sandy Fran Crisco, and Tina Turnover, the Sluts do comedy to raise money for charities such as Project Angel Heart and the Colorado AIDS Project.

Their tongue-in-cheek approach appealed to Westman, who said he has no inclination to cross-dress and no particular affinity for glamour drag queens.

"I didn't take it seriously like a lot of them do," he said. "I was a working rodeo cowboy, just doing the Pearlie May thing for charity and having fun."

The Sluts, he learned, would be holding auditions at BJ's Carousel on South Broadway, so he decided to give it a go. Abandoning Pearlie May, Westman set about creating a new persona with wider appeal.

"My motto," he said, "is 'Always start with the accessories.' I had a metal lunch box I'd picked up in San Diego with the word *Radioactive* on one side, and *Bio Hazard* on the other. So that became my purse."

The purse in turn inspired what would become his nom de scène, Nuclia Waste. Needless to say, Nuclia won the audition and was inducted into the Sluts.

But Nuclia Waste had her sights set on bigger things. Like becoming "the drag queen for all of Denver, not just the gay community." One night, she bought a ticket to a straight charity ball, crashed the party, and stole the show. *Denver Post* columnist Penny Parker called her "Denver's Favorite Drag Queen." The following year, the charity asked her back.

In 2003, Westman was named Mr. International Gay Rodeo Association and has since retired from competition.

"People say I'm a lot quieter as David," he said. "Nuclia's more outgoing. She's all about having fun. She lets my inner child come out and play. Like I always say, it's never too late to have a happy childhood."

PART 3

Worm Farmers, Sign Spinners, and Shopping Mall Santas

Dennis James has an office in the sky

If you've been anywhere near the University of Denver lately, you've probably seen Dennis James hard at work in what he calls his "office in the sky." James, or DJ as he prefers to be called, is the tower crane operator at One Observatory Park, an eleven-story, mixed-use development going up on the SE corner of University and Evans.

"I'm the materials handler," he said. "You tell me what you got, how much it weighs, and where it's going, and I'll get the load there in a timely manner."

Every morning at six, he climbs the 130-foot ladder to his "office," which measures a scant 5 by 7 but which affords him an unobstructed view of the Front Range from Pikes Peak to the Flatirons. He can climb it in ten minutes, but he prefers to take his time, stopping at each of the tower's nine platforms to inspect it for overall condition. Twelve hours later, he climbs down, a descent he said he could do in six minutes if he had to.

A construction worker since high school—he went half-days to Green Mountain, the other half to Warren Tech to learn carpentry—DJ got his first shot at working a tower crane in Steamboat Springs in 1996.

"A company called TCD hired me to help build Torian Plum, this condo project up there," he said. "They asked if I could operate a tower crane. I went up there, got in the seat, and aced it."

It was, for Dennis James, a moment of pure bliss. "This was where I wanted to be," he said, "high above all the testosterone crap that goes on down below on a job site. I never looked back."

For all his enthusiasm, DJ is no tower crane cowboy. He's methodical, painstaking, and careful to a fault. He has to be. Operating a tower crane is, bottom line, an extremely risky profession.

"If something goes catastrophically wrong," he said, "you don't go to the clinic. You go to the morgue."

He should know. He's had his share of close calls. Like the time he exerted some extra line pull to free a form that had frozen around some poured concrete. It jerked loose, and the crane started rocking eight to ten feet forward and backward.

"It took five minutes for that bad boy to settle down," he said. "All I could do was hang on. Cranes have gone over. Operators have been killed."

He keeps a constant eye on the weather. That American flag flying over his cab is there not simply because he's a patriot, but also because it tells him and his crew which way the wind is blowing and how fast.

"Winds are the critical thing," he said. "You can see a storm coming from the mountains like a row of linebackers. The last thing you wanna do is climb out. I weigh 220 and have had my feet blown out vertically while trying to climb down. You get hit with a storm, and it's like being in a ship. The thing's rocking and rolling. You come off it punch drunk."

He's meticulous in keeping his tiny cab neat and tidy. There's a stack of *National G*s and a couple of books on a shelf over his right shoulder, which he studies during downtimes. In case you're wondering, there's no toilet. A Clorox bottle serves the purpose. He sends it down on a rope when it's full.

Tower crane operators earn between $25 and $70 an hour plus lots of overtime. "Top guys can make up to $120,000 a year," he said. "For me, though, it's not all about the money. It's a passion for me, building buildings and walking away safe. I also like mentoring the younger guys. Most operators are quiet. Not me. I demand respect, safety, and steadiness."

Bill Lee still believes in Santa Claus

It was a barmaid at a Glendale disco who first planted the idea in Bill Lee's head.

"She said I had a Santa Clause twinkle in my eye," he remembered.

Okay, so playing Santa Clause in a shopping mall would be a radical departure for anybody, but it was especially so for a guy like Bill Lee who had, up until then, been leading a fairly conventional life.

The Hippy Revolution of the '60s and early '70s had pretty much passed him by. He wore his hair short all through college at Southeast Missouri State, where he majored in biz ad and managed a local McDonald's. (Rush's Limbaugh's brother David was a coworker).

After college, he married and went to work in the food and beverage industry, putting in long hours "to achieve the American Dream." But by 1979, his marriage was on the rocks, he was fifty pounds overweight, and he was rapidly careening toward terminal burnout.

"The divorce really rocked my world," he said. "I finally had to stop and take a good long look at how I was living my life."

He thought about an essay he'd written in high school in which he'd said that he didn't want to live a nine-to-five, rat-race life like his dad. "But there I was, doing exactly that," Lee said. "Going to work, coming home, eating dinner, watching the tube, going to bed, getting up, and doing it all over again."

Lee's first move toward reestablishing a measure of sanity was to walk off the fifty pounds. The second was to quit his job as a bar manager and to take a less stressful position as a bartender. Number 3 was to do the Santa Clause gig at Cinderella City, where he got ten bucks an hour to listen to kids whisper their dreams and wishes into his ear.

His plan at the outset had been to play Santa for just one season, but that was before a lady stepped up with her five-year-old daughter and said, "Santa, this is Angela. Angela is blind." The little girl felt the rabbit fur on his costume and touched his whiskers.

She also touched his heart. Lee resolved to come back the next year, and the next, and the next. He's been doing it so long—this is his thirtieth season—that grown-ups frequently approach him to tell him how much their own annual visits had meant to them as children. Some even bring their own kids to sit on the very lap *they* once sat on.

Playing Santa, however, is not all sponge cake and mistletoe. Mall Santas work six to seven days a week during the holiday rush and, on a particularly hectic day, may visit with as many as 450 kids.

"I try to listen to every child and make it special for them," Lee said. "But the visits can become repetitious, and there's the danger of getting dulled out."

There are an estimated 150 real-beard Santas along the Front Range. A few years ago, Lee and a group of fellow St. Nicks started a professional organization to represent themselves. Society of Santa members are required to undergo an annual criminal background check for insurance purposes.

"A kid falls off your lap and hurts himself or if by accident you touch a wiggly kid in the wrong place and there's a photo of it, you could have a lawsuit on your hands," Lee explained.

The group gets together once a year for a Christmas in July Picnic at Laughing Valley Ranch, Lee's homestead just outside of Idaho Springs.

How has playing Santa changed his life?

"It's made me a more compassionate and caring person," he said. "It's a way for me to enrich people's lives and to open their minds to live more fully. Believing in Santa gives kids a chance to use their imagination. And I do believe in the power of the imagination."

Greg Storozuk: real-time ghost buster

If you had to guess just based on his appearance, you'd probably take Greg Storozuk for a plumber, a tractor mechanic, or a general contractor. In his ball cap, jeans, and T-shirt, he looks like anything but a professional dowser, not to mention a real-time ghost buster.

"I'm old school," he said, "not a New Ager. I got my training from the old-timers. New Age dowsers don't know how to dowse for water, much less to seek out oil."

Storozuk claims a 98 percent success rate in locating underground sources of water and a 75 percent success rate for uncovering potential oil wells. "It's what I do it for a living," he said simply.

He can also clear out your haunted house, but we'll get to that later.

Storozuk spent four years in the US Coast Guard before going to Western State College in Gunnison to earn a degree in municipal recreation. After graduation in 1972, he headed east to visit a cousin who'd just bought thirty-seven acres of prime farmland in upstate New York.

"My cousin happened to mention that he had dowsed for a well," Storozuk said. "I thought that was a bunch of crap, and I told him so."

The cousin handed him a pair of bent brass rods and said, "Here, damn it. You do it!" He showed Storozuk how to hold the rods, told him to visualize an underground stream and to walk 'til something happened. Storozuk did as instructed, and five minutes later the rods, much to his stupefaction, "just flew open."

"*I* didn't do that," Storozuk said to himself. "What the hell just happened?"

He backed up, walked forward again, and this time, nothing happened. He realized he'd forgotten to visualize an underground stream. As soon as he brought the image to mind, the rods once again flew open.

"I played with it for five minutes and zeroed in on a spot the size of a grapefruit."

"Right," said his cousin, "that's it. That's the exact spot I located yesterday. That's where I plan to drill my well."

Storozuk remained unconvinced until his cousin kicked away some dirt, revealing a red-painted stake he'd driven into the ground the day before to mark the spot.

"This scared the hell outta me," Storozuk said. "Just blew me away. They sure as hell don't teach this stuff in college. I had to find out more."

He went to the library, checked out every last book they had on the subject ("Both of them," Storozuk said wryly) and read them from cover to cover.

He heard about a four-day course on dowsing being offered in New Mexico and went to it. He called the American Society of Dowsers and got an invitation to attend their annual convention in Danville, Vermont.

"There were over six hundred people there from all over the world. My mind was on fire. I spent every penny I had on books and supplies and had to borrow money to drive home." Storozuk has attended the convention every year since 1976.

A professional dowser since 1982, he sniffs out more than just water. They don't like to admit it, but oil companies have been known to hire him to help locate potential oil wells.

"On their books," he said, "I'm called a consulting geologist."

And finally, there's the ghost busting. Storozuk said he uses his dowsing skills to uncover what he calls "geopathic zones."

"Geopathic zones are anything potentially hazardous to human health," he explained, "like underground faults, fractures, lightning strike zones, energy fields, mineral fields . . . Ghosts use them as sources of energy. They follow them as you or I might follow a road."

Storozuk said there's a ghost-infested bar in Georgetown, not to mention a couple of haunted hotels in downtown Denver.

"I love going to such places. I don't call what I do exorcism. I request the assistance of 'escorts' to remove the spirits and send them on their merry way. I got a lot of stories," he said. "Damn do I have a lot of stories."

Auctioneer Steve Linnebur is one fast talkin' dude

Some kids dream of being a fireman, others of walking on the moon, but Steve Linnebur knew before he got out of high school that what he wanted to be was an auctioneer.

He grew up on a dryland wheat farm outside of Roggen, Colorado. When he was five, his dad was killed in a farming accident, leaving behind a wife and eight kids. His little brother was born the day after the accident.

"Mom never remarried," Linnebur said. "She stayed on the farm and raised us by herself. We all pitched in, of course, but without a dad, we had to learn the farming business pretty much by trial and error."

After graduating from high school in 1976, Linnebur applied for a two-week course at the Missouri Auction School. They sent him an information packet containing a booklet of drills to work on in advance. Auctioneers, Linnebur discovered, learn to chant by reciting tongue twisters like the kind we all learned as kids.

Betty Botter bought some butter
But she said this butter's bitter.
So she bought a bit o' better butter.
Put it in her bitter batter
Made her bitter batter better.
So 'tis better Betty Botter bought a bit o' better butter.

The packet also contained drills designed to train the tongue and brain to remember number sequences: Ten-ten. Twenty-twenty. Thirty-thirty.

"Basically, an auctioneer's chant is just adding filler words between your numbers," Linnebur explained.

Filler words are phrases like "Dollar bidder. Dollar bid. Would he buy 'em? Wouldja give?" The chant progresses by upping the ante as the bids roll in: "One dollar. Dollar bid. Now two. Now two. Wouldja give two? Two dollar. Now three. Wouldja give three?"

After more than thirty years in the business, Linnebur is still revising and updating his patter, practicing at least two hours a day, often in his car as he drives from one sale to the next.

After the two-week course in Missouri, Linnebur went on to study at CSU, where he earned a master's in vocational agricultural education, a subject that he taught for a number of years at Byers High School in Arapahoe County. His heart, however, was never far from the arena. He volunteered at church auctions and 4H Club livestock sales, gaining experience and refining his technique.

Then in 1980, he and wife Alice put together their first professional auction. "It was a farm equipment consignment sale," he said, smiling at the memory. "We held it in a wheat field south of Roggen."

By 1993, the business had grown to the point where he felt confident enough to quit his teaching job and devote himself to it full-time.

For the Linnebur clan, auctions are a family affair. His daughter Lanay sells food to the bidders out of a catering truck, while his son Stephen, twenty-six, will sometimes take a turn at the podium. Alice, whom he calls "the brains of the operation," runs the office, does the paperwork, and manages the staff.

But it's Steve Linnebur the people come to see, and rightly so. He's extremely good at what he does. So good in fact that he was inducted into the Colorado Auctioneers Hall of Fame in 2008. In 2009, he was named Bid Calling Champion of the Year.

Most unusual item he ever sold?

"That would be the outhouse," he said. "It was an old one-holer, painted white. We picked it up with a front-end loader and stuck it in the lineup. Got $475 for it!"

Biggest day ever?

A horse auction where he grossed over $600,000. Take-home pay on a really good day can be as much as $10,000.

"Auctioneering has been good to us," Linnebur said. "It put my kids through school. I guess the secret of success in this business is just being fair with people and having respect for one another."

Sign spinner Aaron Stuckner gives it a whirl

Drive down any of Denver's major thoroughfares and you're likely to come eyeball to eyeball with a guy in a red shirt doing a "suitcase flip," a "necktie," or an "around the world" with an arrow-shaped sign. That might very well be twenty-three-year-old Aaron Stuckner, one of an elite corps of twenty-five spinners who work for a Denver advertising franchise called Arrow Ads.

Stuckner was introduced to the sport, er, dance, er, job while in college in South Florida.

"I was looking for something to do on Craigslist," he said, "and I saw this ad for a spinner. I'd seen somebody doing it back home in Culpepper, Virginia, where I grew up, and I thought it looked like a great way to make some cash, work on my tan, get in shape, meet girls, and be the center of attention."

He applied and was paired with a spinstructor (spinfluence, spinthusiasm, spinfinite: yes, they really do talk that way in Spinsville) who taught him the fifteen basic tricks and two basic combinations that all spinners are required to master before they're given their first assignment. Having wrestled and practiced karate in high school, Stuckner was in reasonably good shape. Even so, the training was a butt kicker.

"Either it's for you or it's not," he said. "Most kids who've never done sports don't last too long. The sign weighs five pounds, and it takes at least two months to get in shape for an eight-hour shift. My first assignment lasted three hours. An hour into it, I threw up and almost passed out. But I was mentally psyched and just kept on going. I wanted to take it to a whole new level."

Within three months, he was selling ads for the company; and by August of 2009, he was on his way west to become a spinstructor for the Denver franchise. Stuckner estimates he's trained a hundred spinners over the past three years.

Spinners range in age from sixteen to twenty-six.Most of them spin part-time, working ten to fifteen hours a week. A lot of them are already pretty good at some wonky non-traditional sport like skateboarding, BMX biking, or Japanese sword fighting.

"We look for athleticism and stage presence," Stuckner said.

The latter is especially important because spinning is essentially a performance art.

"Each kid brings his own personality and style to the job," he said. "At a busy corner, a spinner will look at fifteen thousand people an hour. You spin when the traffic stops. Freeze and hold when it's moving. You also smile, make eye contact, and point at people. It's very spinteractive."

While a good spinner can earn upward of twenty bucks an hour, there are some less tangible spincentives as well. Like, for example, getting flashed by girls in passing cars.

"It happens," Stuckner said. "Beats McDonalds."

Arrow Ads had a fairly unprepossessing beginning when a couple of San Diego college students got hired by a real estate company to hold up signs on street corners. To pass the time, they started tossing them into the air and spinning them. The moves got trickier, and naturally, they attracted a lot of attention. As business majors, they recognized the commercial potential in what they were doing. They trained a small troupe of spinners and started their own advertising business.

Things really took off when they joined forces with a franchise specialist who renamed the company Arrow Ads and took it spinternational. Arrow has grown to 354 franchises in 5 countries. The Denver franchise has some heavy hitters among its clientele, among them Channel 9, Jiffy Lube, and Phil Long Ford, for whom Arrow claims credit for selling 200 cars in one weekend.

"This job makes me happy," said Aaron Stuckner. "I was in and out of trouble in high school. I hung out with losers, got drunk, smoked pot, and ditched school. Spinning has taught me responsibility, leadership, and how to step up. It's gotta be the coolest job ever."

Spinsperational!

Claude Thompson: Denver's "King of Shine"

Walk past the corner of Sixteenth and Welton on any given day and you're liable to catch an earful about the condition of your shoes from a guy dressed in a crown and purple cape and hollering at you through a cheerleader's megaphone.

"Could be the reason you're walkin' without a woman," he chides the lonesome cowpoke in the battered Tony Lamas.

"Can't close the deals with dirty heels," he admonishes the banker in the pinstriped suit and the tarnished cap-toed Bruno Maglis.

That's downtown Denver's King of Shine, Claude Thompson, talkin' atcha.

Did I say "downtown?" Fogettabadda. Thompson is *God's* King of Shine.

"I was put here for one reason," he said, "to educate man about shoes. I was destined to be God's shoe representative on earth."

Megalomaniacal? Maybe, but let's face it, you don't get to be king of anything by being shy, which Thompson is most emphatically not.

"I don't bite my tongue," he said.

A Denver native, Thompson grew up in Five Points, the middle child in a family of nine kids—four boys, five girls—with a stay-at-home mom and a dad who went out and worked hard every day to put food on the table.

"My parents couldn't afford shoes," he said. "I wore secondhand sneakers my mom would buy for a quarter at Goodwill. You wear other people's shoes, you get other people's problems," which, for Thompson, meant an intractable case of toe fungus and foot odor strong enough to stop a Cape Buffalo.

He graduated from Manual High School class of '68 and went to work selling magazine subscriptions door-to-door in every state in the Union except Alaska, Hawaii, and Florida. Three and a half years later, he was back in Denver, where he would spend the next twenty years moving furniture.

That's where the foot issues finally came to a head. A customer, wishing to preserve her snow-white wall-to-walls, asked Thompson and his crew to please remove their shoes. Thompson balked.

"I told her I'll probably do more damage with my stinky feet than if I keep my shoes on," he said. She went toe-to-toe with the company, and Thompson was given his walking papers.

"I went home crying 'cause I lost my job," he said. "But then God came to me and said he'd cure my stinky feet and that I would be his shoe representative on earth. He educated me on what causes foot odor, which is bacteria and fungus. I believe I know more about foot disease than any other man on the planet. Today I can take my shoes off in confidence. I haven't had stinky feet in sixteen years."

Before he could fulfill his destiny as God's shoe rep, however, Thompson would have to endure a time of "trial and tribulation." He started smoking crack and panhandling on the streets of LoDo. One day, he walked into a Blake Street shoe shine emporium with the idea of hustling the owner, who told him, "I won't give you any money, but I will give you a job."

"I said shoe shine? No way. That's not a respectable job for a black man."

But later, he went home and got a message from the same voice that had shown him how to cure his stinky feet.

"He reminded me that shoe shining was my destiny," he said. "I went back the next day and said, 'I'll take that job.'"

The shop owner showed him what polish to use and how to apply the brush and cloth.

"Anybody can shine a shoe," Thompson said. "It doesn't take a genius. But it took me a year to learn how to do it right. What makes me different from other shoe shiners is that I honor the animal whose skin you're wearing on your feet. God made that animal. That animal didn't shine its skin. Its nutrients kept it shiny. So I don't use wax or silicone. I use cream to put the nutrients back in. I work to keep the skin alive. God didn't mean for us to walk around with dead things on our feet."

Heather Rubald: "Cute with a conscience"

Heather Rubald's designer handbags have the look and feel of high quality Italian leather. But zoom in a little closer and you'll discover something quite unique about her choice of materials. All of her purses are made out of fused, recycled plastic bags.

The black clutch with the blue trim? Garbage bags from ARC/ newspaper bags from the *Loveland Reporter Herald*. That handsome brown hobo tote? We're talkin' King Soopers here. And as for that orange big bow purse? Dude . . . *Denver Post*.

Rubald has been knitting, crocheting, and sewing her own clothes since she was a kid growing up in Loveland. As a theatre major at UNC, she made extra money sewing costumes. The recycled handbag idea evolved over time.

"My mom told me about a friend who'd crocheted a purse out of plastic bags," she said. "I thought, *That's nice*. Two years later, I'm looking for a project, and I had this big pile of plastic bags, so I used them to crochet a big bulky open-weave beach bag."

Now that she had a use for them, Rubald began hitting up all her friends for their plastic bags, which they were more than happy to donate.

"My seven-hundred-square-foot apartment started looking like a landfill," she said. "Maybe a little tidier. My kids liked to roll around in them like they were leaves."

One day, her sister showed up with some interesting news. "Hey," she said, "I saw a video on YouTube on how to fuse plastic bags."

"Super technical," Rubald deadpanned. "You put brown paper on the top and bottom of a stack of four to a dozen flattened bags, set your iron on high, and do a couple of passes on either side. It sounds simple, but it took me a year to perfect the technique." The resulting material looked a lot like leather, but lighter, more flexible, and easier to sew.

Her pallet gradually expanded from basic white and tan to the robin's-egg blue of *Rocky Mountain News* newspaper delivery bags to the multihued disposable tablecloths from kids' birthday parties.

Black was an epiphany. "It dawned on me that people were donating stuff to ARC Thrift in those big black plastic trash bags, and ARC was just tossing them in the garbage. I made a deal with them, and now I get six giant boxes of black plastic from them a week."

Sometimes she lays the plastic out in patterns—plaid, say, or random combinations of Safeway logos—or she'll doodle on them and seal the drawings with a layer of clear plastic.

"I play with it," she said. "It's my new medium."

Aesthetics, sure, but there's also another, more socially conscious side to what Rubald is doing.

"I care about the environment," she said. "It breaks my heart to see birds with plastic rings on their necks. But my bent is really about not wasting anything. It gives me hives to throw away a plastic bottle or a can." She holds up a purse. "This is probably sixty bags that didn't have to go to the landfill."

The concept—"Cute with a conscience"—has begun to resonate with fashion and environmentally conscious women, among them former Colorado first lady Jeannie Ritter, who bought two bags from Rubald at a recent charity run at Harvard Gulch.

That sort of jump-started the business. So much so that last Christmas, Rubald was able to hire a part-time marketing assistant and to start jobbing out chunks of the process.

What happens when they stop making plastic bags?

"Fine," said Rubald. "My work will have been done. But right now I'm having scary fun."

Chris Kermiet: "Square dance calling's in my blood"

Looking back on it, it seems inevitable that Chris Kermiet would follow in his father's footsteps and become an old-time square dance caller. But young Chris had his sights set on a different career. He studied music at the Berkeley School in Boston, composition at CU Boulder and, in the '60s and '70s, played drums behind everything from jazz to rock to country.

"I even played in a Greek wedding band," he said. "I'd have played for strippers if anybody'd asked me."

During the '30s and '40s, his father, the late Paul J. Kermiet, was recreational director at the old Steele Community Center up on 39th and King. In search of wholesome activities to offer at the center, he began holding square and folk dance evenings. His timing could not have been better.

"After the war, there was more leisure time," Kermiet explains. "The soldiers were coming back, and they were looking for family-friendly entertainment."

Square dance fit the bill.

By the early '50s, there was an explosion of interest in it that was driven in part by the availability of recorded dance music. Square dance callers who had done it for fun in the country now realized they could make a living at it in the city. They began travelling around with their record collections, and before long, a fad was born.

Kermiet Sr. went on to found a dance camp at a piece of property on Lookout Mountain owned by a group of "ultraliberal do-gooders" who called themselves the "Lighted Lantern." Open to anyone, regardless of race, creed, or color, the camp offered summer square and folk dance getaways that attracted some of the best dance callers in the nation. Launched in 1946, the camps lasted 'til 1978, when the Lighted Lantern finally closed its doors and bequeathed the property to the Quakers.

Chris and his sibs spent every childhood summer working at the camp. "I grew up in square dance world," Kermiet said. "Part of my job was to dance. I can't remember not knowing how to dance: square dance, folk dance, you name it."

Needless to say, a good number of the Kermiet kids went on to careers in dance. Evelyn and Karen became modern dancers and choreographers and performed at Denver's Changing Scene Theatre with Maxine Munt and Al Brooks. Paula, the youngest, was a founding member of the *Colorado Friends of Old Time Music and Dance* and did square dance calling for the group in Boulder.

One night, she telephoned Chris with an urgent plea. "I'm supposed to call a dance tonight, and I can't make it," she said. "Take over for me."

"Traditional old-time square dances," Kermiet explained, "have a set central figure—dive for the oyster, dig for the clam—but the intro, middle, and end can be changed at the whim of the caller. I wrote some cues down on a piece of scratch paper, whatever I could remember from having done it at the camp, and went on over and did it. I've always had caller skills. I didn't need to be taught."

Evidently, they liked him at Friends because they kept inviting him back. He's been calling dance professionally ever since.

Although the square dance craze of the 1950s, with its increasingly complicated patterns and rigid dress code, has pretty much gone the way of the Edsel, the more traditional community dances using live music, and a living, breathing caller are still going strong in practically every major city in America.

"I don't want traditional community dances to go the way that modern square dance went," Kermiet said. "I want to keep it simple, fun, and easy to learn. I also like the vision and idea of community dances. There's a community-building aspect to it. Plus it's fun. I'm having fun facilitating other people having fun. If you've done the same thing long enough, it's hard to stop. I'm invested in it. I don't want to quit. I guess you could say it's in my blood."

Jennifer Dempsey: Salida Circus "all about the joy"

Jennifer Dempsey is founder and director of Colorado's own Salida Circus. For nearly four decades, she's been performing as an acrobat, stilt walker, unicyclist, knife juggler, and trapeze artist under big tops from Belfast to London, New York, and California.

"The gypsy thing is instinctive in me," she said. "My dad had an on-the-road job, so I was born in a suitcase. We lived in twenty-seven states and finally settled in Fairfax, Virginia, when I was eight."

The move was fortuitous. Dempsey got her first taste of circus life as a third grader at Oak View Elementary School in Fairfax. Her PE teacher, a circus aficionado named Jim Moyer, used to keep the gym open after school in order to teach kids the fine points of unicycling, juggling, plate spinning, acrobatics, contortion, stilt walking, and trapeze. They got so good at it that they began receiving invitations to perform all over DC.

"It was uninhibited, raw fun," Dempsey remembers. "Playful, energetic, noncompetitive: just a total joy. I call it the Oak View Feeling, and it's a vital part of why I do circus today."

Dempsey may have wandered away from that feeling as a teen, but it lay just beneath the surface, waiting to reassert itself. In 1989, she was accepted as an exchange student at Queens University in Belfast, Ireland.

One day, on her way to her Irish lit class, she happened to see a notice pinned to a tree outside the Student Union Building. It was an advertisement for circus workshops at a local Catholic church. She tried not to look at it and did her best not to think about it during class.

As part of their course work, Jennifer and her classmates were reading a book called *The Lonely Passion of Judith Hearne*.

"It was about a spinster who failed to do her own thing out of a simple lack of courage," Dempsey said. "Reading that book, I realized I didn't want to be a student. What I really wanted was to join that circus. The Oak View Feelings were just too strong in me. To this day, I thank Judith Hearne for turning me around."

After class, she went to the church and walked into a scene of utter pandemonium. "There were kids everywhere," she said. "Kids on unicycles. Kids on stilts. Balls flying through the air. I thought I'd died and gone to heaven."

Launched in 1984, the Belfast Community Circus was—is—more than just a school for circus wannabes. It's a government-subsidized community-building tool designed to bring Protestant and Catholic youth together on neutral turf. Dempsey signed on as a volunteer tutor and began performing professionally with the troupe as a stilt walker and acrobat. Despite the "Troubles," she stayed on in Ireland for twelve years, becoming the outfit's artistic director in 1993.

In February 2007, Dempsey moved to Salida to be close to her mother.

"I was thirty-eight, and part of me thought I'd outgrown the circus," she said. "But circus people are my family, and I missed them. So I started the circus workshop in Salida. I know wherever there're kids, there'll be interest."

She got that right. Modeled after the program in Belfast, her trainings attract some three hundred kids a year. Her weekly workshop for adults has evolved into a troupe of ten professional performers.

And then there's Circus Over Sixty, a whacked-out bunch of seniors who entertain at nursing homes and senior centers all over central Colorado.

"Circus injects the Oak View Feeling into an audience and brings it out in individuals," Dempsey said. "It's the spirit of pure joy. That's why it attracts so many people. Life is too short not to be joy filled. If I worried about money, I could never have done this. I'm richer now than I ever thought I could be."

Michelle Baldwin bares all

For Michelle Baldwin—stage name Vivienne VaVoom—burlesque is not only an art form. It's a way of life. An author and visual artist, Baldwin had never heard of burlesque before she happened to catch stripper Jane Blevin's routine at Denver's Mercury Café back in 1996.

"It was fabulous," she remembered. "Blevin's character, Evangeline the Oyster Queen, comes out of a full-sized oyster shell after a one-hundred-year slumber. She looks around for a mate, pulls out a basketball-sized pearl, and does a suggestive striptease with the ball. In the end, it explodes into glitter. I was completely floored. It was suggestive without being lewd. It was fantasy, color, costume, and a three-piece band. People were cheering, and she looked like she was having fun. I liked the aesthetic and creativity of it."

Her interest piqued, Baldwin went to the library and checked out what books were available on the subject. She flew to New York to see a full-scale burley-q with an announcer and a baggy pants comedian and came back to Denver pumped.

"I wanna do a burlesque show," she told her artist friends who caught the spirit and jumped in to help with lighting and sets and props like Venus shells and a rocket ship.

For dancers, Baldwin made the rounds of the local gentlemen's clubs. Accustomed to stark naked pole dancing, the women she talked to were unable to grasp what she was aiming for: a nostalgic recreation of the great strip shows of the '30s, '40s, and '50s.

"Unlike pole dancing," she said, "burlesque is not about being lewd or explicit. It's about attitude and personality. It's flirting vs. hardcore sex. You use your costume to reveal just enough skin to play with the audience and stimulate their imagination. The moves are simpler than pole dance or belly dance. So I had to retrain them in a different language of movement."

The troupe mounted its first production in July 1998. The following year, they travelled to Vegas to check out a burlesque act that was part of a retro '60s garage rock extravaganza called "The Las Vegas Grind." Trouble was, the scheduled troupe never got there. Baldwin offered to pinch hit, and she and her gals threw together a show in twenty-four hours.

There was just one little glitch. Baldwin, a shy twenty-six-year-old who up until then had seen herself as the company's artistic director, had never actually danced in one of her own productions. And now here she was, all done up in a mermaid suit, on stage in front of one thousand people who'd paid good money to see her take it off.

"When I lifted my skirt," she said, "the crowd cheered, and I was hooked. Burlesque broke me out of my shell. It changed my path. For years, I'd been a starving artist doing performance art. And then suddenly I had this platform where people were writing articles about me, and I'm giving talks and presentations and actually making a living at it."

In 2004, Speck Press published her book *Burlesque and the New Bump 'n' Grind*.

"It had five or six printings and was well received," she said. "It was popular in Britain and even got translated into Finnish."

Baldwin said her dancers come in all shapes and sizes, "not just perfect tens," which is probably why her performances tend to attract as many women as they do men.

"Women will often come up after a performance and say, 'Thanks for putting a woman up there who looks like me.' I think burlesque helps women to think of themselves differently," she said. "It shows them that they can be sexy and attractive no matter their age, shape, or weight."

Dr. Rick Clarke builds "drones" in his basement

Ever since his retirement in 2001, Rick Clarke has been building giant remote-controlled replicas of World War II aircraft in a tiny workshop in the basement of his Park Hill home.

"I've always enjoyed working with my hands," he said. "When I was eight years old, an elderly babysitter taught me how to do needlepoint." Pretty soon, he was embroidering dish towels and pillowcases all by himself. Not surprisingly, he chose vascular and general surgery as his life's work.

"Doing clinical rotations my last two years of med school," he said, "I noticed that the surgeons all seemed to be having fun, even in a residency program, where you were on call twenty-four hours a day. It was a lot of work but a lot of fun too. It was also immediate gratification because it gave you an opportunity to help people by getting in there and fixing something."

The model-building hobby started with a gift from his kids.

"They gave me a remote-controlled three-foot-long Kris Kraft speedboat," he said. "The time just flew when I was working on it. Six hours would go by before I'd finally look up. I wasn't interested in playing with the models, but I was definitely interested in building them. It occurred to me that if I could build them for other people, I could pay for my hobby."

The problem, he quickly discovered, is that very few people are interested in remote-controlled model boats. A lot of people, on the other hand, are interested in remote-controlled model airplanes.

"It's a billion-dollar industry in components and kits," Clarke said. "Several thousand people attend Warbirds over the Rockies every year."

"Warbirds," in case you haven't heard, is a remote-controlled aircraft competition that takes place outside of Fort Collins in late September. With upwards of seven hundred competitors and a thousand model airplanes, it's one of the largest in the nation, if not the world.

Clarke caught his first model-building break when a brother-in-law in Amarillo asked him to build a Vought F4U Corsair fighter plane. It had a five-foot wingspan, cost $800 in materials, and took a year to build. Taking delivery, his brother-in-law scratched his head and said, "You know, Rick, I'm never gonna fly the doggone thing. See if you can sell it for me, will you?"

Clarke put it in the window at a hobby shop in Amarillo, and it got snapped up by a modeling enthusiast from Dallas. At which point the hobby shop owner said, "Hey, Rick, can you build me a P-51 Mustang?" and Clarke's second career as a modeleer was off the runway and on its way to bombing Tokyo . . . figuratively speaking.

Clarke has constructed some truly monumental replicas such as a 1/5th scale, fourteen-foot wingspan B-24 Liberator Bomber detailed down to the last altimeter and switch.

"It's equipped with pneumatically controlled retractable landing gears and electric-powered 4 3/4 horsepower engines," he said.

He's currently working on a P-38 Lightning that he estimates will take a year and a half to finish. It's an exact replica down to the panels and rivets, which he painstakingly applies, one rivet at a time, using tiny spots of glue.

On average, a model plane will take him two years to complete and cost close to $6,000. That's just for the materials, by the way. Clarke doesn't charge for his time.

"It's a passion," he said. "I do it for friends as a hobby. The challenge for me is to create a model that is so real that when it's in the air you can't tell the difference between it and a real plane."

Interestingly, Clarke almost never goes to see his models fly.

"I'm always nervous on the maiden flights," he said. "They all crash eventually due to pilot error or mechanical failure. Building airplanes allows me to work with my hands, to use my intellect to solve problems, and to be an engineer. It's rewarding to see the finished product and to have created something that didn't exist before."

Max Donaldson: celebrity grave rubber

Max Donaldson has carved out an unusual niche for himself in the world of public speaking. Each year, he and his wife travel to retirement communities all over the country, giving talks about his favorite subject . . . celebrity grave rubbings.

Never heard of it? Most Americans haven't, though it's a popular pastime in Europe. Donaldson stumbled upon it almost by accident in 2001 while visiting an old friend in Kansas City. His friend happened to mention that jazz legend Charlie Bird Parker was buried in a pauper's cemetery in nearby Independence. "Why don't we go find his grave?" he suggested.

What they discovered was a simple stone set flat into the ground. As soon as he saw it, however, Donaldson realized that somebody'd screwed up big time.

"What?" asked his friend.

"Wrong instrument," he replied. "That's a tenor. Bird played alto. Might as well be a tambourine."

Mistake or no, just being there gave him goose bumps. So much so that he wanted to record the experience. Problem was, neither he nor his friend had thought to bring a camera. They did, however, find some pieces of brown craft paper and a black crayon in the trunk of his car. His friend held the paper down while Donaldson performed his first celebrity grave rubbing.

Wouldn't it be neat, he mused as he drove home, *to start a collection of rubbings of famous people?* A visit to his family in California the following year gave him the perfect opportunity.

"Invariably, somebody famous is buried in a local cemetery out there," he said.

He scored rubbings of pianist Liberace (Forest Lawn), producer Cecil B. DeMille (Hollywood Forever Cemetery), and Mel Blanc a.k.a. the Voice of Bugs Bunny (Hollywood Forever). Needless to say, he was hooked.

His hobby has spawned more than a few adventures and at least one noteworthy misadventure.

"I get to places I'd never go to otherwise," he said. "Like Cole Porter's grave in Peru, Indiana, and Hoagie Carmichael's in Bloomington. Bonnie and Clyde bit the dust on a state highway in Northern Louisiana. I stood on the spot where they got it. Never saw their grave, but it was meaningful just to stand there."

The misadventure? That would be the time he got busted at Westwood Memorial Park in LA after jumping the fence in front of Marilyn Monroe's crypt.

"Some security guards came up in a golf cart and escorted me out"—he laughed—"but not before I got the rubbing."

What began as a quirky pastime has since morphed into a second career. When a friend suggested he start talking about his experiences in front of an audience, "a light went off in my head," Donaldson said. "I started giving fifteen-minute presentations at local Rotaries and Kiwanis clubs."

It wasn't long before he was touring the country with his one-man show, "Stories Under the Stones."

As it happens, Donaldson is no stranger to life in the public eye. For much of his professional career, he was a jazz drummer in lounge acts in Vegas and dance bands in LA, where he sat in with Lawrence Welk and once played a month's worth of gigs with Frank Zappa before Frank Zappa was, you know, Frank Zappa!

The musician's life eventually soured. "I didn't want to grow old in night clubs," he said. "I wasn't a drinker or a smoker. After a while, it got to be a pain in the ass just to be there."

He went to work as a mortgage banker for Western Pacific Financial Corp and got transferred to the Denver office in 1973.

Still, show business was in his blood, and he missed it, which explains why the public-speaking gig turned out to be such a turn on.

"I'm having the time of my life," he said. "I'm seventy-six and feel like I'm forty. It's like I got a second wind, back doing what I wanted to recapture, which was being in front of a live audience. It's a huge gratification for me to see people grinning and laughing. I feel like I'm making a difference in their lives one hour at a time. I call it the 'fastest hour in show business.'"

Sandi Wiese: the straight poop on worm farming

Sandi Weise's poop is popular.

By day, she works as a fingerprint examiner and crime scene investigator. By night, she goes underground to hang out with what some might consider the lowliest form of life on earth—namely, the humble earthworm.

Weise has created a profitable sideline for herself raising and selling worms. A sack of wigglers will set you back $25 a pound, which is, as she likes to point out, "more expensive than a good steak." She also sells worm "castings" (poop) for $9 a gallon, which may seem a tad pricey; but then again, a little goes a long way.

"A gallon is equivalent to a typical bag of compost," she said, "not in volume but in nutritional value."

As of this writing, she's sold out 'til midsummer and has a waiting list as long as your hoe of gardeners clambering to buy more.

She got into worm farming pretty much by accident. A lifelong gardener, she bought a farm in Bennett back in 2007 in order to raise horses, hay, and organic vegetables. But the soil out on the eastern plains, she soon discovered, is pretty poor. To turn it into a proper medium for growing organic veggies, she started raising worms. Lots of worms, as in hundreds of thousands of the squirmy little buggers.

Worms are typically raised in "windrows": fifteen-foot-long, three-foot-wide rows of manure, lawn clippings, leaves, food scraps, shredded paper, and coffee grounds, much of which is donated by her rancher neighbors who would rather give it to her than haul it to the dump.

"Best way I know to bond with a group of people," she said, "is to shovel out a pickup load of poop."

She covers her windrows with old carpet and keeps them watered with soaker hoses in summer. In winter, she lets the snow melt down into them, keeping them moist and toasty, just the way the worms, um, dig it.

Given the right conditions, worms can quadruple their number in a season, so it wasn't long before Weise's windrows were kicking out way more worms than she could use. She placed an ad on Craigslist, and her phone started ringing.

"My original thought was that selling worms was what I wanted to do," she said. "But mainly what people wanted was to talk about how to raise their own. So I started holding verma-culture classes on my farm and also at Denver Urban Homesteading. I'm amazed to this day that people will pay to listen to me talk for three hours about worms."

Weise has written a book on the subject called *The Best Place for Garbage: The Essential Guide to Recycling and Composting Worms*. It's doing well, apparently. Amazon.com has designated it the second most popular book in its category.

"It's number 2 in number 2," she quips, "though I hope to be number 1 in number 2 at some point."

Weise is full of surprising tidbits about her favorite little critters. Like the fact that they possess both male and female genitalia. To make babies, they hook up at the clitella—that red band at the forward end of their bodies—exchange sperm and impregnate each other.

Most worms are not native to North America and are thus considered an invasive species, albeit a beneficial one.

"A worm is really a muscle-covered straw," Weise said. "They suck in their food and poop it out the other end full of nutrients and micronutrients."

Which is, of course, why we love them.

Weise said her greatest satisfaction comes from knowing that she's directly responsible for keeping waste out of the landfill.

"I'll save probably five tons of organic waste a year from the landfill and put it to a greater purpose" she said. "Worm poop doesn't stink. It's a pleasant source of income, and it helps me raise the tastiest vegetables this side of I-25."

Suzanna DelVecchio: belly dance not just hootchy-kootchy

If you think belly dance is just a bunch of hootchy-kootchy, think again.

Suzanna DelVecchio, Denver's premier teacher of Middle Eastern dance, says it's not just some decadent strip tease performed for the amusement of *aghas*, *pashas*, and *sultans*.

"Actually it's a traditional folk dance," she said. "It may look seductive to Western eyes, but in the Middle East, where the sexes are separated, it's mainly performed for other women at wedding celebrations. Historically, it may have originated as a birthing ritual."

Her first glimmer of interest came when she read about it in a book called *Getting Clear: Body Work for Women*.

"It was one of those '70s self-help books," she said, "and there was this interview in it with a belly dancer from New York. She talked about the feminine qualities of the dance and how it had empowered her. You know, 'Dance of the Mother Goddess' and all that stuff I was so enamored of back then."

This was in her hometown of Cincinnati, Ohio, where she was working a dead-end job at Proctor and Gamble and searching for something a little more soulful to do with her life.

One day, her sister came home and told her about a Greek restaurant she'd been to that had a traditional bouzouki band called the Kakasis, and a traditional belly dancer who went by the name Basheeba.

"I went there and had dinner," DelVecchio said. "Basheeba was this blonde white girl in a beautiful costume. She had qualities in her performance that appealed to me. She was soulful, elegant, and sensual without being overtly sexual. She was an artist. As a good Catholic girl, that made it okay for me to pursue."

DelVecchio took a few private lessons, enough to whet her appetite. It was around this time that her then-husband got a job in Seattle and, of course, DelVecchio followed him there. Six months later, she ran across an article in the *Seattle Times* about a school called Beledi Centre for Traditional Belly Dancing in downtown Seattle.

"It involved two ferry boat rides and a bus to get there," she said. "But I was very serious about it." So serious, in fact, that for the next three years, she took formal classes at Beledi. "I discovered that dancing improved my mood, maybe because it put me into the present moment, maybe just from the endorphins." In the process, she also discovered her calling.

DelVecchio wound up in Denver (minus the husband), where she found work as a professional belly dancer at local clubs and Greek restaurants. To augment her income, she delivered "belly grams" at birthday parties and other celebrations.

"At first, I resisted the belly gram thing because I thought it was not artistic," she said. "But it was good money and fun trying to embarrass the guys by getting them up to dance."

By the late 1980s, the allure of performance had begun to wear thin. "I enjoyed the dancing part," she said, "but there was too much smoking and drinking."

So she shifted her focus to teaching and also to producing belly dance workout videos in which she combined Middle Eastern dance moves with yoga asanas, stretch cooldowns, and deep relaxation.

"You're doing movements you wouldn't normally do," she said, "undulating, stretching, and elongating your spine. It's also aerobic. I think of it as the Middle Eastern equivalent of Zumba."

Belly dance has been a satisfying career for DelVecchio.

"I've been able to make a living at it for thirty years," she said. "It's allowed me to be my own boss, and it's given me a lot of personal freedom. It's also a way of expressing how I'm feeling in my body in the moment. There's a contentment and exhilaration I get when I dance. When everything comes together, believe me, it can be a peak experience."

Nick Hodgdon: Crime Scene Cleaners mops up after mayhem

Grandma decomposing in the bathtub? Some guy just blew his brains out in your rental unit and the walls need a good scrubbing? Who ya gonna call? Crime Scene Cleaners, that's who.

"We're the only outfit in Denver that does cleanup after suicides, homicides, and accidental deaths," said company founder and CEO Nick Hodgdon. "We go in, rip up the trauma area, and get rid of the biohazards. A cleanup takes on average about an hour, and we'll earn anywhere from $300 to $500 per job."

Hodgdon has come a long way since 2002, when he was living out of his car and travelling around the country, trying to hawk a line of sweaters he'd had made in Nepal. He landed in Denver, fell in love with the place, and began thinking about starting his own business so he could stay here. Brainstorming with his brother in California over the telephone, the bro happened to mention a guy he knew who was doing crime-scene cleanup. His interest piqued; Hodgdon contacted the man and asked if he could shadow him for a week just to see if he could stomach the work.

"The first job we did was this little old lady in Sacramento who'd been decomposing for a week," he said. "The spot where the body had been was outlined in a writhing mass of maggots, and the place really stank. We put on masks, charged in, rolled up the carpet, stuffed it in a bag, and disinfected the subfloor. The whole scene took twenty minutes to clean, and we made three-hundred bucks."

Which was not a bad little profit margin for twenty minutes' work, and the job was—stench and maggots to the contrary notwithstanding—relatively easy.

"Actually, it didn't bother me all that much," he said. "And also— and this may sound cheesy—I realized I could help people. I would actually be doing something that meant something."

He came back to Colorado, bought a truck and some chemicals, and launched Crime Scene Cleaners.

"I've done everything here from torture homicides to chopped-up bodies in bathtubs," he said matter-of-factly. "Shotgun blasts are usually the messiest, especially if they put the gun in the mouth. That usually takes the whole head off."

During the almost ten years he's been at it, Hodgdon has expanded his enterprise into a "one-stop shop" for all things funereal. He now offers a cremation service for funeral homes that don't have their own ovens, and transports dead humans for the city and county on a subcontract basis.

"We do around fifteen pickups a month," he said. "We go to the scene, wait for the coroner, and do whatever they tell us to do."

Yuckiest job?

"One guy had decomposed in a tub for a couple of weeks. By the time we got there, it was a brown soup full of maggots with hair floating on top. We had to wear full body suits that covered us from head to toe. We double bagged it and took it out to Special Waste in Aurora."

Okay, so how does he process all the guts and gore he sees every day on the job? Hodgdon offered this analogy:

"Two guys from the same small town go off to war. One comes back traumatized and can't get a job. The other guy is fine. I'm the other guy. Generally, I don't take it home with me, although I do feel bad about the suicides, permanent solution to a temporary problem. I think the job has really made me appreciate life. I try to live every moment to the fullest. I ski in winter and hike and ride my Harley in the summertime. I don't think you can be around death and not feel that way."

Hey, it's a dirty job, but somebody's gotta do it.

"Flair" helps bartender Mike Guzman beat back cancer

On the day bartender Mike Guzman moved to Denver, he was diagnosed with stage 4 Hodgkin's lymphoma. Actually, he'd been feeling crappy for months; but when he noticed a lump the size of a grape on his neck, he figured it was time to get it checked out.

"The docs did a biopsy and told me I needed to start chemo right away," he said. "There was a lot of 'Why Me?' I mean, here I was, twenty-one years old, healthy, an avid athlete all my life . . . but these are questions you just can't answer."

Cancer or no, Guzman needed a job. He went to work, tending bar at the TGI Friday's in Lone Tree. As they do for all their bartenders, TGI encouraged Guzzie to learn Flair, which is basically juggling and spinning bottles, glasses, and shakers in the process of mixing a drink. For Guzman, it turned out to be just what the doctor ordered.

"Chemotherapy flattens you," he said. "After a treatment, you can barely move. But I was motivated to get out of bed and practice, and the more I practiced, the more I was motivated to get out of bed. It got my mind off the cancer and gave me enough energy to work full-time while I was being treated."

Guzman learned standard mixology at a country club in Tucson while still in his teens. Flair, however, had always interested him.

"There's a whole show about it," he said. "I used to do theatre and music, so I like being in the spotlight and entertaining people. Most bartenders do."

The guys at TGI gave him some practice bottles, showed him some basic moves—the Stall, the Flat Toss, the Multiplex—and sent him outside to "throw stuff around." Practicing four and five hours a day—plus the eight to ten hours he was putting in on the job every night—it wasn't long before Guzzie was juggling bottles, ice scoops, and martini shakers with the best of them, never forgetting, of course, that the object of the exercise "is to make a drink, and that the drink must be well made."

The brainchild of one Jerry "the Professor" Thomas, whose signature concoction, the Blue Blazer, involved pouring a flaming shot of Scotch from one glass to another, Flair bartending was popular in the New York of the 1880s. A hundred years later, TGI Friday's brought it back into prominence by hosting the first ever World Bartending Olympics in Woodland Hills, California. Two years later, the sport received an additional kick in the shorts with the release of *Cocktail*, a 1988 Flair flick starring Tom Cruise.

The Bartending Olympics has since become an annual event, with competitors coming from as far away as Europe, Asia, and South America. It was at the 2010 Regionals that Guzman met his future business partner, Brad Kaplan, an accomplished Flair artist who'd made it into the world championships four times running. The two started talking about setting up a Flair community to promote the sport in Denver. What began as a Facebook group has since evolved into 5280Flair, a catering outfit that sends Flair bartenders to weddings, parties, and charity events.

"We've been in business a year, so far," Guzman said. "We're doing maybe one or two shows a month for majors like IBM and Sony. We also put on two local bartending competitions a year. It's not your same-old-same-old bartending. Plus we get to meet a lot of celebrities like Puff Daddy and Enrique Iglesias."

Guzman's chemotherapy took six months, his radiation treatments another two. It's been three years since the diagnosis, and so far, he's cancer free.

"Flair helped me more than anything else," he said. "It got me out of the house and forced me to exercise. I don't know if it saved my life, but I *will* say it definitely helped."

Window washer Chris White gets a view from the top

Chris White hangs out for a living—Spiderman style. He's the guy you see dangling in a boson's chair off of some of Denver's tallest buildings—the Four Seasons at Fourteenth and Arapahoe, the Pinnacle at Seventeenth and Fillmore, the Ritz-Carlton at Eighteenth and Curtis. His job? Keeping the windows bright and shiny. It goes without saying that he's good at what he does.

Working by himself, White can do the exterior of a twenty-five-story building in four to six days. That amounts to anywhere from twelve-hundred to fifteen-hundred windows in a dozen drops (a *drop* being one descent from roof to sidewalk). Windows on a high-rise get washed twice a year at upwards of $3,200 a pop. An expert window washer can earn $15 to $25 an hour.

Chris White got his start in Phoenix, cleaning shopping centers on the night shift.

"One of our jobs was to clean the sidewalks out front with high-pressure hoses," he said. "The water would splash up on the store windows. The company was subcontracting out the window cleaning to a daytime crew. Trouble was, they were all out there smokin' pot, so the company had to fire 'em."

This proved to be an unexpected boon for young Chris White, who convinced his employers to let him take over the contract.

"After working all night, I'd pull a couple of hours and do the windows myself," he said.

In 1993, White married a Colorado girl and moved to Denver, where he found work with a local outfit called King Kong Building Services. It was at King Kong that he learned to wash windows from a boson's chair suspended from the roof of a high-rise.

"I had the heebie-jeebies in my stomach the first time I climbed over the wall," he admitted. "It was the same feeling you get on a roller coaster. But with time and experience, it became old hat."

Which is not to say that a good window washer will ever allow himself to get blasé when it comes to matters of personal safety.

"You need to come to work with a clear head," White said. "You need to know how to clean a window so that when you're in the air, all you're thinking about is safety. You also have to be aware of the eternal resting place for all of your equipment. If you drop your cell phone, it could bounce off a wall and hit somebody across the street. Another thing you need to know is how to hydrate properly. I'll drink a gallon and a half of water every day on the job. You don't ever want to get to the point where you're hungry, tired, and angry. That right there is a precondition for an accident."

In addition to great views and a primo suntan, there are loads of perks that come with the job. For one thing, it keeps you sleek.

"Air work is aerobic," White said. "You're constantly moving. You're using the chair, your waist, and your outstretched legs to move you from side to side, so your whole body gets toned."

The job also opened up a world of opportunities for the forty-eight-year-old entrepreneur, who now owns his own cleaning establishment: Chris's Home Improvements.

"Window washing was an avenue for me to be self-employed," he said. "It allowed me to be a single parent when my kids were growing up. I could drop them off at school, get in a decent day's work, and pick them up at the end of the school day. If you give it the proper effort it deserves, whatever your craft, you can make a living at it. I've never advertised. Don't have a Web site. I don't even have a phonebook ad. The Spirit of the Universe provides the work. If you give 'em good service for a fair price, the business will come to you."

Eva Hoffman rides the rails

Right up there at the top of Eva Hoffman's list of fun things to do after retirement was riding the train from Denver to Grand Junction and back, which she now does at least three times a summer. She's not just any old passenger, though. Hoffman works the route as a volunteer interpretive guide for Rails and Trails, a program sponsored jointly by Amtrak and the National Park Service.

As the train climbs into the Rockies and chugs along the Colorado River, passengers come to the lounge car to hear Hoffman lecture on the state's history, wildlife, ecology, resources, and recreational opportunities.

"The National Park Service gives us a script," she said, "but we're allowed to deviate and add our own comments, which makes it fun."

After her talk, she wanders the train, answering questions and pointing out scenic highlights. As a perk, Amtrak provides dinner aboard and puts her up at the La Quinta in Grand Junction.

"We're home by six or seven the following evening, so it's two eight-hour days," she said. "Not a significant investment of my time, but the passengers' comments are so positive it makes us feel like we're making a difference. I love knowing they'll want to come back to Colorado and ride the train again."

The job is a natural fit for Hoffman, who used to ride Amtrak between Denver and Salt Lake when she was working for the EPA as a remedial project manager.

"My job was cleaning up hazardous waste sites in Utah and Wyoming," she said. "I knew a lot about railroad history because it was tied to the mining industry, which was what I was trying to clean up. I used to go to the State Historical Societies and look up old photos, maps, and corporate documents to see where the mines were dumping their waste."

Her dad, also a railroad buff, would sometimes accompany her on her trips, waxing encyclopedic about the route to anyone who showed the slightest interest.

"One time I went off to the club car," she remembered, "and when I came back, a crowd was gathered around my dad, who was pointing stuff out to them."

It was he who suggested she write a guidebook for Amtrak passengers.

"I figured there might be a niche market for it," she said. "So in 2003, I wrote *A Guidebook to Amtrak's California Zephyr: Denver to Salt Lake City.*"

Printed out by her husband on his home computer, the spiral bound, 158-page tome has done surprisingly well for a self-published book.

"We put it up for sale at the gift store at Union Station, and it sold one thousand copies the first year," she said. Ten years later, it's still in print, selling a steady five hundred to one thousand copies annually.

The book opened up a world of unforeseen opportunities for the now-retired Eva Hoffman. One day, she got a call from ColoRail, a local advocacy group interested in encouraging ridership on Amtrak in Colorado.

"It's a very diverse bunch," Hoffman said. "Scientists, engineers, attorneys, CPAs, former railroad officials, retired law enforcement, all of whom share a passion that Amtrak succeed. Their goals fit my goals of wanting to make the ride more informative and exciting. Some of them were doing Rails and Trails, and they asked me to join them."

Hoffman said the job is as enriching for her as it is for the passengers. There's a lot of interaction, and frequently, somebody will have new information or a story to share. Like the time they were going past Ike's favorite fishing hole on the Frazier River and a passenger told the tale of a relative who, at the age of ten, had snuck past the secret service and spent the afternoon fishing with the president.

"It's the best park service volunteer job you could get," Hoffman said. "It certainly beats cleaning latrines and mucking out campsites. And we get to ride the train."

Aiko Kimura honors her ancestors through *Taiko* drumming

If you've been to the Cherry Blossom Festival at Sakura Square or the Dragon Boating Festival at Sloan's Lake, you've probably encountered Denver Taiko, a drum ensemble whose roots run deep in traditional Japanese culture.

In ancient times, drumming was used to scare away enemies and, as a kind of audio scarecrow, to rid farmers' fields of pests. It remains an essential component of many Japanese religious ceremonies. But for Aiko Kimura, Taiko is—first and foremost—a way to pay tribute to her ancestors.

"I play Taiko," she said, "to thank them for giving me the opportunity to do what I love."

That Kimura grew up in Denver was literally an accident of history. Due to Executive Order 9066, which authorized the forcible relocation of Japanese-Americans during World War II, her parents were interned at Camp Amache, not far from Lamar in Southeast Colorado. After the war, the family elected to stay, eventually moving to Brighton, where they established Tagawa Greenhouses and raised carnations and roses for a living.

During the mid-'60s, a Japanese Taiko master named Sensei Seiji Tanaka established a drumming group in San Francisco. Soon, similar ensembles began popping up in places like Los Angeles, San Jose, and Denver, Colorado.

"We're the fourth oldest in the country," Kimura said proudly. In fact, it was her Aunt Caroline Tagawa, along with Mark Miyoshi and Joyce Nakata-Kim, who launched Denver Taiko in 1976. They invited Sensei Tanaka to give a workshop at Tri-State Buddhist Church, where he taught them the three basic elements of Taiko: form, attitude, and spirit.

"Taiko has a stance," Kimura explained. "Just like in karate or judo, you have to find your center or point of balance. You stand up straight but with the knees bent, not tilting forward or backward, not leaning to either side." Form—*Kata*—also has to do with musical technique.

"It's how you hold the sticks and how you strike the drum to produce the best sound," she said.

Taiko training is meant to foster attitudes of self-confidence and respect.

"We show respect to the dojo, the place of learning, by bowing as we enter," Kimura said. "We show respect for the drums by taking proper care of them. And we show respect to our fellow drummers by acknowledging the strength of the group overall. If one person hits louder than the others, that's not Taiko energy."

Known as *ki* in Japanese (*qi* in Chinese), Taiko energy was the third element Sensei Tanaka taught the group. Almost impossible to define, *ki* is variously translated as spirit, energy, life force, or inspiration. It's generated when the group is in harmony with one another.

"When I play, there's a lot of adrenaline," Kimura said. "I'm one with the drum and in tune with the others. It feels good to be here playing. I feel more alive. You want the *ki* to flow through your body and connect with the drum and the audience."

Kimura joined Denver Taiko in 1978, prompted by her Aunt Caroline. At thirteen, she was the youngest member of the group. Her aunt died in 1984, but by then, young Aiko was into it. Thirty-four years on, she's still at it, finding time to practice twice a week, despite a demanding schedule of work (she's one of eight owners of Tagawa Greenhouses) and motherhood.

In the intervening years, Denver Taiko has grown into a popular musical group, in demand not only in Denver, but also in Wyoming, Kansas City, Cincinnati, Memphis, South Dakota, and New Mexico. They opened the new airport in Houston and, in August of 2005, played at Hunter S. Thompson's memorial service in Woody Creek.

"Every performance is special," Kimura said. "It's about giving your all right now. Taiko takes a lot of commitment and dedication. It requires a good and proper attitude. Everything comes together when I'm drumming, but my family is still my number one thing."

Steve Lower: real-life *Magic Mike*

The whole male stripper thing started off pretty much as a joke. Steve Lower was a student at UNC at the time, working on an undergraduate degree in kinesiology. He and a weight-lifting buddy named Todd were sitting around the dorm one day, talking about money, the lack thereof, and how to get more of it.

"Hey, wait a minute," said Todd, "we're bodybuilders. Why don't we put an ad in the paper and advertise ourselves as dancers for bachelorette parties?"

"Yeah, right," said Lower.

Despite the skepticism, Todd went ahead and placed the ad. Next day, the phone rang, and lo and behold, they were booked into their first bachelorette party.

"We had no idea what to expect," Lower said. "I'd done bodybuilding competitions in a bikini, but I had no intention of taking my clothes off."

Todd, however, had no such scruples.

"He got down to his G-string," Lower said, "and the girls just went nuts, screaming and yelling and groping and grabbing. Next thing I know, they're all over me, and I'm down to my Skivvies. That was my intro into the business."

Lower was, shall we say, *intrigued* by what he'd witnessed that evening.

"I mean, you go to a party, they feed you, they give you money, they give you back rubs, they give you their phone numbers," he said. "So I'm thinking, *Hey, this isn't so bad. In fact, this is really great!*"

They took the name Hardbodies, posted ads in the Rocky Mountain News, and soon they were doing three shows a week at $200 each per show—which was a lot of walking around money for a couple of college kids in the early 1980s.

Todd eventually quit the business (he's now an investment banker), but as for Lower, he'd found his calling. He hired a coterie of female strippers and sent them out to do bachelor parties. He hired a crew of male dancers and put together a two-hour revue with the requisite cop, fireman, and construction worker.

"We got real big in Colorado Springs," he said, "doing two shows a week down there."

At thirty-four, Lower was at the top of his game, rubbing shoulders with the rich and famous, doing parties, promotions, and golf tournaments for the likes of *Playboy*, Hooters, and the Denver Broncos. Not only was he running the business, he was still taking it off for the brides-to-be at the bachelorette parties. Needless to say, this did not go down well with his first wife, who was jealous and let him know it.

"To this day I have a hard time in relationships because of this business," Lower admits. "A lot of male dancers have this problem. They're constantly being told that they're hot, and so they start to believe it. They get stuck in this fantasy that they're God's gift to women. But really? The girls assume you're a dummy, all brawn and no brains, even if I almost did get a master's degree."

Lower no longer dances, concentrating instead on the nuts and bolts of running a business.

"I play golf, hire the guys, book the parties. I've lived a life from Hardbodies that most guys would die for: beautiful women, celebrities, tons of money. But Hardbodies consumed my life. It changed my attitude toward people. It undermined my marriages, both of them. I have a hard time trusting women. Most guys wouldn't believe their wives-to-be could do what I've seen them do. I've been doing this now for twenty-eight years. Would I want my wife to go to a bachelorette party? Heck no!"

Jen Kaminski: Pole dancing. It's come a long way, baby

If you've ever been to a topless joint and watched a pole dancer, you were probably unaware (okay, you were focused on other things) of how much muscle power it takes to pull off such a routine.

"Tons of upper body strength in your abs and back," said Jen Kaminski, owner of Denver's Tease Studio at 10th and Bannock. "It blows any other sport away. Women train five to seven days a week to get really good at it."

Contrary to popular belief, pole dancing did not originate in the '60s at strip joints like Shotgun Willy's. It's been around for at least two thousand years. In ancient India, it was a guys-only competitive sport. Chinese acrobats incorporated a second pole, leaping from one to the next, twenty feet off the ground. The more erotic moves you see today in the gentlemen's clubs were initially devised by women—for women—in the rituals of ancient matriarchal societies. As for Jen Kaminski, she discovered it in 2001 at a fitness studio in Broomfield called Flash Dance, where pole dancing was a major part of the curriculum.

As a girl, Kaminski studied ballet and was on track to becoming a professional ballerina. But her parents wanted her to go to college first, and so she wound up studying marketing at CU Boulder instead. Still, the world of dance beckoned, and the offerings at Flash Dance looked like a fun way to keep a toe in.

"Actually, I was looking for a way to transition from ballet to some other form of dance," she said. "I thought of the pole as a vertical ballet bar. I took my first pole dance class and absolutely fell in love with it. After that, I was there 24-7."

Her teachers were all former strippers, so naturally, her friends assumed she'd gone over to the dark side. But Kaminski had a plan.

"I always knew I wanted to do something with dance," she said. "It was a dream of mine to open my own studio."

She started small, teaching classes in other people's gyms, travelling from one location to the next with her own portable pole. In August of 2007, she opened a studio on South Pearl Street, offering night classes while working a day gig at Wells Fargo.

"We grew slowly," she said. "One year after we opened, I got my first teaching assistant." In March of this year, Tease Studios moved to a five-thousand-square-foot space at 10th and Bannock. "I now have fourteen instructors," Kaminski said with justifiable pride.

A typical class begins with ten to twenty minutes of standard warm-up exercises, albeit with a flirty twist.

"So instead of a linear, straight up and down push-up," Kaminski explained, "you start with your booty back against your heels, slide your chest along the floor toward your hands, and then push up. You want your movements to be circular, smooth, and sensuous."

From there, students are introduced to pole exercises of increasing difficulty that are meant to develop core strength and agility. Advanced students are able to extend their bodies parallel to the floor using only the strength in their arms and hands to keep them aloft.

Despite the challenges—or maybe because of them—the sport is attracting adventuresome women, some of them well into their sixties.

"The older gals blow me away," Kaminski said. "Their strength is unbelievable. My oldest was seventy-five!"

Kaminski believes pole dancing's biggest advantage is the self-confidence it inspires.

"I see my students gaining in confidence after their first class," she said. "There's a spring in their step and a new way they carry themselves. It's powerful. It gives you this internal boost. For me as a dancer, it's where I can both lose myself and find myself. It's an honor to be able to give women what I've experienced: the confidence, the community, the workout itself, plus the ability to love their workout as opposed to just a boring walk on a treadmill."

"Trolley Tom" Peyton: reviving Denver's tramway past

A couple of times a month during the summers and whenever the Broncos are at home during the fall, "Trolley Tom" Peyton hops aboard the Platte Valley Trolley and drives it from REI to Mile High Stadium and back. During the half-hour round-trip, he makes stops at Confluence Park, the Downtown Aquarium, the Children's Museum, and Mile High Stadium, all the while offering a running commentary on Denver's storied past, the ecology and wildlife of the Platte, and, of course, the history of the trolley itself.

"We have twenty volunteer operators, both male and female," Peyton said. "The youngest is twenty-five. The oldest is around seventy-seven. Some are history buffs. Some are railroad buffs. Some just like to run a piece of railroad equipment. The uniqueness is the big draw. For me, it's helping to keep Denver's tramway history alive."

Once upon a time in the West, Denver was a trolley town. In fact, the trolley influenced how and in which direction the city grew. Neighborhood commercial centers like Old South Gaylord and Old South Pearl, for example, owe their existence to the fact that they were once major trolley hubs. University Park didn't even begin to blossom until trolley service was established connecting DU with downtown, which, by the way, was how the University got its erstwhile nickname, Tramway Tech. A sightseeing excursion on an open-sided Breezer out to Sloan's Lake, Golden, or Elitch's Amusement Park was a popular pastime and a great way to cool off. But all of that went bye-bye in 1950, when the last of the city's trolleys was replaced by the municipal bus system we've come to know as RTD.

It took nearly forty years before a group of concerned citizens got together to form the Denver Tramway Heritage Society, a 501(c)(3) dedicated to preserving the city's trolley car history and, coincidentally, to bringing trolley service back to Denver, albeit in abbreviated form.

"Burlington Northern owned the track outside of REI," Peyton said. "We managed to buy it cheap. We also leased a trolley car from Comaco Trolley Co. out of Ida Grove, Iowa. It was built in the 1920s in Melbourne, Australia. It was unique because it had its own onboard power generator."

It wasn't long before the society had it up and running. Today it's one of Denver's premier tourist attractions.

As for Tom Peyton, he got involved in sort of a roundabout way.

"I was a member of the Rocky Mountain Railroad Club," he said. "The club had an old wooden interurban trolley stored at the Federal Center that they wanted to restore. A group of us went out to look at it. Mechanically, it was okay, but woodwise it was pretty sad. Darrell Arndt, who was head of restoration, kind of hornswoggled us into restoring it."

It was Arndt who suggested that it might be fun to learn to operate the new Platte Valley Trolley. Peyton jumped on the idea.

"We had to learn safety, bell and whistle signals, how to collect tickets, how to drive it, how to get people off and on. But really, it's not all that hard to operate."

Although he insists that "nothing dramatic has ever happened" in the twenty years he's been at the controls, Peyton has played host to the likes of Governor John Hickenlooper, ex-governor Romer, and former mayor Federico Pena. During the Pope's visit for World Youth Day in 1993, Peyton and his cohorts hauled an estimated ten thousand kids to Mile High Stadium and back.

"It's been fun," Peyton says, "and it's given me something to do in my retirement. Plus I get to be involved with a little bit of history. It's also given me an appreciation of the Denver transit scene, and how people are moved. Before, I never really thought much about it."

Luthier Rock Eggen strives to build the perfect violin

What makes a great violin?

"There's no simple answer," said Denver luthier (violin maker) Rock T. Eggen. "What's most notable, of course, is the sound, but all the details are important. I look for the quality of the varnish. The varnish on a Stradivarius, for example, has all kinds of depth, the most beautiful finish you've ever seen on a piece of wood. It glows. Then there's the wood. The best wood comes from the forests north of Milan in the Italian Alps: spruce for the tops, Yugoslavian maple for the backs. The Italian spruce just works better, produces a better-sounding instrument. The thickness of the wood also plays a part—that and how it's sculpted."

He should know. He's been building violins since he was twenty-three years old. A self-taught musician, he built himself a mandolin and a guitar while still in high school in Salt Lake City. A local craftsman named David Gusset got him started making violins.

"He'd won some international awards for his violins," Eggen said. "We became friends and shared a shop in a farmhouse in the middle of Old Salt Lake. I learned a lot of good skills from him."

His work eventually came to the attention of a Florida violin dealer named Harry Duffy. Duffy had made a name for himself selling high-end violins to some of the great players of the postwar era: Nathan Milstein, Yehudi Menuhin, and Isaac Stern, to name a few.

"Duffy flew me out for a week's trial and then hired me to do restoration work for him," Eggen recalled. "I was in my mid-twenties at the time. It was a fantastic place to work because we saw a lot of the great violins—Stradivarii, Guarnerii—the ones that sell for upward of ten million dollars."

In 1980, he moved west, this time settling in Denver to be close to relatives and the Rocky Mountains, and also to avail himself of the region's cool summers and snowy winters. That year, he established his own business, Rock T. Eggen Violins Inc., eventually locating in a refurbished 1880s Victorian house at 5th and Bannock.

Eggen specializes in creating replicas of the old masters. It takes him around two months to build a single instrument. Varnishing it takes another three weeks.

"That's the worst thing about the process," he said. "I don't think I've ever made the perfect varnish." He mixes his own, combining raw linseed oil with pine resin. "The trick is in cooking it. Temperature is critical. If it's cooked too much, it dries too quickly. If it's cooked too little, it will never dry."

He applies five to six coats of varnish, allowing each coat to dry for twenty-four hours in a drying box fitted with ultraviolet tubing. Prices for one of his violins can range anywhere from $12,000 to $20,000.

Can a Stradivarius be successfully replicated using modern methods? Eggen's response is measured.

"My personal feeling is that some of the best modern violins *could* compete in a sound test if the judges were blindfolded. Bottom line, though, there's a certain cachet to owning a Strad. All I'm saying is there are some great makers working today, but in varnish and appearance, they ultimately don't compare."

Why does he persist?

"I have a love for both music and fine woodworking," he said. "And also a love for the design of a violin. It's a balancing act. You're trying to make something that is thin and lightweight but also very strong. And when it's finished, does it have a beautiful tone and is it easy to play? If so, there's nothing quite so satisfying. There's such a rich history of violins, violin makers, and violinists. To be part of that rich history, that's the thrill in it for me. There are violins that were built in 1564 that are still making music today. That's over four hundred years. It's nice to know you can make something that will outlive you."

Pilot Tom Mace: spreading the word across Colorado skies

Look! Up in the sky! It's a bird! It's a plane! It's a marriage proposal!

No! It's veteran pilot Tom Mace circling Coors Field in his Eagle DW-1 biplane, towing a banner that reads "Laura Will You Marry Me?"

"I've got a 100 percent success rate on marriage proposals," he said. "Laura said yes."

Mace owns and operates Colorado's only aerial advertising company, Drag 'n' Fly Banners. For a hefty $400 to $500 per hour with a two-hour minimum (marriage proposals are a flat $495 for five passes), he'll tote your message across the sky, reaching hundreds of thousands of drop-jawed spectators at a time.

"It's cheap advertising, considering how many potential views there are," he argued. "I can get around Bronco Stadium eleven times in an hour. That's one hundred thousand views per pass if you include the highway traffic. Banner towing is a kind of event. Everyone wants to see it. Everyone wants to read it. Everyone remembers it."

In addition to love-struck suitors, his clients include big-time corporate players like GEICO, and political advocacy groups of any and all persuasions. It was Mace who was up there buzzing the State Capitol building with the "Hick, Do Not Take Our Guns" banner during the gun control debates last March. PETA hired him to fly to Albuquerque trailing a picture of Colonel Saunders holding a plucked live chicken during a KFC corporate convention at the Marriott.

"I was hoping KFC would hire me for a rebuttal flight," Mace joked. "I do have editorial rights. I prescreen all messages: no four letter words, gotta be PG 13. I've only had to turn down one message."

Mace took his first solo flight at an age when most of his high school classmates were just learning to drive. A self-described adrenaline junky, he aimed for a career as a commercial pilot.

"But," he said, "life had other plans."

He got married, had kids, pursued a career in business, moved the family to Colorado, got a job as a fire captain with the Monument Fire Department, and dreamed of flying again someday. Sixteen years would pass before he'd get his chance.

By then, the cost to rent and fuel a plane had risen to an astronomical $105 an hour. If he wanted to fly, he realized, he'd have to figure out a way to make money at it. He kicked around the idea of doing some crop dusting but eventually came to the conclusion that aerial advertising was the way to go. He found a plywood-winged, cloth-covered biplane owned by guy up in Montana who was willing to part with it for $29,000.

"It had a three-hundred-horsepower engine and a fifty-five-foot wingspan," Mace said. "It was built in 1982, but it had always been hangared, so it was in pretty good shape."

Getting a 165-foot-long banner off the ground requires plenty of skill and more than a dash of derring-do. The plane doesn't just race down the runway dragging the banner behind it. Instead, a length of rope with a loop at one end is tied to the banner. The looped end is duck taped to the tops of two ten-foot-tall PVC pipes stuck in the ground 350 feet downwind. Mace takes off, circles back around, goes into a power dive, and connects with the loop by means of a grappling hook attached to the rear of the plane. He pulls up into a steep ascent, yanks the banner off the ground, and climbs to two hundred feet before leveling off.

Face it: it's risky as hell, which is maybe why there isn't a whole lot of competition up there.

"It's a fun business," he said. "I'm usually wound up prior to the pickup. But once I'm in the air, I relax. I'm in my own little world."

And seriously? There's no place on earth he'd rather be.

Ed Ward's marriage ceremonies: "part religious ritual, part Broadway play"

For nearly four decades now, Ed Ward has been making a name for himself in Denver's underground community as a graphic artist, playwright, publisher, storyteller, and promoter of arts both literary and plastic.

In the late '70s he and his wife Marcia inaugurated a weekly poetry reading at the Casual Lounge in Englewood that quickly became a mecca not only for local poets, but also for such nationally known literary lights as Larry Lake and Allen Ginsberg.

In the early '90s he was the driving force behind the Alternative Arts Alliance, a venue in which artists of all media were invited to show their work on an unjuried basis.

For ten years, he emceed the Friday night poetry readings at the Mercury Café, providing a stage for literally thousands of local poets. More recently, he founded Stories-Stories, a monthly forum for prose writers and raconteurs, which celebrated its third anniversary at the Merc last April.

Cultural maven? Most definitely. But there's another side to the man that not many people know about. Ed Ward is an ordained minister in a "religion" known as the Temple of Man. He makes his living as a wedding officiant.

"To be a minister in the Temple of Man, you had to be a practicing artist," Ward said. "You also had to be nominated for ordination. I got nominated in 1981. I started writing poetic wedding ceremonies for friends, and then one day, I realized I could turn it into a profession. I took out an ad in *Colorado Bridal Magazine* and my phone started ringing."

Ward's wedding ceremonies are part religious ritual, part artistic happening, and part Broadway musical.

"Most people today want ritual," he said, "but not in a church or a temple with a religious orientation. I think of myself as a shaman. I try to open doors through ritual and connect people to their deceased relatives. I remember one ceremony where I said the name of the groom's deceased mother and the wind came up. And then when I mentioned the bride's grandmother, a pine cone fell off a tree and exploded. Turned out she used to paint pine cones as Christmas tree decorations."

After the ceremony, a Texas oilman came up to him and said, "I'm on the Houston City Council. I want to join your cult. I've been going to church for forty years, and nothing like this ever happened. But today I come to my niece's wedding, and I finally get it."

For a teller of tales like Ed Ward, the job has proven a veritable treasure trove of incidents and anecdotes. He likes to tell about the time in Colorado Springs, for instance, when he was joining a state trooper (the groom) and a cop (the bride) in holy matrimony, and the best man went and handcuffed the two together and pretended to lose the key. Or that time when the groom arrived on horseback, or the processional where Celtic harpists played the theme from *Jaws*, or the nuptials held in a hotel room where the bride's aunt, a coloratura from New York, "sang an aria that made the hair stand up on everybody's heads."

His fondest memory, though, is of his own wedding to Marcia. "Larry Lake was the officiant," he remembered. "He read a poem and then set it alight."

Lake must have done something right that day. Ed and Marcia Ward have been happily married now for thirty-three years.

Mowing lawns: ideal career for entrepreneur Chet Grabowski

Sometimes the guy who mows your lawn is not just the guy who mows your lawn.

Take Chet Grabowski, for example. Before he began mowing lawns for a living, he'd already had a half-dozen careers and an array of businesses, which, in hindsight, he describes as "professionally successful, but financial disasters."

He launched his career on Madison Avenue in the 1960s, writing jingles and musical logos for small-town businesses such as banks and car dealerships. In 1972, he was invited to Colorado Springs to help establish a magazine called the *Music Scene*. Unfortunately, his timing was off. The state's economy was in the toilet, and the magazine failed.

Undaunted, Grabowski started promoting rock concerts in Southern Colorado, which in turn rekindled his interest in jingle writing and music production. Collaborating with Buck Ford (son of Tennessee Ernie), he wrote the lyrics to the Denver Nuggets' first theme song.

In the late '70s, he launched a small venture capital company to promote local wineries. In the '80s, he got a job selling penny stocks.

"That was an up-and-down industry," he said. "It was all run-and-gun stuff . . . highly speculative. I made a lot of money and lost it all on Black Friday, October 27, 1987. That was the day the DOW dropped five hundred points."

After another mini-crash in 1991, Grabowski walked away from his job as a stockbroker. It wasn't only about the money, either. He'd been diagnosed with prostate cancer, and he was feeling depressed and disillusioned. "I was forty-eight years old, and I was tired."

Midlife crisis or no, he still needed cash, and that's when it came to him that he could make a living mowing lawns.

"I made up some flyers, got some lawn mowers, a trimmer, and a trailer, and I was in business," he said. "I became a grunt guy, outside in the Colorado sunshine, getting plenty of exercise, and making enough to pay my bills. Life was good. I was happy. I'd work from mid-March through October to November, and I had the winter to wander."

Which is really what he'd wanted to do all along. Chet Grabowski is an inveterate traveler.

"I have an inbred enthusiasm for wandering," he said. "When I was just thirteen, back in 1956, I told my mom I wanted to go see my aunt in Savanna. She put me on the train in North New Jersey. I got off in Philadelphia and hitchhiked the rest of the way."

So now every winter, he heads off to a different destination— Europe, Mexico, North Africa, Hawaii—and hitches around the countryside with a backpack, tent, and sleeping bag, crashing on the beaches, in youth hostels, and cheap hotels.

"What a long strange trip it's *being*, not been," he said, "'cause I ain't done yet. I still want to go to Asia, Thailand, and New Zealand."

Whether he gets there or not is anybody's guess. At age seventy, Chet Grabowski is philosophical about the future.

"My concept of God is when *she* points her finger at me and says, 'Not so fast, Grabowski.' My knees are giving out, and I would love to have somebody to travel with. But like I tell my kids, 'Attitude counts. Keep a smile on your face. It's all about the level of energy you bring to living.'"

KUVO's Linard "Scotty" Scott showcases black music "from bebop to hip-hop"

It's two o'clock on Sunday afternoon, and KUVO's Linard "Scotty" Scott is at the mic, launching his weekly two-hour musical exploration with a practiced riff most of his fans probably know by heart.

"Origins/Orgy in Rhythm traces the roots and explores the rich heritage of black music," he intones in accents straight out of hometown Spanish Harlem. "It is a soulful journey and joyous celebration that takes us from Harlem to Dar es Salaam, from Trenchtown to Motown, from Ragtime to No Time, from Bebop through Doo-Wop to Hip Hop and other expressions and destinations. In its myriad manifestation, black music—from ancient to the future!"

"I always wanted to do radio," he said. "My early heroes were the fast-talking black DJs on the radio in New York. Ironically, the most influential of the DJs was a white dude named Symphony Sid. A lot of African American kids would gather around the radio, smoke bud, drink wine, and listen to Sid. In the '50s and early '60s, radio was still a communal thing. I try to recreate that feeling on my show."

He must be doing something right. *Origins* has been on the air now for twenty-five years. While KUVO's format is nominally jazz, Scott makes it a point to showcase a much broader selection.

"I think the contributions of Bob Marley are as significant as John Coltrane's," he said. "The first jazz record I ever bought was a forty-five by Ahmad Jamal called *Taboo*, but I was also listening to salsa: Tito Puente, Eddie Palmieri, Mongo Santamaria. My basis is in jazz, but I like it all."

Although he grew up on the mean streets of Spanish Harlem, he entered all-black Howard University when he was just sixteen years old.

"I was there from 1964 to 1967 during the Black Power Movement," he said. "I lasted three years. I was trying to balance drugs, social life, political activism, and academics. It got to be too much. It was always a thorn in my side that I didn't complete college."

His junior year, he dropped out and eventually found his way into drug rehab.

"Once I got into the program, I took it very seriously," he said. "Some kind of way it worked."

He also knew that if he was going to stay clean, he'd have to get as far away as possible from the drug-infested streets of New York City. Which is why in 1976, he jumped on a Greyhound bus and headed west.

"I knew there was something inside of me, some potential I needed to express," he said, "and if I stayed in New York, I wouldn't accomplish anything. I just said, 'Lord, work your wonders.' And he did."

In Denver, he found work at Gilpin Elementary as a teacher's assistant, a job he's held for twenty-five years. Unintended consequence: "I started feeling like a hypocrite urging the kids to get an education when I never completed college myself," he said. So in 2005, he enrolled at Metropolitan State University of Denver and emerged five years later with a bachelor's degree in African American history. He plans to continue his education, earn a teaching certificate, maybe even an advanced degree.

But his first love and greatest passion remains the work he does at Jazz Radio 89.3 FM.

"It's always felt good to be on the air," he said. "I like the responses I get from people and especially the positive comments about the show during the fund-raisers. The biggest thing, though, is the people I've met."

Legends such as Nina Simone, McCoy Tyner, Wayne Shorter, King Sunny Ade, and Hugh Masekela, have all been guests on his show.

"The Creator's always been on my side and in my corner," he said. "The spiel and the knowledge and the passion that I bring, I always had that. But radio gave me a creative outlet. To me, the station and the staff have been a total blessing."

Tara Spencer takes the road to rodeo royalty

No one could have been more astonished than Tara Spencer when, at the tender age of thirteen, she won her first rodeo royalty pageant.

"My folks were out of town," she remembered, "and a girlfriend called me to say she was going to try out for the Johnstown Saddle

Club queen competition. I said, 'I'll try out with you.' It was a total last minute thing, and I ended up winning it."

The daughter of a PRCA rodeo cowboy and a mom who showed horses, Spencer grew up on a small horse farm in Loveland. She'd been riding and showing horses for years, which was a natural advantage in a competition where horsemanship and equine science comprise 40 percent of a contestant's score.

"Rodeo royalty pageants are a different world from beauty contests," she was quick to point out. "We're not objectivized, and the talent portion tests our equestrian abilities."

Her victory at Johnstown focused her attention and gave her a direction in life. "I wanted to be Miss Rodeo America," she said. "I set my sights on that goal."

Sensing that she might have a winner on her hands, Johnstown pageant director Linda Demaree stepped in to offer her services as mentor and guide.

"I was awkward and gangly when I started," said Spencer. "I had big eyes and knock-knees. On the bus, the kids used to call me Daddy Longlegs and Bug Eyes. But between Linda and my mom, they had me all spit shined and polished by the end of that first year."

Demaree made the rounds with Spencer, escorting her to awards ceremonies and luncheons and to every major parade and county rodeo within a 150-mile radius.

"Linda taught me all the social skills," Spencer said. "How to introduce myself, how to behave in a group setting, how to be ladylike and proper."

She could also be tough when the situation called for it. Once at a parade, Spencer got stung by a wasp. "My parents would have coddled me, got me an ice cream or something," she said. "But Linda just said, 'Suck it up.' So I smiled and rode with tears streaming down my cheeks."

She emerged from the experience a full-fledged public figure, a confident public speaker, and a determined competitor ready to take on the world of rodeo royalty. In 2002, she won the Miss Colorado Lady-in-Waiting Contest. In June of 2005, she went to the state pageant for Miss Rodeo Colorado 2006. By then she was a busy sophomore at UNC, studying communication and journalism and, given everything else on her plate, not at all sure she wanted to devote the time to another pageant. But then at the last minute, she went ahead and entered and danged if she didn't win that one too.

"I'd decided to have fun and just be myself," she said. "We were at a party at the Greeley Stampede and I did a cannonball into the pool. I was later told that I won it on personality."

In her last month as Miss Rodeo Colorado, Spencer went to Las Vegas for the National Finals Rodeo, where she competed in the Miss Rodeo America contest. She didn't win, but she finished in the top ten. It was the last year she would be eligible to compete.

"I was devastated when I didn't win," she said. "You get to live this glamorous lifestyle for a year. And then the rug gets pulled out, and suddenly you're history. It's an ordeal. You know it's coming. You're happy for the new girl, but you're also sad that it's not you."

Of her years in rodeo royalty, Spencer said, "It was a journey that shaped who I am today. It was fulfilling and uplifting. It's also humbling to know there are young women out there who want to follow in my footsteps. I can't think of a single downside."

Phil Tedeschi talks to the animals

Professor Phil Tedeschi talks to the animals, and sometimes they talk back.

"People are lazy communicators," he said. "We rely solely on oral communication. Animals, on the other hand, communicate nonverbally. If you want to communicate with an animal, you have to get along with it." In other words, you've got to make friends.

Tedeschi, who founded the Institute for Human-Animal Connection at the DU School of Social Work, has spent his entire career studying how people and animals relate to one another. In his work, he looks at ways in which animals—dogs, cats, and horses mainly—can be used help cure physical, psychological, and social disorders in humans.

"So in cases of trauma or child abuse," he said, "we'll send in a service dog to promote the early release of oxytocin. That's the same hormone that creates bonding and a sense of safety and well-being between a mother and her infant. Petting a dog releases oxytocin into the brain, thereby reestablishing trust and a sense of safety and well-being in the victim."

Tedeschi became interested in human-animal interaction almost by accident. As an undergrad in 1980, he was enrolled in the pre-vet program at the University of Wisconsin, on track to becoming a large animal veterinarian. To make ends meet, he worked part-time teaching horseback riding.

One day, he got a call from the Mendota Psychiatric Institute, asking if he'd be willing to teach a class to a group of adult schizophrenics. Despite the fact that he had no training in human psychology, he agreed.

"They pulled up in a large van," he remembered, "a dozen of them. At first I was surprised and a little shocked. But in teaching them how to ride, I became fascinated because I could see they were making remarkable progress. Chronic behaviors started shifting as soon as they came into contact with the animals. Patients who couldn't talk began to verbalize. Anxious behaviors like rocking in place started slowing down. I was twenty years old and so profoundly moved by what I was seeing that I exited from the vet track and got permission to write my own undergraduate program in human-animal contact."

What grabbed him most was how such contact could influence human motivation for the better.

"I was working with a three-and-a-half-year-old girl who had spinal muscular atrophy, degeneration of the muscles around the spine," he said. "She was unable to lift her head, and she spent her days looking down at the ground. She had to be in physical therapy six days a week, but it was boring and painful, and she was totally unmotivated. I paired her with a horse. With horseback riding, she was getting all the movement she'd have gotten in physical therapy, the only difference being that horseback riding was an enjoyable activity. What motivated her was coming to see her horse."

This and similar experiences led him to ask the question: "Is it possible to design human-animal experiences to help people become more resilient, overcome trauma, and face challenges more effectively?"

By now he'd moved to Denver and was working at the Emily Griffith Center for Children as a therapist and clinical director. He used horsemanship—riding and jumping over barriers—to help gang kids learn effective strategies for overcoming obstacles in real life, a process he calls "the intentional use of metaphor."

"We're just beginning to explore this," he said. "There are around seventy million companion animals in the US, especially in homes with kids. I myself have two dogs, two cats, two horses, some chickens, two therapy rats, a gecko, three kids, and a very understanding wife. I think people need contact with other living beings in order to have maximum health. Without it, we become unhappy and depressed. Pet ownership may be the best health care plan we have."

Steve "Bite-Size" Carter is bigger than he looks

Steven "Bite Size" Carter is four feet two inches tall.

"I weighed eight pounds one ounce at birth," he said, "and I had a normal childhood. But when I turned twelve, I just stopped growing."

After that, school became a living hell.

"The other kids would crack short jokes or pick me up and dump me into a trash can. I grew up in Hutcheson, Kansas, if that tells you anything. I was a smart kid—talented, energetic, fun to be around—but none of that seemed to matter."

Carter fought back, but by the time he turned fifteen, he'd had enough.

"I hated school, hated the other kids, hated myself," he said. "I finally dropped out and had my mother sign papers, legally emancipating me."

That summer, he got a job with a circus as a sideshow freak. To spice up his act, he learned how to walk barefoot on glass, how to lie on a bed of nails with somebody standing on his chest, and how to climb up a ladder of machetes.

"There're all kinds of tricks to it," he said, "and once you're clued in, you can do it without getting hurt."

He stayed with the circus for three seasons, earning five hundred a week plus expenses.

"We'd tour from March to October and hit all the small towns in Kansas, Oklahoma, Texas, Louisiana, and Arkansas. It was an education."

Carter had itchy feet, and he kept moving west, doing showbiz gigs when they were available, working construction when they were not. He spent a summer at the Grand Canyon acting in a gunfight skit for the tourists.

"I played a character named Deputy Marshall Shorty," he said, "and of course, they put me on the biggest horse they could muster."

It was that skit that finally got him to Hollywood, though he didn't go as an actor. A friend on the show told him there was a job as a roofer waiting for him out there if he wanted it. Carter took him up on it and headed for the coast. Then one day at an LA swap meet, he got into a conversation with a guy who suggested he contact the Coralie Jr. Theatrical Agency.

"The dude was covered with tattoos and his stomach was pierced with like, a walrus tusk or something. He said they were looking for little people for the 2000 MTV Music Awards Show."

Carter made the call.

"That was a real turning point in my career," he said. "Coralie Jr. got me a spot on the show as part of a troupe of dwarves dancing behind Blink 182. The next day, everybody in Hollywood was talking about it."

The MTV exposure led to a bit part in the Mike Myers 007 spoof, *Austin Powers 3: Goldmember*. In 2001, he came to Denver to visit friends and stayed. He started getting jobs locally, doing TV commercials for Erlich Toyota and promotions for clubs like Shotgun Willies. These days he lives in Fort Morgan, where he manages the Tribal Tattoo Shop, of which he is a co-owner.

The situation for dwarves has changed considerably since Carter left home to join the circus in the mid-1980s. The reality show *Little People Big World* on TLC has brought increased exposure and greater acceptance. Advocacy groups like Little People of America Inc. now actively discourage dwarves from taking jobs in sideshows.

"They want us to become lawyers and doctors and such," Carter said. "Before I went to Hollywood, I never thought I'd amount to much. But I learned how to turn a liability into an asset and to be proud of who I am. I came away with a lot more self-confidence and better self-esteem. I've actually done something with my life, which is more than I can say for that bunch of knuckleheads back in Hutcheson."

Mario Cabrera gets his dream car

Driving monster machines is a way of life for Mario Cabrera. For twenty-five years, he hauled freight between Denver and Grand Junction as an engineer for the Burlington Northern and Santa Fe Railroad. His ride? A 4,300-horsepower diesel locomotive. So naturally, when he retired in 2010, he started looking around for something else to drive, maybe not as big as a locomotive, but at least something that would command attention and respect.

He found what he was looking for on eBay: a 1949 Mercury Monarch owned by a customizer in Quebec City. The dude had chopped the roof four inches all around, channeled the body, and lowered it to within millimeters of the ground. With its fiberglass fender skirts, its decorative hood scoops, and its black acrylic metal flake paint job, the car was a Bad Boy by any standard and just exactly what Cabrera wanted.

Fortunately, Mrs. Cabrera agreed to it despite the $40,000 price tag.

"I like to think of it as a retirement gift from my wife," Cabrera said with a wink. "I flew my brother-in-law and nephew up there to get it for me. They put it on a U-Haul trailer and drove it back. It took them nine days."

Introduced to the Canadian market by the Ford Motor Company in 1946, the Monarch incorporated design elements from both Ford and Mercury and originally sold for between $1,400 and $1,800.

"That year, 1949, they only made 11,317 of them," Cabrera said. "No telling how many are left."

And while forty grand might sound like a substantial chunk of change, Cabrera is quick to point out that the car has doubled in value in the three years he's owned it. It also turns heads wherever he goes.

"It's a joy to drive it around," he said. "People holler and get all excited. I've actually had girls try to climb in. And I'm constantly getting notes on it at swap meets from people who want to buy it. But I didn't buy it to sell it. I bought it to drive it."

Maybe so, but he also bought it to show it, and so far he's managed to garner three first place trophies and one People's Choice Award in car shows around the region. At least one of those trophies has an interesting story behind it. It seems that Mr. and Mrs. Cabrera were cruising up Bridge Street in Brighton one afternoon when a cop fell in behind them.

"I turned right. He turned right," Cabrera said. "Then he pulled up next to me at a stoplight. I rolled down my window and asked him how come he was following me. He said, 'I just wanted to ask you about your car.' Turns out he was a member of the Rattle Traps Car Club. He turned us on to a car show at Colorado and Louisiana. I entered, and we took first place."

One of Cabrera's favorite Monarch pastimes is to drive the Golden Super Cruise on the first Saturday of the month from May through October. The Super Cruise is a combination parade, rally, and mobile car show in which as many as five thousand low riders, hot rods, and muscle cars from all over the metro area creep along bumper to bumper in a giant loop around Northeast Golden.

"I'm a refugee from the '50s," Cabrera said. "I'm proud to own this car. I get an attitude whenever I drive it."

In addition to pride of ownership, the car offers all sorts of unforeseen fringe benefits for a sixty-five-year-old retired custom car freak.

"I get invited to all kinds of car shows, so it gets me out of the house and around town," he said. "I'm mechanically inclined, and I like messing around with cars, so it gives me something to do with my time. Best of all, though, my wife likes to ride around in it with me and so do the grandkids. We've been married thirty-nine years, and we're still on our honeymoon."

Medical death examiner Kate Makkai
learns the end of every story

After four years as a paramedic and two as an emergency med tech, Kate Makkai figured it was time for a change.

"Being a paramedic is a rough gig," she told me over a bowl of soup at the Mercury Cafe. "It's like being in prison. Paramedics are some of the most mean-spirited, petty, backstabbing bastards you'll ever meet."

Tall and blonde and flashing a loopy grin, she had arrived at the Merc toting a motorcycle helmet under her arm. She rides a Camelot blue Kawasaki Ninja.

Makkai told me that with all the training she'd received as a paramedic, she had considered going back to school to study medicine. But that was before she was accepted for a summer internship at the Denver Coroner's Office.

One function of the coroner's office is to identify the body and locate the next of kin, and it was to this end of the business that Makkai found herself drawn. She had, she said, an inspiring mentor in the person of her supervisor, the aptly named Tracey.

"Tracey is a profound believer in finding the next of kin," she said, "even when everybody else is telling you it's impossible. She instilled that in me. She really pushed me to track down my first case."

And it was that first case—a homeless guy who'd OD-ed in an abandoned building—that got her hooked.

The cops kind of dropped the ball on this one," she said. "Several homeless people had tried to tell them about the body. But they just laughed it off until it started to stink. When they finally investigated, all they found on him was a small backpack with a couple of empty pill bottles in it. No ID card. Nothing."

Makkai was able to identify him via his fingerprints, which matched those on file with the DPD. But knowing who the dead guy is—or was—is one thing. Finding out who his relatives are is another altogether. Makkai began phoning around to area homeless shelters. "Who were his friends?" she wanted to know. "Did he have any kids?"

As it happened, one shelter had a bag in their storage closet containing a duplicate birth certificate with the guy's parents' name and the county where he was born. Makkai managed to locate his second wife, who put her in touch with his sibs, who in turn informed her that their long-lost brother had a couple of grown-up kids out there in the ozone somewhere. It took her three months to put all the pieces together, but in the end, she reunited the family.

"I went home that night feeling like I'd really done something," she said. "It was my first taste of it, and it was addictive. It's become an obsession."

The idea of uniting a family has a certain resonance for Makkai, and it forms part of the complex mosaic that comprises her motivation for doing this job. Her mother was adopted, and as an adult, Mom had hired a private investigator to find her birth parents. He not only found the parents, but also four sibs she never knew she had.

"Now I'm the PI," said Makkai, "and it's gratifying for me to be the one who does that for people."

Makkai said that solving that first case was a turning point for her. For one thing, it led her to realize what she wanted to be when she grew up, and it wasn't a doctor.

"I have a passion for this job," she said. "There's a sense of completion in it that I never got as a paramedic. I was always pestering the emergency room nurses to find out how things turned out. Now I get to know the end of every story. I get to sit through the credits."

The job has also given her a healthy perspective on death.

"I think you live a more complete life when you embrace it," she said. "It's not so frightening when you look it in the eye. Death is final and relentless, but it's not cruel."

Yakov Neyman serves up snappin' dogs and sage advice

Go to the University of Denver's north campus on any given school day, and you're liable to run into Yakov Neyman vending hotdogs from a stainless-steel pushcart. A Belarusian who immigrated to this country with his wife and daughter in 1992, he's been at it ever since the air bag factory where he worked moved to Utah. They gave him a TV set and a $6,000 severance check, but at sixty, he was too old to look for another job. His brother suggested the hot dog business.

"What is hot dog?" Neyman asks as he opens a fresh bun, lays in a buffalo pup, drips on some melted cheese, adds glazed onions and jalapenos, and hands it over to a DU prof who is one of his regulars. "In Russia, I never see. I don't even know what is hot dog."

The severance check went to pay for the cart.

In the six years he's been at DU, he's managed to attract a loyal clientele with a taste for his exotic menu of elk, buffalo, turkey, veggie, beef, pork, and chicken sausage dogs with mozzarella, artichokes, and roasted garlic.

"I have good food," he said. "All natural. No antibiotics. No preservatives. No MSG. No fillers."

Neyman has caught more than a few barbs from fellow émigrés who wonder why someone with his credentials—a PhD in engineering and a string of patents in Russia for his innovative work in the field of plastics technology—would stoop to such a "lowly occupation."

"When you get older," Neyman explains, "you understand that life is short. Money isn't everything. You want to satisfy people. I feel better when people feel good."

Neyman also can't stand to be idle.

"Engineering guys, we're stupid," he said. "We have to be doing something all the time."

Born in the town of Babruysk in 1939, Neyman was a refugee by the time he was eighteen months old. The Germans had invaded, and word spread quickly through the Jewish community that their plan was to wipe out every Jew in Belarus. With Neyman's father away at the front, his mother put little Yakov on her shoulders, took his brother by the hand, and headed for the nearest railhead a week's walk away. They stayed with a family in Siberia for the duration. By the time the war was over, Yakov's father was dead, and the town of Babruysk lay in ruins. Twenty thousand of its Jewish citizens lay buried in mass graves on the outskirts of the city, murdered in batches of thirty by Hitler's minions.

"It was hard time for my mother," Neyman remembers. "It was hard time for everybody. In Russia, they don't have time to build houses for the people. Maybe two families live in one-room apartment. You want to make boom-boom you have to ask everybody to go to kitchen."

There was also the thorny problem of Russian anti-Semitism, which Neyman says persists in that country even to this day.

"With Jewish last name," Neyman said, "they won't hire you. We all know about it, so we don't even try."

In 1980, when it became possible for Jews to expatriate to the US and Israel, Neyman went to see his mother.

"Should we go?" he asked her.

"There's no future for you or your kids in this country," she replied.

She packed her bags and moved to Denver. But Neyman hesitated. He'd finished his education, had married, and was working as an engineer in a chemical manufacturing plant in Leningrad. Twelve years later, he and wife Tatiana followed his mother to the US.

"Life is better here," he said. "There is future for your kids if you're not lazy."

Any words of advice? "Yes," he said, fishing a can of root beer out of his ice chest for a young student who's just rolled up on a skateboard, "don't complain for yourself."

Jim Wagenlander fosters friendship between Mongolia and Colorado

Denver attorney Jim Wagenlander likes to point out the unlikely similarities between Colorado and Mongolia. Take the terrain, for instance. Mongolia has mountains, prairies, and arid deserts. So does Colorado. Both economies are based primarily on mining, agriculture, and tourism. Our mutual governments are struggling to balance economic necessities with the need to protect the environment. And finally, Mongolians and Coloradans share, in Wagenlander's estimation, a way of being in the world.

"A certain personality type develops under a big blue sky," he said. "Mongolians are open, hospitable, competitive, ambitious, independent, and self-reliant. But what I like most about them is their self-deprecating sense of humor."

Wagenlander knows whereof he speaks. He's been involved with the Central Asian republic since 1989. That was the year he began steering his law firm, Wagenlander & Heisterkamp LLC, in the direction of international practice.

"We examined a bunch of countries and finally settled on Mongolia because of its similarities with Colorado," he said.

His timing could not have been better. The country was in the process of sloughing off sixty-five years of Communist rule and instituting a free-market economy. A flood of Mongolians had begun heading west to study at Colorado School of Mines.

"We wanted to expand on that," Wagenlander said. "We started an organization called the Colorado Mongolia Project to provide the Mongolian community here with a formal association to promote economic, political, and cultural ties between our two cultures."

By the year 2000, Denver was playing host to the largest population of Mongolians in the Americas. Today the country has the fastest-growing economy in the world, and the standard of living is booming.

"It's gifted with extraordinary natural resources and a bright, well-educated population," Wagenlander said. "Some of the world's biggest mining players are there now. Rio Tinto, an Australian mining concern, has spent $5 billion in developing what is now the largest copper mine in the world. Mongolia also has the world's largest undeveloped coal field."

Part of Wagenlander's mission has been to encourage local firms to invest in Mongolian development.

"I've taken 160 people to Mongolia over the years," he said. "We bring delegations to Mongolia and the countryside, helping Coloradans to identify with the Mongolian people."

His efforts have not gone unnoticed. In 1999, he was appointed honorary consul by the Mongolian government. By then he was already on a first-name basis with some of the country's major players, including Tsakhiagiin Elbegdorj, who is the country's current president.

"I first met him in 2000," Wagenlander remembered. "He was one of the first leaders to challenge the Communists. He was here in Colorado studying, so one day I called him up and invited him out for a beer and some chicken in City Park. I introduced him to the music of Bob Marley, and he became a fan. He's got connections with Colorado, a special relationship more than anywhere else in the Americas."

In many ways, there could have been no one better suited for the job than Jim Wagenlander. He's always had a passion for international issues, not to mention a yen for travel to exotic destinations instilled in him by a globetrotting father.

"I had five sibs, and he always took us with him," he said. "Dad promised us that he'd take us anywhere we wanted to go after high school. My choice was Russia and Eastern Europe. It was still the Soviet Bloc back then."

Reflecting on his more than twenty-year association with the people of Mongolia, Wagenlander remains in awe of what they've been able to accomplish.

"The strongest experience for me was to see the terrible period they had to endure during the transition from Communism to a free-market economy," he said. "I saw their strength and endurance and their ability to survive. Their economic deprivation during the early '90s was extraordinary. So it's great to see them become so prosperous. This year they surpassed Qatar in terms of GDP. I and my family are so much better off for having been exposed to these people whom we once knew so little about."

Nadia Solsbery and Samuel Henderson: professional balloon benders

If you spend any time at the Cherry Creek or Aurora malls during the Christmas season, you'll probably run across Sam Henderson or Nadia Solsbery frantically twisting balloons. Balloon sculpting is their principal means of support, and they're doing quite well at it. It's not only keeping a roof over their heads, it's putting them through school. Sam's finishing up his certification as a personal trainer. Nadia studies art and business at Metro State.

Sam picked up the craft while doing volunteer work for an organization called Take Action Foundation in Cuernavaca, Mexico.

"We were working at an orphanage and juvenile detention center, putting on a puppet show to teach the kids morals and values," he said. "After the show, we'd twist balloons and hand them out."

As for Nadia, she'd been doing it since she was a kid of nine or ten.

"My parents used to do balloons at parties and volunteer charitable events," she said. "I'd go with them to help out. I discovered I had a knack for it. It's artistic and creative. It makes people smile, and it puts me in touch with kids."

The two met through Take Action Foundation and quickly discovered they had much in common. As children of nondenominational Christian missionaries, both had lived abroad for much of their childhoods (Nadia was born in India, Sam in Peru). Both are fluent in Spanish. Each comes from a gi-normous family (Sam has seven brothers and sisters, Nadia has ten). And then of course, there's the balloon thing.

Turning it into a business was Nadia's idea. She was twisting balloons to raise money for her volunteer work when it dawned on her that she could probably make a living at it. Two years ago, she and Sam started Amazing Balloon Creations.

"We sell it as a free attraction for restaurants such as Sbarro's Pizza and IHOP," Nadia said. "Pretty much anywhere that's family oriented."

In restaurants, they twist for tips. In other venues—carnivals, street fairs, daycare centers, and the like—they charge anywhere from $2 to $5 depending on the intricacy of the piece. They have a basic repertoire of around thirty sculptures—Smurf, Mermaid, Elmo, Spider Man—but they've been doing it for so long they can invent stuff on the spot.

"Our customers like to get a rise out of us by asking for the impossible," Nadia said. "One time at a bachelorette party, we put together a giant wedding cake. Plus hats with babies on them."

On average, the couple works twenty-five hours a week in restaurants and then puts in an additional eight to ten hours on weekends at birthday parties, grand openings, and fund-raisers. Christmas is, of course, sheer lunacy.

"You have to be fast," Nadia said. "One day I did two hundred balloons. I had a line of forty or fifty kids. It was nonstop."

"Your fingers get really sore," Sam added. "I've got tennis elbow."

The couple especially likes working with kids.

"We're not just some grumpy old guy in a clown suit," Nadia said. "We're young and presentable, and we're kid friendly. That's our edge. We remember their names, and if somebody comes up crying 'cause his balloon popped, we'll make him a new one."

"I can't imagine having a nine-to-five job," Sam said. "This is so much better. I can work my own hours. It gives me flexibility and cash."

"I like that I can interact and talk with all different kinds of people," said Nadia. "And it's portable. I literally can go anywhere and make a living at it. Plus it's not just some boring, dead-end job. I look forward to going to work every day. I can't imagine how my life would be without it."

Susan Atkins: learning through sequential monogamy

"My problem was that I could never decide what I wanted to be when I grew up," said Lakewood resident Susan Atkins. "I think it was fear of commitment. If I chose one thing, I'd have to give up everything else. So in college, I took all the General Ed courses and then dropped out when it was time to choose a major."

Atkins traveled, did secretarial work, waitressed, and cleaned houses. Then she met and married John Atkins, and together they established a tree farm and settled down to raise a couple of kids. Home alone for much of the day, Atkins began writing and submitting articles to magazines.

"It was a hard way to make a living," she said, "but a good way to spend your time."

It also gave her the "generalist variety" she craved.

"I was fifty years old before it finally dawned on me that what I really wanted to be when I grew up was a generalist. I had this epiphany: why not indulge my myriad interests one at a time for a specific period and then move on to something else?"

She called her approach "sequential monogamy." Here's how it works.

Twice each year, in January and June, she picks two subjects she'd like to know more about. Usually, but not always, one subject is theoretical, the other practical: astronomy and camping, online gaming and French, computer science and classical music.

Atkins established six ground rules for her new learning enterprise.

Be Sequential: "Sequential means that one project will lead to another," she said. "I won't stay with one thing forever."

She carries a notebook around with her and keeps a list of things she might want to study in the future: Colorado history, the xylophone, dream analysis, Shakespeare, jazz, Egyptology—the list keeps growing.

Be Monogamous: "I make a commitment to stay with a subject for at least six months," she said, "but no longer than a year."

Resolving to stick with it, come hell or high water, helps her get across some of the rough spots.

"Geology was the hardest thing I ever tackled," she said. "I couldn't find a retired geologist who was leading field trips or anything. I really wanted to quit, but I hung in there. The monogamy part is definitely the biggest challenge for me."

Keep It Simple: "I usually go to the children's section of the library to get my books," she said. "I'm also into the *For Dummies* series, and I order educational videos from Netflix. This keeps it easy and fun."

Be Cheap: "I try not to spend a lot of money," she said, "because I know I'll be moving on in six months."

So instead of buying books, she borrows them from the library. And if she needs a piece of equipment such as a telescope or some camping gear, she rents it.

Be Brave: "I'm trying to be like my one-year-old granddaughter," Atkins said. "When she falls down, she just laughs and gets up. I'm learning that it's okay to make mistakes. It's okay to admit to your ignorance. That's the most important thing I've learned in this process. We expect ourselves to be competent in all things, so we shy away from things we're not good at. So these learning adventures prod me to move out of my comfort zone and try things I have no natural ability for . . . such as juggling, for instance."

Celebrate: Atkins gives herself a "graduation party" at the completion of every study. She went to the Tucson Observatory at the end of the astronomy segment, and she and John traveled to Paris in '06 to celebrate the completion of her French lessons (and their twenty-sixth wedding anniversary).

"When I start a new subject, it's like a new love affair," she said. "Everything's fresh and exciting and maybe a little scary. When you start learning something new, suddenly you see it everywhere. It's all in your vision. It's all out there, but you won't see it until you start looking."

Dr. Dongming Fan needles his patients back to health

Dr. Dongming Fan radiates cheerfulness and confidence as he needles his patients, many of whom have given up on more conventional methods of treatment. As a matter of full disclosure, let me state here that I am myself a recipient of Dr. Fan's ministrations. I went to him after being told that I would need total knee replacement, both legs, no question. The pain had become so severe that I needed a cane to walk. After a couple of months of acupuncture and a thrice-daily infusion of bitter Chinese herbs, I'm happy to report that I am walking, climbing stairs, and riding my bicycle with little or no pain. Best of all, I've pitched that wretched cane.

Dr. Fan and his wife, Dr. Junou Cheng, came to the US in 2003 as guests of the Colorado School of Traditional Chinese Medicine where they taught acupuncture and herbal medicine. They've since opened their own clinic in Cherry Creek. Both have brought with them a wealth of knowledge and practical experience unparalleled anywhere else in the United States today.

Dr. Fan is a third-generation practitioner of traditional Chinese medicine (TCM). Born in 1966 in Heilongjiang Province, he learned the craft initially from his grandfather, who began training him when he was just seven years old. He went on to earn a doctorate at Heilongjiang University, where at thirty-two he became the school's youngest professor. He was also invited to join what was known as the "Expert's Clinic," a facility staffed by some of China's most illustrious healers.

"I was seeing forty to fifty patients a day, three days a week, and another hundred on the weekends at my parents' clinic in Mingshui County. I was also writing (he's the author of eleven books), teaching, and doing research," he said. "We treated everything. Heart disease. Cancer. In China, patients can choose either TCM or Western medicine or both. I noticed that the cancer patients following Western protocols were not lasting as long as those we treated with acupuncture and herbs. We saved a lot of lives using very ancient methods."

I asked him how his life has changed since coming to the US. He laughed and quoted an American maxim. "'It's a free country.' Here you can do what you want. In China, to start a business, you need to get eighty or a hundred official stamps. It takes forever. It's so much more efficient here, and I appreciate that."

Any difficulties?

"I'm definitely Chinese," he said. "I miss traditional Chinese culture. I also miss my parents and teachers. They gave me my life and knowledge and taught me how to be a human being. I would love to be there to help them in their old age. Maybe we'll go back to China when we retire."

Dr. Fan's prescriptions for a long and healthy life are simple if not downright grandmotherly: protect your body from extremes of heat and cold, eat your vegetables, get at least eight hours of sleep a night, and try not to worry.

LeeAnna Jonas: spirit realm investigator

It's a question as old as time itself. Where do we go when we die? Is death the end, or is there something more?

Spirit Realm Investigator LeeAnna Jonas suspects there is, and she uses technology—digital recorders, infrared cameras, electromagnetic field detectors, and something called an *Ovilus*, (a device for converting spirit energy into words)—to prove the existence of spirits or ghosts.

Jonas leads what she calls a "Three-girl Paranormal Investigative Team" (her partners are Lolli Hughes and Allyson McNeil) to try and communicate with spirits from the other side who have either been trapped or who have unfinished business and have decided to stay.

"None of us are scientists," she said, "but we try to debunk everything before we acknowledge it as actually paranormal. We look for every possible explanation before we accept it as genuine."

Calling herself "a beacon for this kind of stuff," Jonas saw her first apparition at the age of ten in the basement of a friend's house.

"We were playing with a Ouija board and performing a séance," she said. "We called upon a spirit we had heard about on the news, a babysitter who'd killed a baby and herself. We looked up and saw a misty apparition in a rocking chair, with a baby in one arm and a knife in the other. We all three saw it, and we ran upstairs screaming and told the mother of one of the girls. Ever since, I've known there was another side and that there are unknown questions that need to be answered. I knew immediately that I was different and that I had this capacity."

She's had a number of paranormal experiences since then. One particularly hair-raising event took place at the World War II exhibit aboard the *Queen Mary* in Long Beach, a ship that is widely believed to be haunted. She noticed the knob on a closet door jiggling back and forth and tried to communicate with the spirit behind it. Later, in the elevator on deck 3, she pressed the down button and felt the elevator descending. But when the doors opened, she was still on deck 3.

"This happened something like five times," she said.

Incidents such as these sparked a desire in her to know more about "the other side." She started watching TV shows like *Ghost Hunters* and *Most Haunted* and eventually came across a program called *Paranormal Challenge* in which teams of spirit realm investigators compete to see who can gather the best evidence for the existence of a ghost in a certain location.

In July 2011, she and her team appeared on *Paranormal Challenge* aboard the allegedly haunted USS *Hornet*. Although they didn't win, they were able to detect indentations in the beds of the ship's sick bay as well as changes in the electromagnetic field around them.

In March of 2013, her team appeared on *My Ghost Story*, investigating paranormal activity at the Gilpin County Court House in Central City.

"We caught EVPs (electro voice phenomena) and picked up actual voices on a digital recorder," she said. "To me what this means is that spirits are amongst us at all times. It proves that not everyone crosses into the Light. Our job as spirit realm investigators is to prove to skeptics that spirits do in fact exist. Our team is also there to help them if they ask for it . . . If they want to get unstuck, then we will try to cross them over."

Bill Chapman: Golden treasure hunter

The most valuable item treasure hunter Bill Chapman ever found was a diamond platinum ring worth a cool five grand. It belonged to a young woman who, needless to say, was desperate to get it back. Chapman returned it to her with his compliments.

"There are those in the hobby who say 'finders keepers,'" he said. "I'm not one of them. It's a double reward for me if I can find a lost item and return it. I get a story out of it plus the joy of the hunt without expectation of reward. It just makes me feel good."

Ironically enough, it was finding his own lost ring that launched Chapman's treasure-hunting career. In 1964, he was serving as a junior assistant scoutmaster at a Boy Scout Camporee in Jefferson City, Missouri. When he got home, he realized he'd lost his Eagle Scout ring, probably, he surmised, in a field somewhere back at the camp grounds.

His dad had a friend in the National Guard with access to a clunky old World War II minesweeper. The following weekend, out in the field with the sweeper, his dad asked him where he'd spent most of his time. They went to the spot, drove a stake into the ground, and began sweeping around it in ever-widening circles.

"On the third pass, we found the ring," Chapman said. "But by then we were having so much fun we kept on looking. In addition to the ring, we found coins, a pocket knife, some Boy Scout emblems, and a neckerchief slide."

More important, Chapman had unearthed what was to become a lifelong passion.

"When I got out of the military in 1971, before I even bought bedroom furniture, I bought a metal detector. It was a Heathkit from a magazine ad that I had to build myself. I'd go to the local parks and sweep. I started finding jewelry and old silver coins, usually just enough to go to Radio Shack to buy more batteries."

Eventually, he upgraded to a more sophisticated model with a "discriminator" on it that sorted out the sounds of unwanted target types like nails, bottle caps, and foil. As a general rule, something that's been on the ground 50 years will be buried 3 to 4 inches below the surface; 100 years, 6 to 8 inches; although there are exceptions. Chapman said he's found 150-year-old coins just lying in the grass.

"Whenever they re-sod the parks, that's when you'll see metal guys out there," he said. "We call this Park Hunting. That's how most people get started."

But there's another dimension to the hobby called Relic Hunting that in recent years has been consuming a lot of Chapman's attention. Relic hunters research areas where historic events took place and then sweep them for coins, brass buttons, insignia, weapons, spoons, bullets, pottery, glassware, horseshoes, railroad spikes, and C-ration cans from the old cavalry units. Walking the old Santa Fe Trail, he once found a complete brass bed.

Chapman, who hated history class in school, said he now devours history books in search of locations where relics might be found.

"Sometimes it's a chance to rewrite history," he said. "Metal detectors changed our understanding of what happened at Little Big Horn, for example. The best relic find is one we can associate with a specific individual. I have something I think belonged to Tom Custer, George A. Custer's brother."

The item in question is a love token, a seated Liberty quarter that was given to Tom by Custer's wife Libby, with whom he was reputed to be having an affair.

"When a loved one went away," Chapman said, "a family member would scrape off the back of a coin, inscribe it with their initials, and turn it into a pin. There's an 'L.C.' on the back of Tom Custer's pin. Libby Custer? I can't prove it was Tom Custer's, but it makes for a great story."

Tom Fry: man of a thousand voices

You've probably heard him in commercials for everything from Arby's, to Coors to the Colorado Lottery. Tom Fry is what's known as a "voiceover artist," one of those *basso profundos* you hear every day in radio and TV commercials, movie trailers and documentary films.

But what separates Fry from your run-of-the-mill announcer is that he doesn't just use his own speaking voice in a commercial or video. Instead, he brings into play an arsenal of accents, celebrity impressions and cartoon voices to create characters appropriate to the venue.

Needless to say, he's good at what he does. Very good. He can switch from one British accent to the next—Liverpool, to Cockney, to upper-class—without missing a beat. The voices of good ol' boys, surfer dudes, Latinos, East Indians, Russians and African-Americans roll off his tongue with the greatest of ease. And if the script calls for an old man, or a pirate, or for that matter Ronald Reagan or Yosemite Sam, Fry is on it. Recently, in what has to have been a tour-de-force for a voiceover artist, he played all the male characters on the video game APOX.

Bottom line? The boy can't help it.

"When I hang out around people with accents," he said, "I just find myself imitating them. It's in my blood. My mom was a TV personality and voiceover artist when I was a kid growing up in Detroit. She was the voice you heard when you called Directory Assistance at 555-1212 . . . ' The number is . . . 'The New York Times called her 'the most heard voice in America.'"

Fry may have come by his talent naturally, but he has also honed it through years of study and practice. He majored in telecommunications and theatre at Indiana University in Bloomington, and while still a student there did a morning drive-time show for a radio station in nearby Evansville.

After a stint as an announcer and production guy at a radio station in Maryland, he moved to L.A., where he spent 8 years taking intensive voiceover classes from some of the best in the business—guys like audio book narrator Frank Muller and "Voiceover God" Pat Fraley, best known as the voice of Krang in *Teenage Mutant Ninja Turtles*.

"They taught me the difference between announcing and voiceover acting," Fry said. "Working with these guys, I realized I could do this."

He came to Denver in 2004 and went to work as an on-air personality at 99.5 The Mountain. These days he does a nationally syndicated classic rock show on Westwood One that plays in 150 markets from Hartford, Conn., to Trinidad, Colorado.

His first love, however, remains voiceover acting. So much so that in 2011 he built a recording studio in his den and launched his own home-based audio production business. Voiceovers are now his main source of income. He works at it four to eight hours a day, 50 hours a week.

"I probably do ten auditions a day, through leads that come to me via my website and through networking," he said. "I book between three and 10 jobs a week. I may do five or six takes. Then I edit out breaths, mouth sounds, and mis-pronunciations. A 15 second tag might take a half hour to produce. Nothing leaves my studio unless it's perfect."

It's a busy life, but Fry loves his work and wouldn't have it any other way.

"This is a job I can do 'til I die," he said. "When I'm 90, as long as I can pull up to a mic in my Rascal Scooter, I'll still be doing this job. I never get bored; it's always something different; different energy, different attitude, different characters. I'm a born entertainer and if I can't entertain a crowd on stage or in front of a camera, I can at least entertain myself."

PART 4

Painters, Poets, and a Dog Who Wants to Direct

Charles Parson: "framing an epiphany"

Charles Parson makes his art out of industrial strength materials—I beams, granite slabs, steel cables, and assorted nuts and bolts the size of manhole covers and fire hydrants. In a career that has spanned nearly four decades, he's had fifty-five one-man shows in cities all across the country. His Earth Gate, a six-thousand-pound steel and stone tower, looms three stories above N. Wadsworth Boulevard at the entrance to the Arvada Center for the Arts and Humanities.

Working on such a gargantuan scale has extracted its measure of blood, sweat, and tears and, on one occasion, nearly cost Parson his life. In 1996, he was teaching at Rocky Mountain College of Art and Design (RMCAD) when it was located on East Evans near Monaco. RMCAD had an outdoor sculpture studio perfectly suited for the fourteen-foot-tall structure Parson had it in mind to build. He decided to take advantage of a two-week summer break to work on it.

He was using a moveable A-frame hoist to suspend two steel panels that together weighed in the vicinity of seven hundred pounds. The hoist was positioned on a concrete slab. Somehow it migrated to the edge of the slab, and one wheel slipped over, throwing the whole apparatus out of kilter. The steel panels pivoted ninety degrees, and the hoist toppled over, striking Parson in the head and knocking him out cold.

"I never saw it coming," he said.

He awoke in shock, unable to see out of his left eye, the left side of his face swollen and bleeding. He was pinned under the hoist, and there was no one within hollering distance to help him. Somehow he managed to wriggle out from under it and get back on his feet. He knew he'd have to drag himself out of the building and get across Evans to the RMCAD Offices, where someone could call an ambulance.

Out on the street, dazed and confused, he looked around to try and orient himself and saw the address on the Fine Arts Building.

"Just to the left of it," he said, "I saw—or sensed—a bright white light. It was beckoning me, offering me comfort and safety. A feeling of quiet acceptance came over me, and I wanted nothing more than just to surrender to it. Then I thought, *If I die, I'll miss my wife and kids*, and my whole attitude shifted from acquiescence to belligerence. It was as though I was challenging death to come and get me, and at that point, I knew I would live. I lay down on the sidewalk and felt huge waves of pain and fear.'"

X-rays later revealed that Parson's skull had been crushed around his left eye. He underwent corrective surgery and, three months after the incident, was back at work in his studio. He has not forgotten the encounter with the White Light, which he says continues to influence his life and inform his art.

"I'm much calmer now, a little less career oriented and more inclined to be reflective in my art," he said. "The experience has intensified my desire to know more about life after death. I also find that emptiness has become more important in my work. I see my sculptures as framing emptiness, which may not be tangible, though it is perceptible. It's like trying to frame an epiphany. How do you frame an epiphany?"

Poet Bill Tremblay: "a place without guardrails"

When Colorado poet Bill Tremblay was thirteen years old, he and his parents took a road trip from their home in Southbridge, Massachusetts, to San Francisco, California, to visit his sister and meet her new baby.

"We rode out there in a 1951 Buick four-door sedan," he remembered. "It was black with a ton of chrome on it."

One night, they stopped at a motel in Salina, Kansas; and when they left the next day, the plan was to drive all the way to Wendover, Utah, in one straight shot, twelve hours, dawn to dusk.

"My dad drove an eighteen-wheeler for a living," said Tremblay, "so he was used to going long distances."

They drove through Denver and headed up into the mountains on Route 40, past the buffalo herd, and on into Empire, where they stopped for lunch.

"Just past Empire on the way to Berthoud Pass, there's this huge hairpin turn," said Tremblay. "We rounded it and came upon a small gathering of people looking over a cliff." They pulled over to see what the matter was. "Some of the women were crying, and the men were talking in hushed tones."

Tremblay peered over the edge into the vertiginous abyss. At the base of a sheer three-hundred-foot drop, two cars had landed one on top of the other.

"There was steam still coming out of the radiators," he said. "The one on the bottom was crushed like a sardine can."

They learned that the first car had been carrying six sailors on their way East from California. The driver had apparently fallen asleep at the wheel. In the second car, a station wagon containing a family of four, the driver had been so mesmerized by what had just happened to the car in front of him that he followed it over the cliff, lemming style. Ten people were dead down there.

Shortly thereafter, the highway patrol arrived, trailing ambulances, tow trucks, and a team of mountain climbers who rappeled off the cliff, hooked cables to the cars, and hauled them up with the bodies still inside.

Later, Tremblay sat in the back of the family sedan and listened as his parents tried to make sense of what they'd seen.

"This is a dangerous road," his mother said.

"It's not dangerous if you know what you're doing," countered his father, the professional trucker. "There are rules of the road that you live by, and one of them is that you don't push yourself. If you feel sleepy, pull over."

That was the life lesson he meant to impart to his impressionable son, but young Tremblay came away with a different understanding.

"Colorado is a place without guardrails," he said. "There's still some wildness to it. The positive value of no guardrails is that you have to pay attention. I believe that the quality of life is a direct result of the quality of your perception. When you're forced to pay attention, the quality of your experience goes up. There are so many people walking around out there with dazed expressions on their faces like they're a million miles away. They aren't paying attention. They're not fully alive."

Tremblay dates his decision to become a writer to that horrific experience on the road to Berthoud Pass in 1953.

"I went back home that summer, resolved to become a writer," he said. "Life can go in an instant. Might as well try to tell its stories before the thread is cut."

Twenty years later, Tremblay and his wife Cynthia moved to Fort Collins, where he'd been hired to teach creative writing at CSU.

"We arrived in a sun shower with double rainbows," he said. "We took it as a sign that we'd made the right choice."

Painter Sam Morreale's second act

This one is about my brother Sam, who, at the age of sixty-seven and after a ten-year hiatus, has returned to his first love, abstract expressionist painting. Over the past three months, in very quick succession, he's produced twenty new works.

Three years ago, it was by no means a foregone conclusion that my brother'd be around today to lift a paintbrush. In July of 2007, he was diagnosed with a rare bone marrow condition called myelofibrosis. The disease turns healthy bone marrow to fibrous scar tissue. Before long, the marrow stops producing red blood cells altogether and the patient dies. Astronomer Carl Sagan had it. So did children's author Roald Dhal (*Willy Wonka, The Fantastic Mr. Fox*). It's sometimes referred to as an 'orphan disease' because it affects such a small number of people (about one in 150,000) that Big Pharm is reluctant to "adopt it." There's no financial incentive, you see.

The only viable treatment is a complete bone marrow transplant (BMT), which is an iffy proposition for guys over sixty-five. BMT either works or it doesn't. If it doesn't, you're history. If it does, it'll still only prolong your life by a few years.

"My decision," Sam said, "was that if it's terminal either way, why bother? I'm not afraid to die, and I don't want to spend my final days hooked to a machine. I'd just as soon die at home and skip the aggravation. Worst case scenario, your energy is low and you're tired most of the time. I can live with that."

In June of last year, Sam and his wife Cyndy went to the Mayo Clinic in Rochester, Minnesota, for a definitive diagnosis. The news was not good.

"They offered no hope and no alternatives," Sam said. "They said I'd be dead by Christmas. The irony is that I've always taken good care of myself; watched my diet, took my supplements, avoided sugar and junk food. But after that diagnosis, I went out and bought myself a Coke. I hadn't had one in thirty years, and you know what? It tasted damned good."

By last fall, Sam was getting whole blood transfusions every one to two weeks and platelet infusions every other day. When he wasn't sleeping, he was reading or watching the tube.

"That got old pretty quick," he said. "I was bored and restless, and I started thinking about maybe painting again. I hadn't picked up a brush in ten years. Now I wasn't sure if I *could* pick up a brush. My hands were arthritic. My shoulders were killing me. And I couldn't keep my arms up for long enough to paint in front of an easel."

To compensate for the weakness in his arms, he placed his canvases on a table top and painted looking down. Soon he was spending five or six hours a day at it, taking time off to sleep when he needed to.

"Painting," he said, "brings me into a meditative state where I lose all track of time. It's given me an opportunity to reflect on my life—where I've been, what I've done, what I'd do differently."

What *would* he do differently?

"I'd spend more time painting and less time chasing a buck," he said. "Being this close to death, I've come to see that success isn't just about accumulation. Life is short, just a nanosecond, really."

A couple of months ago, Dr. Mike Bergman of the Rocky Mountain Cancer Center started Sam on Vidaza, an experimental drug designed to make the blood cells work more efficiently, thereby reducing the need for blood transfusions. It seems to be working. It's been three weeks since Sam's last platelet infusion, and last Friday, his numbers were high enough that he was able to forego a blood transfusion. Dr. Bergman is optimistic.

Note: Sam Morreale passed away on December 28, 2011.

Actor Paul the Dog: from wags to riches at the DCTC

There are some interesting parallels between Paul the stray Chihuahua turned actor and Laika the Soviet space dog, whom he portrays in *When Tang Met Laika* this month at the Denver Center Theatre Company. Laika was found on the streets of Moscow and launched into space on November 3, 1957, aboard Sputnik, thus becoming the first earthling ever to orbit the planet.

Paul was found last December at the intersection at twenty-sixth and Decatur-cold, scared, hungry, and limping from an injury to one of his hind legs. He was picked up and brought in to Maxfund, Denver's no-kill animal shelter at 10th and Galapago.

Laika died approximately seven hours into the launch when Sputnik's cooling system failed and the cabin temperature rose to 104 degrees F. The Soviets had no intention of bringing Laika back alive anyway. The plan was to euthanize her with poisoned food at the end of the mission. Her death sparked a worldwide protest over animal experimentation, a reaction with which Maxfund would have sympathized.

"We don't euthanize animals here," said shelter director Tony Willemse. "We never turn away a sick or injured dog or cat. We treat them and keep them safe until they're adopted. That's our mission."

At around the time Paul was brought in, theater director Terry K. Nolan was beginning a search for a dog to play Laika.

"He was looking for a small dog with a calm, attentive demeanor," said Ward Duffy, who plays Soviet cosmonaut Yuri Gagarin in the show. "Jack Russells (terriers) are the right size but way too energetic and feisty. So are Chihuahuas for that matter, but Paul is not your typical Chihuahua. He's very placid. Not at all yappy. He'd sleep eighteen hours a day if he could."

Nolan's search led him to Maxfund, where one look at Paul told him he'd found his star.

The problem was that by then Paul was already spoken for. Patrick Schaetzel, proprietor of the Celtic Tavern in LoDo, had just adopted him. "My girlfriend, Nikole, and I were in the market for a French bulldog. But then I dropped by to discuss a fund-raiser we're doing for Maxfund, and Tony showed me Paul, who immediately snuggled into my second and third chin. I was a goner. Love at first sight. We decided to adopt him."

Tony Willemse worked out a compromise between Schaetzel and the Denver Center in which Paul bunks in with Ward Duffy at

Brooks Towers during the week and goes home to Patrick and Nikole's on Sundays and Mondays. The arrangement seems to be working, although as Schaetzel puts it, "There's still a month of shows left, and every Monday, it gets harder and harder to let him go. He brings a lot of life into the house."

Paul appears on stage in a space costume for a total of twenty minutes every night.

"When the show starts and the costume goes on," Duffy said, "he becomes very focused. He can totally sense my energy. If I'm calm, he's calm. If I'm nervous, he's nervous. Loud noises don't seem to bother him. He's interested in the scene changes and in the other actors."

Paul's a male, Laika was female. Does he have a problem playing a girl?

"Well, he was fixed . . . ," Duffy said, "but no, he's cool with it. He's a character actor, you know, so he likes the challenge of playing a female."

Maxfund is using the occasion to promote adoption, and Paul, never one to rest on his laurels, has become its official celebrity spokes-dog. You'll sometimes find him in the theatre lobby after performances greeting fans and giving out "pawtographs." To date, four additional animals have been adopted due to his newfound notoriety.

Is he a one-hit wonder, or is there a future for Paul in show business? "Absolutely," said Duffy. "He's got the temperament and charisma to go right to the top."

Plans? "Well," Duffy said, "acting's great, but I think he really wants to direct."

Choreographer Garrett Ammon: "dancing the imperfect self"

When choreographer Garret Ammon was named artistic director at Ballet Nouveau Colorado in 2007, he and his wife, Associate Director Dawn Faye, wasted no time in updating the company's approach to both performance and marketing.

Classical music? No way. Ammon sets his dances to rock 'n' roll. He also fosters collaborations with artists from other disciplines— poets from Lighthouse Writer's Workshop, for example, and musicians from local bands such as Paper Bird. As for marketing, he keeps his audiences abreast of upcoming performances via Twitter feeds, Facebook posts, and YouTube videos.

His approach seems to be working. In his first two years as BNC's artistic director, 61 percent of his audiences were first-time attendees at a ballet—no mean feat considering the results of a nationwide study by the National Endowment for the Arts which pegged dance right behind grand opera as the least popular art form in America. By Ammon's second year, the company was seeing a 33 percent jump in ticket sales.

The son of an Arizona crop duster, Ammon grew up in Tucson, where he sang Broadway show tunes in his junior high chorus and studied hip-hop moves on MTV. For his fourteenth birthday, he asked his mom for a year of dance lessons. She enrolled him in a once-a-week jazz class, which—and I quote—"Totally blew my mind."

He went on to study ballet fundamentals with former ballerina Kim Swimmer, who one day said to him, "There's nothing more I can teach you, Garrett." She sent him on to Ballet Etudes in Mesa for more advanced study. There he took ballet lessons five days a week from 3:30 p.m. to 9:00 p.m. and all day on Saturdays.

"It became a complete obsession for me," he said. "It was what I lived for."

After a six-week summer intensive in Richmond, Virginia, Ammon began auditioning for a place in the ballet school of a major company.

"That's how it works," he said. "You find the company you want to work with and try to get into their school. That's the most direct route."

Virtually every school he auditioned for—American Ballet Theatre, New York City Ballet, Pacific Northwest Ballet/Seattle, Pittsburgh Ballet Theatre, and Houston Ballet Academy—wanted him. Ammon chose Houston because, as he said, "Male dancers were in demand there, and they were offering a full ride—scholarship, housing, air tickets, the works."

At seventeen, he became the youngest dancer at Houston. Two years later, he was hired as an apprentice and then as a member of the company's corps de ballet.

But there is, as Ammon was soon to discover, no job security for a young dancer in a big troupe like Houston.

"One day, three young guys showed up who'd been training since the age of five," he remembered. "They were huge and very advanced."

Ammon was sent packing.

"I was devastated," he said, "but in the end, it turned out to be a good move. Large companies like Houston with forty-eight members was not a good fit for me. It's a machine, and you're a cog."

That season, he was hired by Oregon Ballet Theatre in Portland with a cast of fourteen, "which meant that everybody got to be part of the creative process." Added bonus: Trey McIntyre, whom Ammon had known in Houston, became the company's resident choreographer.

"He saw my potential and invited me to learn his work," Ammon said. "I got a lead role in a major new McIntyre ballet, which was a big deal for me. McIntyre opened my eyes to my own potential as a choreographer."

The following year, Ammon joined Ballet Memphis where, on his own initiative, he choreographed a series of short pieces he called *Interior Works*. It wasn't long before he was creating dances for the main stage and getting serious attention in the dance world.

"It was at Memphis that I really began thinking in movement," he said. "Movement became my vocabulary, my medium, my language for expressing what was going on in my head and heart. My dances are about less-than-perfect relationships and being stuck with an imperfect self and learning to be okay with that and in the end to revel in your imperfection and to embrace it. Those are the ideas that are compelling and worth exploring for me."

Sculptor Ira Sherman: going to the places that scare you

Late one summer afternoon in 1979, there was a loud knock at the door of Ira Sherman's storefront, Alva Studios, at the corner of Louisiana and Logan. Named for his boyhood hero, Thomas Alva Edison, Sherman made his living there creating handcrafted jewelry. He'd just closed for the day. But now peering in through the window was this young kid, maybe sixteen or seventeen, wearing a watch cap, a long shirt, and baggy pants.

"He seemed really nervous," Sherman recalled, "deranged even, like he was on drugs or something. I shouted through the window, 'What do you want?' at which point he raised a very large and deadly looking .357 Magnum and shouted back, 'Open the door, motherfucker, or I'll blow your head off!'"

What Sherman describes as a "hum or a buzz" came over him. He unlocked the door, and the kid stepped through and pointed the gun at his head.

"Open the safe," he demanded.

"Maybe it was an accident," Sherman said, "but as I was bent over the safe, the gun went off, and a bullet whizzed past my ear and blew a hole in the floor."

The thief quickly filled his pockets with the safe's contents, grabbed the money from the cash drawer and, on his way out, swept Sherman's keys and some gems off the countertop. Fearing that he might return, Sherman did not sleep at the studio for the next ten days.

He planted a small white flag in the bullet hole ("My flag of surrender") and spent some time reflecting on the life he had come so close to losing. He was twenty-nine years old, and he'd never traveled, never been outside the country.

"I'd seen the movie *Midnight Express*, and I just assumed that the rest of the world was dangerous and the US was safe. But after the robbery, I knew this was a total illusion. How many people do you see getting shot on television every night? It's part of our culture to just shoot your way through a problem."

It was time, he decided, to go travelling.

His journeys over the next several years took him to Europe, Israel, India, Nepal, Thailand, Burma, and Japan. "I felt totally at home wherever I went," he said. "I was never, ever concerned for my safety."

Back in the States, Sherman continued making jewelry, but he also found himself drawn to larger and larger pieces. He went from earrings and bracelets to wearable mechanized art, to public sculpture on an architectural scale. One such piece, a half-ton kinetic, neon and stainless-steel piece called *Strange Machine* hangs from the ceiling at the light-rail station at Louisiana and Pearl, just three blocks from the storefront where he was held up.

"I was born trepidatious," he said. "But after the robbery, I decided the best way to handle my fear was to go to the places that scare me. That's exactly why I started taking on projects that were beyond my technical ability. I learned to break them down into small, manageable segments, and I picked up the skills I needed as I went along. Anything I can imagine I can build."

His work has been shown in exhibitions in Canada, Europe, Israel, and Japan. The Renwick Gallery at the Smithsonian Institution owns a piece of his art. Both *Wired Magazine* and *Popular Mechanics* have featured his work.

"Sometimes I think that without the robbery, none of this would have ever happened," he said with a wry smile. "I'm still trepidatious. But I've learned that it's how you deal with your fear that makes the difference."

Slam Poet Josiah JahLion: "ain't nothin' but a love thing"

No one could have been more surprised than Glenn McKinney (who has renamed himself Josiah JahLion) when the universe saw fit to bestow a poem upon him as he was making his way through City Park one September day in 2005.

"I flunked every class in high school," he said. "I hated English, and I really didn't like poetry. You couldn't get me to sign a birthday card much less write a poem."

Which is not to say that he lacked intellectual curiosity. He read political tracts from the Black Panther Party and the Nation of Islam and anything he could find on Rastafari. He also spent the better part of thirty years travelling the globe, soaking up wisdom, and learning what there was to learn.

"I didn't like school," he said, "but travelling gave me knowledge."

JahLion went home and wrote the poem down. He's been writing "stories that sound like poems and poems that sound like stories" ever since.

"I have no preconceived idea of what I'm going to write," he said. "I just sit down to a blank piece of paper and let it come up."

He writes every day, all day, under any and all conditions: "middle of the night, with kids around, when I'm tired. Doesn't matter. I've never had writer's block. I don't even know what that means. For me, writing's an improv, like jazz. Guys like Coltrane? They never knew what they were gonna play before they played it. I write like that."

His younger brother told him in a phone conversation that he should recite his pieces in front of an audience. Before that, JahLion had never heard of spoken word and knew nothing of performance art.

But it sounded like a good way to get his stuff out there, so he memorized a dozen poems and went to the Mercury Café, where every Sunday at 9:00 p.m. there's a slam poetry session. In May of that year (2009), the Merc was holding a poetry contest with a first prize of $25 cash. JahLion entered and damned if he didn't win it. It was only the second time he'd ever performed a poem in public.

"Now there's some buzz," he said. "I'm getting a lot of positive feedback. I'm gaining confidence. I realize I can do this."

JahLion works hard at polishing his pieces and getting them ready for presentation. Practice, he said, starts the minute he wakes up in the morning. He carries with him the poems he's memorizing and works on his delivery as he goes about his day.

"It takes me three days to a week to memorize a poem," he said. "But to get my feelings into it, it'll take a month or two to where I feel I'm ready to perform it."

So far he's memorized fifty poems and has set himself the challenge of learning a total of one hundred. He performs three or four nights a week at various venues around town, most notably at the Merc. Though his poems are written with a black audience in mind, "twenty- to thirty-year-old white kids seem to be my biggest boosters."

"I'm part of the generation of black men who spoke out," he said. "I never learned restraint of speech or to be politically correct. My poems are raw, and curse words are part of the rhythm and cadence of the pieces. Sometimes I look out at the audience and think they couldn't possibly handle my stuff. Ninety percent of the time I'm wrong."

Writing and performance have given Josiah JahLion a new lease on life. At sixty-two, he says he feels like a twenty-year-old just starting out in life. "I'm surprised at how things have come together. I believe in past lives. I feel like I've done this before. There's magic in my life, and for that I give credit to the Creator."

Painter Bob Ragland: "nonstarving artist"

There's a fine line between "doing it for the money" and getting properly paid for what you do. That's the razor's edge artist Bob Ragland has been walking his entire artistic career.

"'Selling out' is nonsense," he said. "To heat and eat and get your work done, you need to get paid. Real artists don't starve."

A firm believer in Malcolm Gladwell's 10,000-Hour Rule (i.e., that you have to do something a minimum of 10,000 hours to get good at it), Ragland works hard at his craft. In a career that has spanned nearly five decades, he's produced close to four thousand pieces. But he works equally hard at promoting and selling his work, sending out letters to potential buyers and handing out postcards wherever he goes.

"I haven't had a gallery show in years," he said. "I do all my own wheeling and dealing. I've become really adept at raising my own profile."

As a self-described "working class, journeyman artist," Ragland keeps his prices within range of the average consumer. His Shoe Box Paintings, so-called because they're small enough to fit into a shoe box, go for between $50 and $100 apiece.

There have also been, over the years, some really big scores. In 1996, the EPA paid $10,000 for one of his landscapes. Kaiser-Permanente has a Ragland at its Franklin Street location. A painting of his was on display at the White House during the Carter years and now graces a wall at Atlanta's Jimmy Carter Presidential Library. And Denver's Kirkland Museum has thirty of his works in its permanent collection.

Ragland got his first big break in the early 1960s doing paste-up and layout on weekends for a freelance commercial art shop at Eighteenth and Gaylord.

"We did brochures, ads, and menus," he said. "It was all done by hand in those days. I learned a lot from those guys on how to get work done quick and dirty."

The rest of the week, he worked at the post office, painting and drawing in his spare time, and wondering how to make a living at it full-time.

"Art school teaches you how to paint the barn," he said, "but not how to sell the barn. What I needed to learn was the business side of art."

He sought out mentors.

"There weren't a lot of artists of color, at least not locally and very few nationally, who were getting any ink," he said.

He did, however, manage to connect with two prominent black artists who were supporting themselves via their work. One was social realist Charles White, who taught at LA's Otis Institute of Art. The other was *Life Magazine* photographer Gordon Parks, whose portrayals of ghetto life and the civil rights movement brought him to national prominence.

"I met both those guys and sat and talked with them," Ragland said. "They told me I should always have a source of regular income and to perfect my promotional skills."

A teaching job at the Career Education Center at 26th and Eliot provided the former, at least until last year, when the fine arts program there was discontinued. Other than that, Ragland has supported himself almost entirely by marketing his work directly to his audience, often in novel and creative ways. Like the time he threw a buy-one-get-one-free art sale at his house in City Park West.

"Two paintings for $300," he said. "Within three days, I made enough to pay off my mortgage. Dick Kreck, who was the city side reporter at the *Post*, even wrote a piece about it."

Ragland lives a frugal life, averaging around $10,000 a year. Still he wouldn't have it any other way.

"I have a gift," he said. "I try to serve it. There's nothing else I want to do. I've been an artist my whole life. It's an honorable and noble profession."

Painter Dan Ericson: "Signtologist"

Signtologist Dan Ericson paints monochromatic portraits of his favorite rap artists on old traffic signs. His paintings resemble stencils, the kind of sophisticated pictorial graffiti you sometimes catch on concrete walls, though Ericson is quick to point out that he is no graffiti artist and that once a sign is painted, it does not reappear on the street.

"I've had friends go to jail for graffiti," he said.

Like many an artistic epiphany, Ericson's signature use of old signs began as a mistake. He was taking a course in painting at Arapahoe Community College and was working on a series of four portraits.

"I messed up the last canvas," he said. "It was supposed to be a painting of Ice Cube. But the perspective was off, and the lines were all wrong."

The project was due the next day, and it was too late to go out and buy another canvas. Rummaging around in the carport, Ericson found a No Parking sign.

"It was old and faded. I decided to paint on that. I turned it in the next day and got a D on it. It didn't make sense. I mean, three canvases and a No Parking sign?"

He destroyed the three canvases but kept the sign.

"It was kind of cool," he said. "There was something unique about it. I started dabbling with it, painting portraits of the musicians I was listening to at the time."

Pretty soon, friends were dropping by with old signs for him to paint on. He began going to government auctions and cultivating relationships with the various municipalities around Denver to get their scrapped street signs.

"This gave me access to how signs are made," he said. "I started picking up bits of reflective material and adding them back into the paintings."

A major turning point came as he was rendering a portrait of rapper Biggie Smalls on a bullet-riddled stop sign some friends were using for target practice. (Smalls was killed in a drive-by shooting in 1997).

"It showed me that I could use the message of the sign as a commentary on the subject," Ericson said. "That was really the piece where I found my voice."

The *Smalls* painting was picked up by a hip-hop zine called *XXL* and reproduced in its December 2007 issue.

Ericson makes it a point to give away much of his art to the musicians who have inspired him. In fact, his paintings often serve as an oversized backstage pass, getting him past security to talk to the musicians in person.

"It's like completing the circle of inspiration," he said. "They've inspired me, and the paintings inspire them."

Ludacris, Spike Lee, John Legend, Sting, Nelly Furtado, and Cee Lo Green all own works by the Wash Park artist.

The sobriquet Signtologist was a gift from Black Thought, lead singer of the Roots.

"He wrote it on the sleeve of a CD, and I asked him if I could use it," Ericson recalled. "He needed a ride to his hotel, so we made a deal."

Equally intriguing as his art is the manner in which Ericson shows and markets it. Imagine walking into a stark white gallery with nothing but QR codes on the walls. (QR codes, in case you didn't know, are those ubiquitous little black boxes you're seeing on billboards, magazine ads, and Web sites. Encoded in them are all sorts of interesting data: text, URLs and, in Ericson's case, photos of his work. They're read by means of a scanner in your smart phone). Last summer, Ericson mounted a show at the Mac Spa on Wyncoop in which gallery goers were invited to scan wall-mounted QR codes to see the art.

"It was totally digital," enthused Ericson. "An artless art show. No more lugging heavy artwork around. We had it set up so you could click on PayPal, buy it on the spot, and have it sent directly to your home."

An artless art show? Think of it as a sign of the times.

Lori Kanary's Lite Brite panels break Guinness Book records

There's a childlike quality to the work of Denver artist Lori Kanary (pronounced "canary," as in the bird), but it has more to do with the materials she uses than with the images she creates. She makes her art out of Lite Brite.

Lite Brite?

Back when Kanary was just starting to chirp, Lite Brite was a popular kids' toy. It's basically a light box covered with a screen into which translucent plastic pegs are punched to form glow-in-the-dark patterns.

"It was considered high-tech in the early '80s," she said. "You could sit in a dark room, plug it in, and let your imagination go wild."

Fast forward to 1999. The Denver Art Museum has mounted a show of French Impressionist paintings, and the whole city is going bazingas with Impressionist-inspired shows at local galleries and commemorative French specials at area restaurants. Swept up in the madness, Kanary gets the, uh, brite idea of creating a giant replica of Monet's *Impression Sunrise*. Not in paint, mind you, but in Lite Brite.

"I wanted to make the toy bigger than life," she said. "It'd be the first work of its kind in the whole country."

She approached Red Shift Gallery at 22nd and Broadway with her idea, and they jumped in big time, even contributing a five-by-seven aluminum light box to the project. Kanary, for her part, went out and scored an appropriately sized sheet of aluminum with the same hole pattern as the toy. Her initial plan was to project an image of the original onto the screen, but instead, she wound up freehanding it.

"I got so focused that I can't even remember doing it," she said. "I was like a robot. I'd look at the picture and insert the pegs. My fingers were bleeding, but I loved the idea so much I was determined to get it done."

Her efforts did not go unnoticed. The Denver Art Museum mentioned it in their official brochure. They also contacted the *Guinness Book of World Records* who in turn called Kanary.

"I was working at the Auraria Book Store at the time, and it was a total surprise," she said. "But at 62,856 pegs, it was the largest Lite Brite painting in the world."

Now on permanent display at the Hollywood Guinness Museum, the piece is no longer the world's biggest. Her record was shattered in 2007 by artist Mark Beekman, who produced a Lite Brite replica of Leonardo da Vinci's *Last Supper*.

"It was twice as big as mine," Kanary said. "Five by eleven and 120,000 pegs. But by then I'd pretty much had it with Lite Brite."

Well, maybe; maybe not. Because later that year, she was approached by an ad agency wanting to know if she'd do a Lite Brite for their client, Asics Running Shoes. Asics would provide the image, a Lite Brite-inspired running shoe plus an eleven-by-fourteen aluminum frame, which would make this particular Lite Brite hands down the biggest on the planet. Kanary couldn't resist. She rented a studio, hired a half-dozen art students, and flat got after it.

Working day and night with her peg pushin' posse—not to mention Mom and Dad and the ninety-year-old father of her technical assistant—Kanary managed to complete the piece in just under two months.

"I was really stressed," she said. "I may have just been allergic to the epoxy we were using, but I broke out in hives."

Guinness flew to New York in August 2008 for the launch party and actually counted every freakin' one of the 347,004 pegs it had taken to build the piece. Once again, Lori Kanary was the undisputed world champion of Lite Brite humongousness.

She's philosophical about the fact that her record was broken three years later. Performance artist Rob Surette built a 9/11 tribute that was 20 percent bigger and used over a half-million pegs.

"Guinness records are meant to be broken," she said, "no matter what."

Yeah, but would she do it again?

"Maybe for a million dollars," she said. "I dunno. I might try to beat the record. You never know."

Composer Laura Mangus: her music graces *Argo* film score

If you've seen *Argo*, Ben Affleck's film about the rescue of American hostages during the 1979 Iranian Revolution, you might remember the scene in which Affleck's character, CIA operative Tony Mendez, sits alone in his hotel room, contemplating what will be the most dangerous part of the mission. The hostages, masquerading as a film crew scouting locations in Teheran, are to leave the protection of the Canadian Embassy for the first time. Nothing actually happens in the scene, but what gives it its punch is the musical score: a lone female voice singing what sounds like an Islamic chant.

But the language is not Arabic, the content is not Islamic, and the singer is not Iranian. She's Boulder's Laura Mangus, who composed the melody to go with a traditional Aramaic version of the Lord's Prayer.

"Aramaic is a Semitic language close to Hebrew and Arabic," Mangus explained. "It was the language spoken by Jesus of Nazareth. There are still a small number of people who speak it today in Syria."

As if all of that isn't irony enough, there's an additional twist which has to do with the fact that the song cuts off in mid-prayer with the words "thy will be done." One might interpret this to mean that Mendez has come round to the understanding that he must act, even though whether the mission succeeds or fails is entirely out of his hands.

"I have no idea if the placement was deliberate," Mangus said, "but it's still significant."

Although music is her principle spiritual practice, Mangus said she would not describe herself as a professional musician. In fact, other than some stress-inducing violin lessons as a kid, she's had no formal musical training at all. She does see herself, though, as a lifelong spiritual seeker. As a child of seven or eight, she remembers having lucid dreams in which she would encounter "older and wiser beings who'd take me on adventures." She also remembers hearing voices that the adults in her life could neither hear nor explain.

"I was both curious and distressed by these experiences," she said. "Part of me just wanted to be a normal kid. Another part of me wanted to understand."

Her search eventually led her to Boulder's Naropa University, where she took courses in Buddhist philosophy and Christian mysticism. It was at Naropa that she was introduced to the music of Krishna Das, a *kirtan* (devotional) singer in the Hindu tradition.

"Listening to it was like an arrow that bypassed my rational thinking mind and struck my heart directly," she said. "It had the effect of opening up my voice and connecting it to my heart and to the Divine. *Kirtan* definitely opened up the path for me."

It was her Sufi teacher, the Aramaic scholar Neil Douglas-Klotz, who suggested that she set the prayer to music.

"He had a retreat space in Edinburgh," she said. "I was there studying with him. I asked him why no one had ever set it to music, and he said, 'Maybe that's your job.' Over the course of a year, the melody came to me in its present form."

How has her recent cinematic success changed her life?

"No great offers from Hollywood," she joked, "though it has had a definite impact on my family and on the Sufi community. But I think the biggest effect has been on me personally. It's given me an infusion of confidence and strength, and I can see there's a lot more music inside of me. This is something that the world embraces."

Arthur Jones deciphers Negro spirituals' hidden messages

African American spirituals like "Joshua Fit the Battle of Jericho," "Go Down Moses," and "Wade in the Water" are so much a part of the American songbook that we tend to take them for granted. Few of us are aware of their origins, much less the hidden messages contained within them.

"Most people conflate them with Gospel songs, but they're a different genre," said Dr. Arthur Jones, professor of culture and psychology and associate dean at the Women's College of the University of Denver. Jones is also the founder of the Spirituals Project, a nonprofit organization dedicated to preserving the sacred songs of African American slaves.

As a psychologist, Jones specializes in African American mental health issues, but it wasn't until he began studying the Spirituals from a psychotherapeutic point of view that he began to see a connection between music and the psychological well-being of the black community. Black culture, he maintains, is oral culture. Its history, mythology, and values are transmitted through song.

"That was how we passed on our stories, how we passed on the black experience," he said.

The trouble was that African slaves, newly arrived and thrown together without regard to family tie or tribal affiliation, found themselves cut off from their ancestral roots.

"The creative solution," Jones said, "was to borrow ancestors from the Old Testament, all of whom just happened to be freedom fighters."

Moses, who led his people out of bondage in Egypt, is a case in point.

African American spirituals abound with hidden social justice messages. "Swing Lo Sweet Chariot," for example, is an oblique reference to the "Underground Railroad." "Wade in the Water," sung by slaves as a baptismal rite, contains secret instructions for potential runaways to go by water to avoid leaving a trail for the bloodhounds to follow.

Arthur Jones's passion for music first flowered when he won a place on the New York All-City High School Chorus.

"It was very competitive to get in," he said. "There were kids from all 120 of the city's high schools. Singing in that choir was the highlight of my high school life. I lived for the rehearsals on Saturday mornings."

But in college and up to his ears in coursework, Jones was forced to set his passion for music aside.

"I was only the second person in my family to go to university," he said. "It made no sense for me to major in music. So I followed in my older brother's footsteps and got a PhD in clinical psychology."

Jones credits a midlife crisis with rekindling his interest in music.

"I had a yearning to sing again," he said. "I started working with a voice teacher who taught me how to breathe and project and a performance coach to learn music performance."

He auditioned and won a place in the chorus of Opera Colorado, toured with the Colorado Springs Symphony, and, in 1990, was approached by the Denver Museum of Natural History to do a recital in honor of Black History Month.

"Without thinking, I blurted out, 'I'd like it to be about the hidden meanings in Negro spirituals.' Trouble was, I had only surface knowledge of the hidden meanings in Negro spirituals, so I had to dig deeper. This was the first time I did a concert exclusively of Spirituals, and I was overcome with emotion. I was really drawn into it."

So much so that he began a serious study of the spirituals and eventually wrote a book on the subject called *Wade in the Water: The Wisdom of the Spirituals*. It was while writing the book that he came to understand the connection between music and mental health.

"I finally felt centered in my professional life," he said. "I've always been meant to do this, to be at the center of a national movement to preserve and revitalize this important cultural tradition. For me, it's become a spiritual calling."

Paul Briggs: Denver's most famous unknown artist

If his friends have anything to say about it, the late Paul Briggs may someday be remembered as Denver's Most Famous Unknown Artist. In April 2013, they pooled their resources to mount a posthumous exhibition of his work at Denver's Sketch Food and Wine.

An artist of unusual skill and imagination, Briggs was a master draftsman, printmaker, photographer, photo-quilt maker, cartoonist, and digital imagist. Although few outside of his immediate circle had any idea of the scope of his artistic endeavors, Briggs created literally thousands of images over the course of his sixty-four years.

To support himself, he ran lights and managed props for the Colorado Symphony and the Denver Stagehands Union, getting jobs off the bulletin board as they became available. Any suggestion that he try to make a living off his art fell on deaf ears. He wouldn't even discuss it. He wanted nothing to do with gallery owners, artists' representatives, or the commercialization of his work. The whole point, as far as he was concerned, was to make art and have fun doing it. He never sold any of it and, in the end, gave most of it away to his friends.

He had no interest in showing his art publicly, although there were some exceptions. In the early '70s, a photo quilt he pieced together made it into an exhibition of Colorado artists at the Denver Art Museum. On a couple of very rare occasions, a drawing, a print, or a quilt might make its way onto the walls at Pirate Gallery. The only one-man show of his entire career took place in the lobby of the old Changing Scene Theatre in November of 1991. It caused a sensation.

Briggs had a long list of idiosyncratic interests, which naturally found their way into his art. Tattoos, Native American regalia, cowboys, bucking broncos, jackalopes, cacti, motorcycles (of which he owned one badass 1,300 cc Harley Softail that was pimped to the max in turquoise and white) were all grist for his creative imagination. He loved postcards and kept an extensive collection in his living room on a revolving carousel. He was fascinated by UFOs and the possibility of alien abduction. Or more to the point, he liked the *imagery* of UFOs and alien abduction and, as a photographer, made several composites of fake flying saucer sightings.

Possessed of an encyclopedic knowledge of Colorado history, geography, and geology, Briggs was an avid camper and hiker. He could tell you the names of the plants and grasses growing alongside the trail and knew which mushrooms you could eat, which ones could get you high, and which ones would kill you dead.

He kept a pool table in his garage and practiced enough to be able to compete in the taverns and biker bars he liked to hang out in. He spoke passable Portuguese, a language he picked up over several trips to Brazil and from Brazilian friends who stayed at his house whenever they were in town. He had a tin ear and an atrocious singing voice, but he loved music, especially jazz, salsa, and anything Brazilian. He knew—and could play well enough to turn heads—exactly one song on the piano: "Maria," from *West Side Story*.

What survives of his oeuvre are the drawings and prints he gave to his friends, plus somewhere in the neighborhood of five hundred digital images retrieved from his computer after his death. Nobody knows what happened to the quilts.

Painter Gary Michael tries his hand at narrative fiction

Fifty was not a walk in the park for Denver artist Gary Michael. "That was my toughest birthday," he said. "It seemed like, 'Now I'm old.'"

Part of the problem, as he saw it, was that his family had a history of Alzheimer's, and the prospect of losing his wits was anathema to him. To stave off dementia, Michael devised a program of mental and physical conditioning for himself.

"My resolution was to try something different every year," he said. "That included travel. One year I went to the Galapagos and on other years to Croatia, Mexico, and Nepal."

He started climbing mountains to stay in shape and studied Spanish to keep mentally fit. One year, he painted a 120-foot mural of whales on the wall that surrounds his property at 10th and Milwaukee.

"And every year I paint a self-portrait and try to make each one different," he said.

There was, however, one project he'd been putting off for years, and that was to write and publish a novel. Then one afternoon on a hike along the western edge of Fort Collins, he happened to walk by a prairie dog colony and suddenly something clicked inside.

"I'd always liked the book *Watership Down*," he said, "and I started wondering what it would be like to write a book like that, but about prairie dogs instead of rabbits."

He consigned the project to the backburner where it simmered until the day he walked into a bookstore and was struck by the sight of row upon row of novels.

"Some by people smarter than me, others by those not as smart as me. So I asked myself, *Why not me?* I didn't want to go to my grave without at least having tried it. So I went home, sat down, and started writing."

The story he devised has to do with a prairie dog colony threatened by human development. Ten of its denizens go in search of a new place to burrow. Along the way, they cross a river on a raft with the aid of a helpful beaver, fend off an attack by a vicious badger, and learn to trust one another in pursuit of a common goal. Ultimately, they arrive at their destination, an idyllic meadow where they establish a new colony.

"I learned a lot about prairie dogs," Michael said, "like that their language actually has a grammar. They can distinguish between a man *with* a gun and a man without one. They also have the most complex underground habitat in the animal kingdom, with air conditioning and rooms for different purposes."

It took him two years to complete the manuscript, at times working with a professional editor who encouraged him to seek out a publisher. But as anyone who's ever tried it can tell you—writing a novel is one thing; getting it published is another altogether.

"I started sending out proposals to publishers and got nowhere," Michael said. "They all told me, 'We're not talking to new authors.'"

In the end, he made the decision to self-publish. He hired a book designer, did the cover art and interior illustrations himself, and had a dozen copies printed through Snowfall Press out of Monument, Colorado.

He started small, consigning just three copies to the Tattered Cover. After they'd sold a dozen, he approached them about doing a public reading. They ordered another fifty copies and sold forty-nine of them at the event. He put it out as an eBook on Amazon and Nook for $6.99 and so far has sold close to one hundred copies.

"If I were younger, I might have gone the traditional route," he said. "But I'm not a patient man. I didn't want to have to live with the regret that I didn't even try. I learned that I could do it, and others are taking delight in something I created. Even if I don't sell another copy, it will have been worth the effort."

Cartoonist Ed Stein on life after the *Rocky*

At the height of his career, cartoonist Ed Stein's work was featured on the editorial pages of 450 newspapers nationwide and occasionally graced the pages of the *NY Times*, the *Washington Post*, *Time*, *Newsweek*, and *Playboy Magazine*. He was the editorial cartoonist for the *Rocky Mountain News* from 1978 to the fall of 2009, when the much-loved daily bit the dust.

"The collapse of the *Rocky* was devastating in a number of ways," Stein said. "When you lose that audience, it's not the same. I always depended on the sense of having a conversation with my readership. The cartoons continued to be syndicated, but now there was no sense of feedback. My editorial cartoons lost their vibrancy."

At the time, Stein was also drawing a comic strip for the *Rocky* called "Denver Square." With an entirely local focus, the strip featured wry comments on life in the Mile High City. After the paper's demise, he took the basic format and characters from "Denver Square" and gave them a national focus. Rechristened "Freshly Squeezed," it's now a family-oriented strip with a dad, mom, kid, and two grandparents who have lost their retirement savings and are forced to move in with their children.

"The humor," Stein said, "is derived from a family squeezed in together in a house that's too small."

Ed Stein has been drawing since he was a kid in third grade.

"It was a revelation to me that I could do something the other kids couldn't," he said. "I started drawing compulsively and looking at cartoons in magazines, trying to figure them out. I fell in love with writing something funny and illustrating it. It was the fusion of humor and art that appealed to me."

Figuring he'd probably have a hard time making a living as a cartoonist, he went for a major in graphic design at DU.

"But then the '60s happened" he said. "Some friends of mine started an underground newspaper on campus called the *Student Free Press*. I did a cartoon for the first issue. It was about Chancellor Mitchell. He'd kicked some students out for participating in a sit-in on campus despite promises he'd made to work with the student council on disciplinary matters. The cartoon showed him making promises with his fingers crossed behind his back."

Stein walked into the Student Union on the day the paper came out and found everybody talking about his cartoon.

"That's when I realized I could be a bad boy and get rewarded for it, which is basically what editorial cartooning is," he said, "making fun of people in authority and getting rewarded for it. People take you seriously. It's bizarre."

After graduation, he spent nine years copyediting, doing paste-up, and drawing cartoons on a freelance basis for anybody who'd publish him—*Cervis Journal*, the *Lafayette Leader*, *Straight Creek Journal*, and the *Broomfield Star*—all the while looking for that elusive job as a full-time political cartoonist.

"I kept talking to the *Rocky*," he said. "I must have walked in there a dozen times. They started publishing me on a freelance basis."

The paper finally hired him full-time in 1978, and he stayed with them 'til they closed.

It's not surprising that Stein is pessimistic about the future of newspapers in this country.

"We're seeing increasing layoffs on newspapers across the US," he said. "I think democracy depends on a vigorous newspaper press; not bloggers, not TV news, not cable. Newspapers are the only thing with the power and authority to hold our political and economic leaders accountable. Some of what we see going on in politics now is a direct result of the decline of newspapers. I don't know what's going to replace them or even if they *can* be replaced. Who's left to call the politicians bluff? Where are the truth tellers?"

Dan Johnson: one-man band for the digital age

Musician Dan Johnson is not the kind of one-man band you think of when you think of a one-man band—the rumpled old guy on a street corner with a bass drum on his back, a banjo at his belly, and a complicated array of horns, whistles, and harmonicas around his neck. Thanks to a computer program called MIDI (Musical Instrument Digital Interface), Johnson can sound like anything from a country and Western band to a symphony orchestra. He provides the guitar work and sings in a voice that sounds a little like Willie Nelson, though ask him and he'll tell you it's the other way around.

Here in Denver, Johnson has managed to carve out a niche for himself playing gigs at nursing homes, senior centers, and rehab facilities.

"The old folks appreciate you comin' in," he said. "I call what I play twentieth-century music: rock songs, pop tunes such as "Jeepers Creepers" and "Johnny Be Good," a lot of Perry Como, Frank Sinatra, and Chuck Berry. I try to give a history of the song, or I'll ask, 'Where were you in '52?' and then play a tune from that era."

He averages four to eight jobs a week and last year played over 240 gigs.

He's been at it since he was a kid. At age twelve, living in Southern France where his dad was stationed in the military, young Dan heard an English rock band playing "Chain Gang."

"It hit me that I should be a guitar player," he said. "My dad bought me a Sears-Roebuck electric guitar. I hung out with the GIs down at the servicemen's club and learned a lot of different styles."

In 1966, he joined a Denver rock band called the Wild Ones.

"We opened for Herman's Hermits, Charley Rich, and the Dave Clark Five," he said. "We almost got the gig opening for the Stones, but we were out of town that night."

A tour of duty in Vietnam interrupted his budding career as a rock 'n' roll musician, and when he came back, he went to work for the postal service. But his love for music remained undimmed, and he continued to play guitar and sing in rock, country, jazz, and night-club-style pop bands all around the state. In the mid-'90s, he was sent to Gunnison to supervise the local post office, and it was there that he learned the MIDI system.

"I built a rig in the back of my pickup with amps, microphones, and speakers," he said. "It was like a mobile stage. I'd go out to the campgrounds and offer to play for the tourists for free. I came home that first night with a whopping six bucks in tips."

Not a particularly promising start, but by Labor Day, he'd played ninety gigs at the campgrounds and earned enough in tips to pay for his gas, a new stove for his wife, and a year of college for his son.

"I was having the time of my life," he said. "I got better at arranging and playing. Plus it was something to look forward to. I did it after work and met lots of folks in their RVs."

It also saved him from going postal working eleven-hour days at the Gunnison Post Office. In 2005, he retired and moved back to Denver.

If it wasn't for music, I think my mental health would have suffered," he said, looking back on nearly fifty years as a professional musician. "Music takes you away from reality. You can go to places in your head in a song you can't go otherwise. I'm always learning new material. You can never learn enough."

Quilting pieces together Michael Gold's life, memories

Michael Gold is a Renaissance man: an interior designer, a visual artist, an educator, and a singer/dancer/actor with a Broadway credit to his name. He's also a world-class quilter.

Quilter? You're thinking "Grandma," right?

But real men can—and do—quilt. In fact, there's a whole show of quilts by men on display right now at the Rocky Mountain Quilt Museum in Golden; and if you haven't seen it, it's worth a visit. A piece by Michael Gold called *In My Father's Ties* is prominently featured.

Gold had already been machine sewing theater costumes for ten years by the time he was introduced to quilt making in 1987. He went to a hand-piecing and quilting class at a place called *Quilts in the Attic* on Old South Gaylord.

"I was the only guy in the class," he remembered. "The teacher was one of my mom's best friends. She taught us this pattern called

Grandmother's Star. I fell in love with it. I made a quilt out of all the scraps from ten years of sewing: my nephew's Halloween costume, curtains from my college dorm room, fabric from costumes I made at the Country Dinner Playhouse. To this day, I can tell you where all the scraps came from."

Gold soon realized that quilt making could serve as a medium for storytelling. *In My Father's Ties* is a case in point.

"When my dad died in 1993, I inherited his ties," Gold said. "He had over sixty ties, a lot of them from the '70s and '80s. They were big, wide, colorful, and bold. He was a businessman who sold fluid mechanical controls like water valves and meters. He was also a hobbyist oil painter, a great sketcher, and a devout Catholic."

In 1997, Gold was performing in the Broadway revival of *Annie* when his dresser (herself a quilter) suggested that he incorporate the ties into a quilt to honor his dad's memory. He cut them into 2-inch pieces and appliquéd them onto fabric squares—576 of them—which he pieced together into a traditional pattern known as cathedral windows. For the backing, he sewed together cotton squares in the form of a color pallet.

"The overall cathedral-window pattern represents Dad's Catholic faith," he explained. "The ties represent his business career. The multicolored backing represents the artist in him."

Gold estimates it took him fifteen thousand man-hours to complete the piece, working on it four to ten hours a day. The work, he said, ultimately turned into a form of grieving not only for his own father, but also for the fathers of his friends in the show's cast and crew.

"My dad was my best friend," he said. "I was only thirty-eight when he died. I would work on it in my dressing room, and folks would drop in and tell me stories about their fathers. It became a way for all of us to process our stories."

Over the years, his friends and relatives have called upon him to tell *their* stories through his quilts. Four of the panels on the National AIDS Quilt, for example, were created by Gold. He did framed quilt squares for a client and her three sibs fashioned from their bathrobes, pajamas, dresses, and jackets. His best friend lost both parents six weeks apart. Gold created two quilts for him and his sister, fashioned from their parents' clothing. They were displayed at a Christmas open house where friends and relatives reminisced through tears and laughter.

"Quilting allows me to express who I am and what lies in my heart," Gold said. "It's so powerful in the way it ignites and moves people's emotions, and yet it's just fabric."

Lisa Rooney plays the *nay*

Like almost everybody else in the Middle Eastern band Zaruna, Lisa Rooney has never been to the Middle East.

The group is made up of four Americans and one Arab Christian from Haifa. In the band, Rooney plays a species of bamboo flute called the *nay*, which she took up while working in Argentina as director of the Bridge Spanish Language School in Buenos Aires.

"First thing I did when I got there was to seek out a belly dance class," she said. In addition to dance, the teacher was offering a course in the intricacies of Middle Eastern drumming. Rooney signed up.

"The rhythms are different," she said, "not your standard Western 4/4 time, but odd meters like 5/8 or 7/8 or even 10/8 time. Middle Eastern rhythms make you want to get up and dance!"

What really turned her on, though, was the multicultural bouillabaisse of the class.

"I loved the mix," she said, "an American in Buenos Aires learning Middle Eastern drumming from the Argentines."

One night at a recital of Sufi music in somebody's living room (again, Turkish music in Buenos Aires with nary a Turk in sight), she became entranced by the *nay*, which sounded to her very much like the human voice. After the performance, she approached the flautist.

"I want to play the *nay*," she said. "Where can I learn, and how can I get one?"

He volunteered to teach her and sold her an instrument he'd made himself. "Call me when you can get a sound out of it," he said. That took three days of trying.

"The *nay* is held at a forty-five-degree angle," she explained. "The air is blown both into and across the hole. I studied with him for six months. Then I got transferred to Denver."

Before she accepted the assignment, though, she googled "Middle Eastern Music in Denver" and came across an ensemble called Sultanah. The group was led by an Australian woman named Kylie, and Chakid, her Moroccan husband. A multi-talented musician, Chakid played violin, keyboards, the *nay*, and a pear-shaped lute called an *oud*.

Rooney e-mailed them, requesting information. They wrote back with a simple invitation: "Come play with us." Rooney joined the band as its official *nay* player.

"I could only play two songs," she said. "But I learned a lot from them about improvisation and performance."

Kylie and Chakid departed for the East Coast in 2011, leaving behind a small coterie of Western devotees who, like Rooney, had become entranced with Middle Eastern music. Together they founded Zaruna and began playing regular gigs at the Phoenician Kebab and the Mercury Café. They also make it a point to join forces with an all-Jewish klezmer band called the Lost Tribe for an annual concert they call Salaam/Shalom.

"Everyone in the band feels like we're knocking down stereotypes and misconceptions," Rooney said. "It's important for us to show that people are just people. The concert is another way symbolically to show that Muslims and Jews can coexist."

Zaruna gets together once a week in somebody's living room to rehearse and learn new songs.

"It's a social gathering with a sharing of food," she said. "We play a wide variety of music including classics from the '30s and '40s, traditional dance songs, folk songs, and *Samai*, a musical form with four distinct movements and a refrain. In terms of personal fulfillment, this is where my passion lies. Music is like an escape from reality. It takes me into a different dimension. It's very much like meditation. It clears your mind, relaxes your body, gives you energy, and generates feelings of happiness. I also like the bond (known as *Tarab* in Arabic) that happens between the performers and the audience. You know it's a good show when they're clapping and dancing or when they fall silent and are mesmerized."

Mezzo soprano Jennifer DeDominici's "love-hate thing" with opera

Mezzo soprano Jennifer DeDominici said she "never heard an opera 'til I was in one."

"When I was a kid, we'd take these long car rides where the whole family would sing," she said. "Me especially. I loved academics, played sports, and had no idea that people could make a living as a musician or singer."

As a prerequisite for graduation from Gorham High School in East Central Maine, students were required to complete one fine arts credit. Young Jennifer signed up for the school chorus, an experience which she said opened her eyes—and her ears—to a whole array of new musical possibilities.

"I'd never heard four-part a cappella harmony before," she said. "I had no idea the human voice was capable of making such beauty on its own."

She and her choir pals took to bursting into song—flash-mob style—whenever the impulse overtook them, knocking out barbershop chordal progressions between classes in the hallways and after school on the bus.

As valedictorian of Gorham's class of '95, DeDominici got a full navy ROTC scholarship to Holy Cross in Worcester, Massachusetts. There she joined the Campus Chamber Singers, won an understudy role as Eliza Doolittle in *My Fair Lady*, and found herself getting more and more deeply into the music and less and less interested in a career in the navy. Decision time.

"The deal with ROTC is that they pay for your first year free," she said. "After that, you owe *them* four years' service or all back payments for however many years you've gone to school. It was navy vs. music, and I couldn't decide."

To give herself time to mull it over, DeDominici attended a weeklong silent retreat offered by a priest at Holy Cross who just happened to have heard her sing in *My Fair Lady*.

"At the orientation meeting, he asked me to sing something," she said. "So I belted out a few bars of 'I Could Have Danced All Night.' He said, 'My dear, you have a gift. It's your responsibility to use it.' I couldn't have asked for a better sign. I decided to leave Holy Cross and not do the ROTC thing."

She enrolled at University of Southern Maine.

"I still had never had a voice lesson," she said, "and for the audition, I was supposed to sing a solo classical piece."

She sought help from her old high school choir teacher, Mr. Christopher Peterson. Peterson suggested she sing Giuseppe Giordani's "Caro Mio Ben" and advised her to "Pretend you're an opera singer." It worked. DeDominici won a full tuition scholarship and graduated four years later with a degree in vocal performance and music education.

In 2001, she moved to Boulder to work on a master's in vocal performance. That year, Opera Colorado was auditioning for an outreach ensemble to perform in schools, hospitals, and senior centers in an effort to expand its audience. DeDominici auditioned and was hired.

"That," she said, "was my first professional job as a solo opera singer."

Since then, she's appeared in a variety of roles for Opera Theatre of the Rockies, Opera Colorado, and the Santa Fe Opera Company. But a starring role in a major production is not easy to come by.

"There just aren't a lot of roles out there for mezzo sopranos," she said. "I'm in my early thirties. I feel like I'm just coming into my full voice, but I still don't have a career that can pay the bills. Opera is a love-hate thing. It's like you've got a dysfunctional relationship with your career. It keeps telling you no but gives you just enough to keep you coming back for more. There's nothing I love doing more. But I want to be honest enough with myself to be able to quit when I no longer love it."

Laurie Gibb's VW van: a rolling work of art

One thing Denver fabric artist Laurie Gibb chose not to do when she turned sixty-five was kvetch.

"I didn't want to just sit there and complain about aging," she said. "I wanted to celebrate by taking some risks and doing something really unusual."

The question was . . . *What?*

She kept thinking about a journey she and her husband and kids had taken around the Pacific Northwest in a VW van in the late '60s. And then there was that weird dream she'd had where she was forced to leave home with only what she could fit into one suitcase. The dream, she realized, was an invitation to reflect on what was most meaningful to her in life.

"I always loved creativity," she said. "I was driven by that. That was what was most important to me."

So . . . art and travel. Those two elements eventually coalesced into a plan to take off for a year, drive around the country, make art, visit local art museums and installations such as Carhenge, outside of Alliance, Nebraska, and do her best to live in and enjoy each moment as fully as possible.

"Once I committed to the journey," she said, "everything just seemed to fall into place."

To finance her travels, she found a tenant willing to rent her house for a year. Then she bought a new VW Eurovan that would serve as both shelter and transportation. And finally, she was able to land three artist residencies at schools around the country: New Jersey in November, Georgia in February, and New Mexico in April, destinations and time constraints that would lend her voyage structure and purpose and enable her to make art in a university setting. By mid-August 2006, she was ready to go.

But now with the bustle of preparation behind her, she had to overcome one last hurtle, and that was her fear of being a woman alone on the road. As an artist, she came up with a novel solution.

"I created what I like to call my Man-in-a-bag," she said. "It was a sack filled with odds and ends to make it look like I had a man travelling with me. Stuff like men's magazines, a pair of huge flip-flops, and a Sturgis T-shirt, which I would set out on the dashboard whenever I spent the night at a campground. As the trip progressed, I stopped doing it. I don't think it fooled anybody."

Man-in-a-bag or no, there was at least one genuinely scary moment at a campground in Upstate New York. Gibb was snug in her van and drifting off to sleep when she heard footsteps approaching. Whoever it was paused, tried the door, found it to be locked, and walked away, leaving Gibb wide awake, thumb poised over the car alarm button on her key chain.

As the trip progressed, Turtle, her VW van, became the love of her life.

"That van was my home, my studio, my safe haven, and my constant companion," she said. In the twelve months they spent together, she and Turtle logged twenty thousand miles and covered thirty-seven states, one Canadian province, and the District of Columbia.

Once they were safely back in Denver, Gibb spent the next two years making art quilts inspired by the journey's special moments and places. It was while sewing these quilts that a radical concept occurred to her. Why not turn the van into a work of art by covering it with quilts?

"It was a way to honor my beloved Turtle and also a means of exploring how the journey had changed me." (Gibb's quilted car won her a blue ribbon at this year's Denver County Fair.)

Gibb said the journey taught her life lessons in self-confidence, spontaneity, simplicity, and tolerance.

"I learned I can take on something scary and make it work," she said. "I don't get bogged down in fear and anxiety. I've gotten rid of a lot of clutter, and these days I'm more able to live in the moment. I've also learned to be more accepting of other people's limitations. You know, in the end, everybody's just trying to do the best they can."

Aztec dancer Carlos Castañeda:
"holding the door open for the next generation"

One of the more colorful experiences you're likely to have in the streets, parks, and museums of Denver is traditional native dance performed by Grupo Tlaloc Danza Azteca (*Tlaloc* is the Aztec god of rain, fertility, and water). The troupe was founded in 1980 by a handful of Chicano students interested in learning more about their indigenous heritage. Carlos Castañeda, the company's principal dancer and current director, has been with the group since 1984.

The son of beet and onion farmers, Castañeda was born in Delta and grew up in Trinidad and Rocky Ford. His grandfather, who was part Tarahumara Indian, came up from Chihuahua in search of a better life, though his parents had threatened to disown him for making the move.

"We had to fit in," said Castañeda. "So we left our culture and ways behind. My grandmother told us we had native and Mexican blood in us. She wanted us to know that this is who we are."

Castañeda came to Aztec dance—and a deeper understanding of his culture of origin—in a roundabout fashion. His older brother had participated in the occupation of Wounded Knee in the early '70s and had made friends among the Lakota Sioux.

"He was going up there pretty regularly," Castañeda said. "I joined him on the Rosebud Reservation in '78 for the Sundance Ceremony. I've done it every year since then."

Sundance is an intense four-day ordeal that includes fasting, song, dance, and body piercing. Dancing in the heat of the late summer sun, participants are said to enter a meditative state that allows them to communicate directly with the Creator.

"We go without food or water for ninety-six hours and dance from sunup to sundown," Castañeda said. "On the first day, you think about the world. On the second day, you think about hunger and thirst. On the third day, you stop thinking about hunger and thirst. On the fourth day, the spirit leaves the body. At that level, almost anything is possible."

Castañeda said that Sundance changed his life. "As a teenager I was drinking and drugging and in trouble. Today I'm healthy, and my family is in good shape."

While there are direct benefits to the dancers themselves, Sundance is ultimately done for the benefit of others.

"[When I dance] I forget about *my* needs and dedicate myself to the welfare of those I pray for," Castañeda said. "We do it so our people will survive. I sacrifice myself so my children and future progeny will have a good life."

Perhaps the greatest benefit for Castañeda personally, however, was that Sundance put him in touch with his own cultural heritage. "I'm not Lakota Sioux," he said, "but Sundance has opened doors for me. I've made connections with others from my own culture, other native people from Mexico and the Southwest who come to the Lakota dances."

Eight years after Castañeda joined Grupo Tlaloc, its founding teacher returned to Mexico, leaving the directorship in the hands of his protégé, Carlos Castañeda. Castañeda immediately set about learning—and teaching—the spiritual and ceremonial aspects of *la danza*. The group now consists of thirty members, with a core of fifteen experienced performers.

"We were at one time the only Aztec group this far north," he said. "Now it's done all over the US, Canada, and even in Europe. Through dance, we're reviving a once-dormant culture."

Castañeda wants to correct some of the misconceptions that mainstream America has about the history of his people. "In the old days, history books only mentioned Cortez and human sacrifice," he said. "My hope is that we can establish a ceremonial site or a cultural center here in Denver, where we can store our archives, watch videos, and hear audios. I see my role as holding the door open for the next generation."

Poet SETH Harris explores the plus side of breaking the rules

Most poets write for the page. Denver poet SETH Harris writes for the stage.

"I think most poets start out as closet poets," he said. "I wrote poetry for years without sharing it. I didn't even think of it as poetry.

But after several years of jotting things down in a notebook, I decided to start reading it at open mics."

At his first public reading (Muddy's Java Café, 1988), he met a local poet and musician named Woody Hildebrand, who in turn introduced him to actor/poet/musician Tupper Cullum. As it happened, all three were interested in exploring nontraditional ways of presenting their poetry. Together, they formed a performance troupe called Poets of the Open Range.

"We called ourselves the Open Rangers because we were open to all ways of presenting poetry," Harris said. "We were also open to whoever wanted to participate. It wouldn't be just us. We brought in musicians, poets, dancers. The whole idea was to make poetry entertaining. For me personally, it became a substitute for having my poetry in print. Actually, I was never really interested in having my stuff published. But performance was a way of getting my words out there and of polishing my poetry. Even today, performing anything I write is the best way to polish it. My ear and the audience tell me when a line hits the mark."

Harris grew up in Huntington, Long Island, and studied English and liberal arts at Indiana University near Pittsburgh, Pennsylvania. His senior year, he served as editor-in-chief of the school newspaper, for which he wrote a popular weekly satirical column.

"I left college interested in writing novels," he said. "But then a whole evolutionary process took place."

While visiting friends in Denver, he managed to land a couple of jobs, writing PR for both ArtReach and Eden Theatrical Workshop.

"I learned from these two jobs that every genre of writing can teach you something about the art of using language," he said. "But what attracted me to poetry was that it allowed me to break the rules of syntax and grammar. By breaking the rules, I learned more about why the rules were there. By writing poetry, I also developed more dexterity in my use of language."

As a writer-in-residence for the Denver Public Schools, SETH teaches his students the creative side of rule breaking.

"I show them how they can break the rules of grammar and syntax and come up saying some amazing things," he said. "There's no such thing as a bad poem. Some are better than others, but none are bad. There are ways to make a mistake sound or seem refreshingly original. In Jazz, for example, one of the techniques of improv is that if you make a mistake, repeat it, then go on from there."

At sixty-one, SETH has returned to his first love, narrative fiction.

"My main priority now is getting my novel finished and published," he said. "I believe the role of the writer is to be a journalist, no matter what kind of writing you choose to do. You look at the world and strive to understand it as honestly and accurately as you can, and then reflect that in everything you write. I don't believe there's salvation for the collective, but there is salvation for the individual. I don't think you can change the world, but you can help this individual and that individual understand things a little better, and therefore improve their lives. I figure if I can help others heal themselves, then that will be the greatest service I can do with my life."

Angelique Olin: ex-cop turned photographer maps landscape of human body

Last March, Angelique Olin was named Denver Photographer of the Year by RAW Natural Born Artists, a national organization that offers support to fledgling creatives. Although she did not go on to win the national title, the award was a feather in her cap, considering the fact that she's only been taking pictures professionally since 2010. Before that, she was a cop running calls in a patrol car and field-training new recruits for the Fort Myers, Florida, Police Department.

"There were moments when I liked being a cop," she said. "Mostly, though, it was a thankless job. We were always under pressure. I saw so many things no human being should ever have to see, like car accidents and having to tell the next of kin that their child had just died."

And then there was that time she came this close to shooting a fifteen-year-old who'd escaped from juvenile and claimed to be holding a gun behind his back. Fortunately, somebody tackled him before Olin had to pull the trigger. But still.

By the time she was mustered out after sixteen years on the force, she'd developed a tremor in her right hand and could no longer shoot straight. Unlike a lot of people facing early retirement, though, Olin had absolutely no doubts about what she wanted to do next with her life.

"For me, retirement was like a door opening," she said. "I knew I wanted to be a professional photographer like my dad. He tried to instill a love for it in us kids, but I was the only one who ever really went for it."

At age thirteen, she was already serving as his personal assistant on wedding shoots.

"I always loved it," she said. "It's one of the few things that has never bored me."

She enrolled at the International Academy of Design and Technology in Tampa, where she studied digital photography, graduating magna cum laude in 2010 with a portfolio that garnered the highest mark ever recorded at the school.

"What I wanted to shoot were artistic nudes," she said. "I've always been fascinated by the human body, both inside and outside. I believe everyone has something that's beautiful about their body. That's what I look for when I shoot."

Here's what's different about Olin's nudes. They don't look like naked bodies, they look like landscapes: hills, valleys, sand dunes. The topographical impression is augmented by the fact that she rarely includes faces in her photographs.

"I can take your picture and put it on the wall and nobody would ever know it's you," she said.

As a sidelight and to make a living, Olin also does what's known in the industry as boudoir photography. Women hire her to photograph them either nude or in their negligees as a gift to a significant other.

"Most women are not comfortable with how they look," she said. "So generally I photograph the body and not the face. It starts out as a typical sexy boudoir shot and gradually becomes more abstract. Looking at the photos, you see the art before you see the nudity."

After she graduated from art school, Olin's husband, Curt, sent out resumes and landed a job as a computer programmer with the Federal Government in Colorado. The couple moved here in January 2011, and Olin began showing her work First Fridays at Don Campbell Gallery on Santa Fe. She credits the RAW Denver award with kick-starting her career in her new home.

"Florida was hell hot and oppressive," she said. "As a cop, you knew where all the dirt was. Being a cop was never me. I love not having to carry a gun. I love being able to look out and see the mountains. For the first time in my life, I feel like I've got something that's really mine. What I do now is from the heart.

Christy Honigman celebrates the power of art
to heal and transform

Christy Honigman woke up feeling like hell the day after the 2004 election, and it wasn't only because George W. Bush had managed to secure a second term.

"What the election said to me was that it was now okay in America to be mean spirited and intolerant toward outsiders. It was all about denying asylum to political refugees and putting up a fence on the border to keep the illegal aliens out."

As a consultant to the Rocky Mountain Survivor Center, Honigman had a heightened sensitivity to the issue. "One of my clients," she said, "was a victim of torture who was seeking asylum. So it was important to me as an artist and a citizen to convey a more inclusive message to people with different backgrounds and personal histories."

Professionally speaking, Christy Honigman wears two hats. By day she's a consultant to nonprofit organizations. By night she's an artist whose work is represented in more than fifty private and corporate collections around the country.

Honigman approached Denver's Mizel Museum with a proposal to create a work of art around the theme of *Tikkun Olam*. The phrase means "heal the world" in Yiddish, but in recent years, it's been expanded to embrace notions of social justice, peace, freedom, equality, and the restoration of the environment.

What Honigman envisioned was a collaborative piece in which participants would interpret the universal values of world repair in pictures, poems, and stories. The overall conception was simple: twelve, seven-foot-tall columns painted black, each bearing five panels created by members of the city's immigrant and refugee communities expressing their thoughts on the topic. The Mizel liked the idea and agreed to sponsor it.

"We set up tents at events around town like naturalization ceremonies and UN International Day and invited people to etch their poems and stories into wet artist's plaster spread over the panels," Honigman said.

When the plaster dried, Honigman painted them in limes, violets, magentas, azures, yellows, tans, and grays. There's an archeological feel to these pieces. It's like looking at graffiti scratched onto ancient walls. The messages they convey are powerful in their stark simplicity.

Like this one in Serbo-Croatian: "Live. Forgive. Love. Think sometimes that your life is not only for yourselves."

Or this one from Ghana: "Sow the seeds of peace into the hearts of the young."

Or this fragment of unintentional poetry from Sierra Leone:

> The Heart
> The mothers of mothers.
> The mothers of mankind
> The god of happiness,
> The god of sadness and peace.

"Many of the people who worked on this project are survivors of torture and exile," Honigman said. "They not only lent their personal expression to it but in the process of creation also experienced the power of art to heal and transform."

Was Honigman healed and transformed as well?

"I started with a sense of hopelessness," she said. "But working on this project, I learned something about our interconnectedness and mutual interdependence as human beings. Let's just say I'm a little more hopeful than I was."

Annie Zook's puppet theatre: not just another roadside attraction

The brainchild of artist Annie Zook and her husband Dave, the Denver Puppet Theatre represents the happy confluence of their individual dreams.

Annie had been putting on puppet shows for years at shopping malls, libraries, local museums, and kids' birthday parties. "This involved a lot of schlepping," she said, "and I decided I was getting too old for that." Her dream was to someday have a permanent puppet theatre.

"On our vacations, we liked to drive country roads in the Midwest, stopping off at roadside attractions," Annie explained. "Dave always thought it would be fun to own a tourist trap."

They started looking for a combination theatre, living space, and roadside attraction and found their dream home in a ramshackle old building on 38th Avenue, a block and a half west of Federal.

"It was flooded, it stunk, and the windows were boarded up, but we could see past all that," Annie remembered. "It was a good location, and there was ample parking. What made it work, though, was that it was big enough to cater to school groups."

It was also big enough for them to live in, although during the renovation phase they found themselves camping in the courtyard. The puppet theatre finally opened in October of 1996, but by then their vision had evolved into something much, much bigger. "We wanted it to be part of the community," Zook said, "a kind of family farm in the city."

They now offer a mixed bag of activities like a family improv group and a craft area where kids can make their own puppets. There's space for town hall meetings. There's a recording studio on the premises managed by their son, and a hair salon operated by their daughter-in-law. Not long ago, the Zooks put in a coffee shop where Dave serves as barista, baker, and "carrier of heavy objects." Meanwhile, the courtyard has been turned into a peaceful oasis where people can hang out and eat their lunch.

This heady mix of activities and services to the contrary notwithstanding, the puppet shows remain the central focus of Annie Zook's attention. She writes the scripts, builds the sets, makes the puppets, pulls the strings, does the voices, and operates the lighting via a preset light box that she works with her feet.

Her scripts are reinterpretations of traditional fairy tales such as *Jack and the Beanstalk*—tales that "stick in the mind." In her updated version, Jack learns to be resourceful and self-reliant.

"I want to convey to kids that they can figure out their own problems," she said. "They have their own resources, and they can empower themselves. That's the story's takeaway for our times."

The shows grow and change based on feedback she gets during and after each performance.

"I'm listening to their comments," she said. "I'm also listening for a certain rustling that tells me when they're losing interest. I try to have something crazy happen every ten minutes. A puppet falls or burps or can't find something that's right in front of their face. Or they'll try to count and can't, so the kids have to help them out. They shout out solutions: 'Turn around! Climb the beanstalk!' You don't get these opportunities with flat things like TV."

As hectic as it can sometimes be, Annie Zook loves what she does.

"Our roadside attraction is a dream come true" she said. "If I had to do it all over again, I'd turn around and do it in a minute. I realize I am rich, though not in the commonly accepted sense. I get to be with kids, and I get to do my artwork. Where's it all going? We have no plan. I guess I'll just keep doing it 'til I die."

Namita Khanna: architect brings classical Indian dance to Denver

In a poem entitled "Among School Children," W.B. Yeats asks, "How can we know the dancer from the dance?" That would be an appropriate question for classical Indian dancer Namita Khanna, who's been doing it since she was three years old, and teaching and performing it since moving here in 1990 to study architecture at CU Denver.

Performance is in her DNA. Her father, Kishan Khanna, was a Hindi playwright and theatre director, her mother, Aruna Khanna, was an actress and a classically trained Indian singer.

"There was always music in our household," she said. "Grandpa would be drumming on the breakfast table, and I would dance. My first time ever on stage, I was one year old."

Sensing her interest and natural talent, her parents found a dance guru to teach her *Bharata Natyam*, a classical dance style that originated in the South Indian state of Tamil Nadu.

"It's the oldest form of dance in India," she said. "Very angular and squatty. Very precise. There's a lot of eye rolling, neck movement, and hand gestures in it. Dance in India originated as both worship and celebration. The dances tell the stories of the gods. We believe that Shiva puts his energy and passion and anger in us when we dance."

At age eleven, she was introduced to another form called *Kathak*. Less angular and more flowing and graceful than *Bharata Natyam*, *Kathak* involves a lot of spinning and intricate footwork.

"It's like a conversation between the tabla player and the dancer," she said. "They try to match each other's rhythm. It's almost a competition."

Her choreography combines elements of both and is seasoned with Indian folk dance and a dash of Bollywood. In February of 1991, while still at CU, she was invited to perform in a show for the local Pakistani community.

"Two weeks later, I got a call from an Indian lady who'd seen me dancing. She wanted to know if I'd teach her two daughters. I was flattered and excited but unfortunately too busy with schoolwork to accept."

A year later, though, she managed to find the time to start a class for the two daughters and one other girl in the basement of her Arvada home. Within a month, five more students had found their way into the class, and it wasn't long before her fledgling Indian dance academy had outgrown the basement.

Over the years, Mudra Dance Studio has had to move to ever larger spaces. Its enrollment now tops 138 students.

"Sixty to seventy percent are Indian," she said. "The balance are whites, blacks, and mixed ethnicities. Also a lot of adoptees. The point is you don't have to be any particular shape or form or age or color to learn Indian classical dance."

In addition to the classes, the school maintains a professional performance group of eight dancers and two drummers, with a hectic schedule that last year exceeded one hundred performances.

"One day last November," Khanna said, "we did a performance in Littleton and then had to rush all the way up to Greeley for a second performance on the same day."

Khanna maintains that her work as an architect and her work as a choreographer are of a piece.

"My architectural training enables me to get a sense of the design and color and geometry of a performance," she said. "It helps me visualize the whole scene in 3D."

Having a second career as an architect also means she doesn't need to worry about supporting herself through dance.

"It was important to me from day one not to make dance about money," she said. "It's not about money and has never been about money. For me, dance is the raw and honest expression of my soul. When I'm on stage, I'm able to transfer the joy I'm feeling to the audience. I can see it in the smiles on their faces. That to me is beyond satisfaction. It's beyond any payment in the world."

Country singer Rudy Grant: some things matter more than a shot at the big time

Maybe the big time is not all it's cracked up to be. That's the conclusion country singer Rudy Grant came to when Columbia Records offered him an audition back in 1975. The record companies were vying with one another to discover the next Charley Pride, and somehow word got back to them about an African American country singer in Denver who might just fit the bill. At the time, Rudy and his band, the Uncommon Herd, were gigging at a joint called the King's Loft in Aurora. The reps Columbia sent were none other than Sonny Wright and his wife, Loretta Lynn's little sister, Peggy Sue.

Grant turned them down flat.

"I had two young daughters who needed a father," Grant said by way of explanation. To support his family, he was working three jobs: one as an optician at Fitzsimons Army Medical Center, another as a passenger services agent with United Airlines, and a third playing gigs in honky-tonks from Aurora to Golden to Boulder. To him, a recording contract looked like so much pie in the sky.

"Mr. Wright said the only reason he was even talking to me was because of Charley Pride's popularity," Grant said. "That pretty much made my mind up for me right there."

Rudy Grant was born on a farm outside of Shreveport, Louisiana, the seventh son in a family of nineteen brothers and sisters. The family moved to a farm near Bastrop in the northeast corner of the state, where they picked cotton, raised vegetables, and hunted, trapped, and fished for food.

"At age fourteen, something got into me," Grant said. "I started feeling restless, like there's gotta be something else out there."

Late one night, he packed a bag, climbed out of his bedroom window, and hitchhiked into Bastrop. He spent his first night away from home sleeping under the front steps of the local pool hall.

He got a job at Scott's Groceries in Bastrop, stacking shelves, pumping gas, fixing flats, changing oil, delivering groceries, and running errands for $25 bucks a week plus meals.

A year and a half later, he figured he was ready to move on. Tricked out in a green cowboy hat, mirror sunglasses, and a clean pair of overalls, he boarded a Greyhound bus to Denver, where he had an uncle willing to take him in. In Denver, he earned his GED and took a civil service exam that led to a job as an optician at Fitzsimons.

All through this time, he was teaching himself to play the guitar and acquiring an extensive repertoire of country songs. Apparently, he got pretty good at it because at a Christmas party at work one year, a banjo-pickin' co-worker heard him and invited him to a Sunday evening open stage at a bar called the Four Seasons. Grant got up and knocked out an old Conway Twitty tune. Less than a month later, he was fronting his own band.

"We played covers of Johnny Cash, Merle Haggard, Hank Williams, Jim Reeves, and, of course, Charley Pride," he said. "This was in 1965. I was the closest thing people could see to Charley Pride."

Now retired after more than thirty-three years in government service, he's put together a new band called Rudy Grant and the Buffalo Riders.

"We play twice a month at White Fence Farm, once a month at the Blossom in Windsor Gardens, and a dinner show every Friday night at Lupita's in Aurora," he said. "In May, we go on tour in England with a British group called the Salt Creek Band. Country music at this stage in my life is the one thing I'm truly passionate about. The biggest joy in my heart is when I look out at the audience and see a nodding smile on their faces. The big time doesn't interest me, but boy I do love the local scene."

Barb Donachy: involved in the bigger picture

If you were around during the 1980s, you may recall that the Reagan Administration caused a dustup when it was revealed that our government was putting theater nukes and cruise missiles in Europe. Denver artist Barbara Donachy and her boyfriend and future husband, Andy Bardwell, were travelling there at the time.

"Everywhere we went, people were talking about our government's plans for fighting a limited nuclear war on European soil. They were asking us questions that we had no answers for."

Later in the journey, Donachy had what she describes as "a life-changing dream."

"I was back in Denver, standing at the corner of Speer and Logan facing Cherry Creek. Overhead a huge bomber filled the sky, and when I looked down, I saw that Cherry Creek had become a boiling tidal wave that was rolling right toward me. I knew I had to do something quick, and I woke with a sense of relief that there was still time."

Donachy joined the Nuclear Freeze Movement and began doing research on the actual size of America's nuclear arsenal.

"The numbers were staggering," she said. "I couldn't visualize them. So I decided to replicate them in clay."

With the help of a dedicated crew of volunteers, she produced a thirty-two-thousand-piece clay replica of the American nuclear arsenal that included warheads, submarines, bombers, and missiles. The

Amber Waves of Grain Exhibit helped to focus international attention on the issue of nuclear proliferation.

Flash forward twenty-five years. Today the exhibit is stored at the Peace Farm in Amarillo, Texas, and Donachy's life has taken a surprising turn. She's no longer making art. Instead, she's pursuing a career in public health.

On second thought, maybe it's not so surprising.

"My involvement in art was never divorced from social issues like war, civil rights, and the environment," she said. "I see war and nuclear annihilation as health issues, so I've always been on that track."

In 1997, Donachy became the US coordinator for a group called Potters for Peace (PFP), which was at that time working to help impoverished Nicaraguan potters to market their wares. But in 1998, Hurricane Mitch seriously compromised the country's fresh water supply. PFP began making ceramic water filters at a factory that employed both local potters and international volunteers. By 2001, they'd manufactured an estimated five thousand filters, and they were given a grant from USAID to study the effectiveness of the device.

"Of course, nobody bothered to read it," Donachy said of the finished report. "Andy and I were down there, and we found a copy of it on the desk, and Andy, who tends more toward left-brain thinking, picked it up and studied it. He turned to me and said, 'Have you read this?' And I said no, and he said, 'Well, you should.'"

The study revealed that the Nicaraguans were washing their filters in contaminated river water. Moreover, while the devices were eliminating 99.9 percent of the bacteria, in a tropical climate like Nicaragua's, the remaining tenth of a percent was growing back at an alarming rate and contaminating the purified water in the storage tanks.

"It was exciting for volunteers to make water filters," Donachy said. "But wanting to do good is not enough. We needed to train the end users of our filters. We needed to monitor the results of our efforts. We needed to start looking at the big picture."

Donachy now holds a master's in public health from CU Medical.

"Artists are great right-brain thinkers," she said. "I went back to school to learn the left-brain side of the equation. I wanted to be involved in the bigger picture."

PART 5

Panthers, Tigers, and Buffalo Soldiers

Bob Fuchigami: Camp Amache a bitter legacy for
Japanese Americans

Pearl Harbor Day—December 7, 1941—marked a turning point in the life of eleven-year-old Bob Fuchigami, though he would not begin to understand the full impact of the day's events until the middle of the following year.

"Up until the attack on Pearl Harbor," he said, "we were living a normal American life on a truck farm in Yerba City, California." Fuchigami was the seventh of eight kids. "We were Nisei, the first generation born in the USA. At one end of the dinner table, all of us younger kids spoke English. At the other end, the older kids and my parents spoke Japanese."

Six months later, they were ordered to report to the train station in nearby Marysville for transport to a relocation center somewhere in the Western United States. They were given six days to pack their belongings and settle their affairs. A local high school teacher leased the farm with an option to buy.

"He made so much money on fruits and vegetables that he was able to buy it within a year," Fuchigami said. "We lost everything: our farm equipment, our orchards, our home, and its furnishings."

Before they left, Fuchigami turned his pet rabbits loose. The family dogs were simply abandoned. A train, packed with Japanese Americans and a detachment of soldiers assigned to guard them, took them east to Grenada Relocation Center near Lamar, Colorado. The camp was still being built when they arrived. The barracks were divided into six rooms apiece, each lit by a single lightbulb and heated with a coal-burning stove. The Fuchigamis, a family of ten, were allotted two rooms.

"There was no furniture. Everybody got a canvas cot, a thin cotton mattress, and two GI blankets. That was it."

Apart from the Spartan accommodations, what struck Fuchigami most forcibly about Camp Amache, as it came to be called, was the high barbed-wire fence that surrounded it. That and the guard towers manned by armed American troops.

"The guard towers represented our complete loss of freedom," he said.

The 640-acre facility soon became home to 7,500 inmates. It was a self-sufficient community.

"They kept people busy," Fuchigami said. "Everybody had a job."

Some staffed the mess hall; others did office work. There was a fire department and a camp newspaper. The kids went to a makeshift school where they sat on wooden benches with their notebooks on their laps.

Fuchigami's father, a farmer by trade, worked in the camp's farm. One day, he fell off a truck and injured his back. Fuchigami's mother suffered a stroke. Neither ever fully recovered.

"He was sixty when we went in," Fuchigami said. "Mom was fifty-four. They had struggled through the Depression. They should have been able to retire in comfort. I'll never forgive this government for what it did to them."

They were released in September of 1945, having spent three years at the camp. Everybody got $25 and a train ticket back to where they came from.

"Why were we there?" Fuchigami asks. "Who made the decision to imprison us? I've spent my entire life trying to figure that out. I came away at age fifteen, feeling like a third-class citizen, wondering how to fit back into society."

The camp experience also instilled in him a deep-seated mistrust of authority.

"The government lied to us," he said. "There was no reason for us to be locked up."

Upward of 118,000 American citizens of Japanese ancestry were incarcerated in facilities such as Camp Amache. Which is a lot,

Fuchigami points out, when you consider that there were only 126,000 Japanese Americans living in the US at the time. Over 90 percent.

"I have no qualms about calling Camp Amache a concentration camp," he said. "'Relocation center' was just a euphemism they used to get us to go. We were prisoners. That's what a concentration camp is, a place to keep political prisoners, dissidents, and minority ethnic groups."

Jack Welner, holocaust survivor

Jack Welner, his mother, a younger sister, and her friend hid behind a china cabinet in their apartment, determined to avoid transport to Hitler's extermination camps. It was August 1944.

Two months earlier, the Allies had landed on Normandy Beach and were fighting their way toward Poland. Those Jews who had survived the past five years of starvation and slavery in the Lodz Ghetto were being evacuated by the Germans.

The Welners lasted two days in hiding before their food ran out and they were forced to give themselves up. They made their way to the train station and were loaded into boxcars. Several nights later, the train came to a halt, and the doors were finally opened.

"Those were the doors of hell," Welner said.

They had arrived in Auschwitz. Outside, the guards were screaming, "Men, this side! Women, that side!"

Welner's mother handed him her last crust of bread. "You take it, son," she said. "You'll need it."

"That was the last time I ever saw her," he said, his eyes welling. "She was immediately taken to the gas chambers and murdered. My sister and her friend were sent to Bergen Belson. I stayed behind in Auschwitz."

Jack Welner was nineteen when the Germans marched into Poland in September of 1939. In his home town of Lodz, the SS turned the poorest part of the city into a ghetto surrounded by barbed wire with a sentry box every 90 feet. Some 164,000 Jews were evicted from their homes and forced into the compound.

"We were completely cut off from the rest of the world," Welner remembered. "Even our radios had to be turned in under penalty of death."

Originally intended as a temporary gathering point for Jews and gypsies bound for the camps, Lodz became an industrial center for the manufacture of materiel for the German Army. Anyone unable to work was immediately sent to an extermination camp. It wasn't long before starvation and disease were running rampant.

"I used to go to the fields and pick grass for my mother to make soup out of," Welner remembered. "There was an epidemic of typhus, and the lice were eating us alive. We were hungry, dirty, cut off from the world. Every night, I prayed, 'God, don't let me wake up in the morning.' We really wanted to die. I still have nightmares from that time."

A week after he arrived at Auschwitz, Welner was again transported, this time to Dachau.

"We were each given a piece of bread, a bit of blood sausage, some salted margarine, and a couple pots of water," he said.

Sealed into box cars, the trip to Dachau took four days and four nights. A selection of men from Lodz was then sent on to Camp Number 10 at Utting am Ammer-see.

"We were just walking skeletons by the time we got there," Welner said. "The German's really made animals out of us. They would give us soup in a pot for five men. No spoons. We would fight over the scraps in the pot."

He was put on a work crew, unloading long heavy sections of rebar from boxcars. In his weakened condition, Welner realized he could not survive the ordeal. In desperation, he approached the German foreman of his work detail and offered to help him. Luckily, the man was a "Good German." He gave Welner a job as his assistant, and every few days, he would sneak food to him.

Welner remained in Camp Number 10 through April 1945. By then it was obvious even to the SS that the Third Reich's days were numbered. They assembled the remaining prisoners and sent them on a death march into the surrounding mountains. Though it was springtime, there was still snow on the ground. By May 1, the bedraggled band found themselves in the middle of a forest where, unable to take another step, they fell into the snow and went to sleep. They awoke early the next morning to discover that the SS men and most of the guards had fled.

Those few guards who remained led them to a barn in a nearby town and disappeared. Welner buried himself in a bale of hay and went to sleep. Later that day, someone tapped him on the shoulder. "The Americans are here," he said.

Welner eventually made his way back to Lodz, where he was reunited with one of his younger sisters. He found another sister in Bergen Belsen later that year. The rest of his family was dead. Sponsored by an uncle, Welner emigrated to Denver and found work as a carpenter.

Today at the age of ninety, Welner gives talks to Denver school children about his experiences in the camps.

"I'll never forgive them, and I'll never forget," he said. "But I don't hate their children for what their fathers did. I tell the kids never to let hatred into their hearts. If you do, it will ruin your life. You should never let the past ruin your future."

Lauren Watson: rise of a radical

The anger started early for activist Lauren Watson who, in the late 1960s, founded the Denver Chapter of the Black Panther Party.

"Out in Sacramento when I was in the first grade, they used to have us sing songs like 'Old Black Joe,'" he said, "and I could see that the other kids were snickering. I went home and told my mother, and she came down to the school and lit the place up. She was just five foot five, but she had that principal up on his desk, threatening to take the issue to the school board."

The old songbooks were replaced.

In 1950, Ruth Watson moved her family to Denver. While it may have had a reputation for racial tolerance, Denver was still a segregated city in those days.

"Blacks had to sit in theatre balconies," Watson recalled, "and we were never seated in restaurants, at least not in downtown. So we didn't go downtown. We stayed up on the north side of Twenty-third." By the time he entered Manual High School in 1954, the boundary line had moved south to Colfax, and schools such as Manual had become predominantly, if not exclusively, black.

"A handful of white kids used to be bussed in from Adams County, where there was no high school," Watson said. "I began to notice that the white kids, who were even poorer than us and not any smarter, were getting on student council and being placed in advanced classes. Most of the teachers were white, and they had very low expectations of us. If you look at the history textbooks from the time, there was maybe one page with a picture of blacks in bandannas working the cotton fields."

Much to the dismay of his mother, his teachers, and his sister Saundra who was Manual class valedictorian in 1955, Watson started ditching school and raising hell.

"Basically, I didn't give a shit," he said. "My grades were terrible."

Despite the rebellious attitude and lackluster academics, Watson did manage to graduate. He applied and was accepted at Denver University on a provisional basis. To get to school, he would take the York Street bus south and then walk home in the afternoons. That was when he started noticing the cops circling and keeping an eye on him.

"Occasionally, they'd stop and question me," he said, "and I'd wonder, *What's this all about?* But the reason was obvious. I was a black boy in a white neighborhood."

Watson lasted one quarter at DU before blowing it off and heading out to LA, where the discrimination was neither subtle nor covert.

"Most of the women were employed," he remembered, "but not the men. They'd drive the women to work and go back to the block where they stood around all day, drinking and lifting weights."

To make matters worse, the LA cops were downright brutal.

"They'd bust you for jaywalking and beat the hell out of you," Watson said. "There was a lot of rage building in the community, and the Black Muslims were starting to talk about fighting back."

The anger and frustration finally boiled over one hot summer evening in 1964, when a guy named Marcus Fry got into it with the cops at a neighborhood liquor store.

"Word spread like wildfire that Marcus had been beaten up," Watson said. "So we all jumped in our cars and went over there."

By the time they arrived, the police had cordoned off the area, and the Muslims were throwing bricks and bottles and chanting slogans. The situation quickly escalated into a full-scale riot.

"This really impressed me," Watson said. "People in LA were standing up to the cops, and I thought we should be doing this back home. I came back to Denver with a serious attitude. I joined CORE, and started hanging out with SDS and the Young Socialist Alliance."

A few years later, he met Huey Newton who, along with Bobby Seale, urged him to found a Denver chapter of the Black Panther Party.

Now seventy-one and bedridden with complications from back surgery and chemotherapy, Lauren Watson makes no apologies for his revolutionary past.

"I sacrificed my life for what I believed in," he said. "I have no regrets. I'd do it again if I had the chance, but I'd do it better."

Phil Martinez: learning the lessons of war

Phil Martinez speaks with the dead-eyed seriousness of someone who has seen the worst the world has to offer and lived to tell about it. Of his tour of duty in Iraq, he said simply, "It was hot. It smelled like trash, and the people hated us. Even the people we were trying to help would shoot at us if they got the chance."

Just exactly how much the troops were hated became abundantly clear three weeks after he arrived in country.

"We had just dropped off some school supplies to a village south of Baghdad," he said, "in an area known as the Triangle of Death. There was a loud explosion, and I saw a plume of smoke coming up out of the lieutenant's truck ahead of us. We stopped. I thought, *IED* (Improvised Explosive Device)."

The front of the vehicle had been blown off, and there was debris scattered everywhere. Looking inside, Martinez saw his friend Choat lying on the floor, wounded and unconscious, the medics working frantically to save him.

"When he came to, he couldn't stand up, and his speech was slurred," he said. "We called in a heli and evacuated him. He survived but lost his spleen and had long-term brain damage."

On the trip back, nobody spoke.

"I saw my whole life flash before my eyes," Martinez said. "In one second, I had to grow up and quit being a punk kid. I was afraid, but I realized I had a responsibility to the other guys in my unit. Before, I thought life was a big joke. Now I knew I was not invincible, and I had to make some serious changes. I owed it to my family to straighten up. How do I want to be remembered? Not as a troublemaker but as a good person. I reevaluated my life."

It was a reevaluation long in coming. By his own admission, Martinez was a hell-raiser in high school (Thomas Jefferson. Southeast Denver).

"We were into stealing cars, breaking into places. Lots of drinking, getting in fights, playing hooky," he said.

Needless to say, he got kicked out and was reassigned to the Alternative Life Skills Center at Ninth and Cherokee. He did manage to earn a high school diploma there, but just barely.

"I had horrible grades, no money, no job prospects, and I'm thinking, *What's next?*"

When his best friend went to jail for kidnapping and attempted murder, Martinez realized it was time for a course correction. He called a recruiter, enlisted in the army, and went in a week after his eighteenth birthday.

"I did very well in basic," he said. "That was the first time I wanted to learn and do my best."

He was assigned to the Tenth Mountain Division at Fort Drum, New York, and deployed to Iraq as a cavalry scout in August 2006.

Once or twice a month, some vehicle in his convoy would get hit. But fortune favored Phil Martinez. He returned unscathed.

Now six years later, he has mixed feelings about the war.

"When I first joined up, I thought it was a good thing," he said. "But after seeing it firsthand, the experience changed my outlook. We tried to do the right thing, tried to help them out, wanted to help them build schools and feel safe. I hate to see all that time and effort wasted, but I think we were misled. The whole experience kind of sucked."

Which is not to say that he learned nothing from it.

"War puts things into perspective," he said. "You learn to respect the small things: a hot shower, clean water, a full night's rest. You learn to love your family and friends and to put others before yourself. All the guys had one another's back. I wouldn't trade that for anything."

Bob Kirtdoll: he was there for *Brown v. Board of Education*

It wasn't all that long ago that racial segregation was common practice all over these United States.

"There may not have been official segregation," said Denver resident Bob Kirtdoll, "but we knew where not to go. You couldn't be in a white neighborhood after dark. You couldn't get served in restaurants. We'd buy food at the lunch counter and take it away to eat. We had to sit in the balcony at the movie theatre. We were supposed to sit at the back of the bus."

Segregation in the public schools, on the other hand, was a matter of settled law. In 1896, the Supreme Court had ruled in *Plessy v. Ferguson* that as long as separate facilities for blacks and whites were *equal*, segregation did not violate the Fourteenth Amendment.

"That was all just natural bullshit," said Kirtdoll, who speaks from personal experience.

In the early '50s, he was a student at Pierce Addition School on the outskirts of Topeka, Kansas.

"There were just two rooms for all eight grades," he said. "The lighting was poor. It had a coal-burning furnace and a tiny playground with two or three swings. Our textbooks were old, worn, and out of date. We definitely got an inferior education."

On Monday nights, Kirtdoll would attend something called Downbeat at Monroe Elementary which, like *Pierce Addition*, was a segregated school.

"Downbeat was held in the gym," he remembered. "We'd go there to dance and play ping-pong. I used to see Linda Brown there all the time."

The Linda Brown he refers to was the eight-year-old daughter of Reverend Oliver L. Brown, who became the lead plaintiff in a landmark case that would eventually overturn *Plessy v. Ferguson*. Reverend Brown and Bob's father, the Reverend Ruby Kirtdoll, were fellow ministers. They knew each other well.

The Brown family lived seven blocks from Sumner Elementary, a school built in 1936 for the exclusive use of white children. To get to all-black Monroe, Linda Brown was forced either to walk a mile across a dangerous railroad switchyard, or to travel more than an hour by bus.

In 1952, under the auspices of the Topeka Chapter of the NAACP, Reverend Brown attempted to enroll Linda at Sumner Elementary. She was, of course, refused admission. A class action suit against the Topeka Board of Education was brought by Brown and the parents of twelve other children. The case eventually made it to the Supreme Court, which rendered its decision in favor of the plaintiffs.

"Segregation of white and colored children in the public schools has a detrimental effect upon the colored children," wrote the Supremes. "The impact is greater when it has the sanction of the law, for the policy of separating the races is usually interpreted as denoting the inferiority of the Negro group. A sense of inferiority affects the motivation of a child to learn."

It was a finding borne out by Bob Kirtdoll's own experience.

"I knew I wasn't dumb," he said. "I was good at math. But English, history, and science I just didn't get. There was zero black history. We did get a little bit about George Washington Carver, but not enough to believe in his ability or to help us believe in our own capabilities."

Kirtdoll dropped out of school in the tenth grade, joined a union, and went to work in the construction industry.

"The education system reinforced the idea that we were inferior," he said. "The purpose of education for black people was to keep us in our place."

The changes wrought by *Brown v. Board of Education* were slow in coming. It would be another twenty years before the nation's schools were fully integrated.

"Sure there's been some progress," Kirtdoll said. "You can sit where you want and live where you want if you can afford it. But the biggest stumbling block to equality is still poverty. That's what keeps black people down. It breeds ignorance, defiance, and crime. We got A, B, C, and D, but we ain't got money. You get money, and you can do what you want."

Modern-day Wyatt Earp reenacts his great-grand uncle's life story

Wyatt Earp found out about Wyatt Earp the same way most Americans discovered him in the mid-1950s: he saw him on TV.

"One night, my dad and I were watching this show called *The Life and Legend of Wyatt Earp*, and he turned to me and said, 'That's your family, y'know.'"

Starring Hugh O'Brian and billed as the "first adult Western," *Wyatt Earp* was the most popular show on TV from 1955 to 1961. As it happens, today's Wyatt Earp is the great-grandnephew of the legendary lawman. Bearing his famous forebear's moniker, however, has been something of a mixed blessing. For one thing, he's had to put up with more than his share of lame jokes. Example: "Why did the man put a bowl in front of his TV set? He wanted to watch Wyatt Earp."

When he lost his first scrape to a kid who'd taunted him with 'Earp, slop, bring the mop, and don't forget the bucket,' Wyatt's dad enrolled him in a boxing class.

"I had the arms of an orangutan," he said, "so I could keep my distance. Boxing taught me the virtue of two left jabs and a right-cross."

It also taught him how to, well, roll with the punches.

"I developed a self-deprecating sense of humor among my friends," he said. "As a kid, you either learn people skills or you wind up a very bitter critter."

Earp went on to a successful thirty-five-year career with New York Life. Meanwhile, his wife, Terry, was making a name for herself as a writer of situation comedies. One day, she got a call from none other than Hugh O'Brian—yes, *that* Hugh O'Brian. Would she, he asked, be interested in writing a one-man bio-drama about the life of Wyatt Earp? The play would serve as a fund-raising vehicle for Hugh O'Brian Youth (HOBY), a foundation that provides leadership camps for promising high school sophomores. Terry spent the next six months researching and writing the play, but when she sent it off to O'Brian, he'd already moved on to other things. The script sat unproduced in her file cabinet for a year until it finally dawned on her, "Well . . . duh. Why don't I just have *my* Wyatt do it?"

"*Her* Wyatt" liked the idea. He spent the next two months memorizing the forty-one-page monologue.

"I put it on tape and played it over and over again 'til I could puke it," he said.

Wyatt Earp: A life on the Frontier, is a two-act play, the second act of which "lasts exactly twenty-eight minutes, thirty seconds," said Earp in a sly nod to the Gunfight at the OK Corral, which took place, he is quick to point out, "not at the OK Corral, but in a vacant lot a block and a half away." The showdown lasted all of thirty seconds.

Arizona Territory in the late eighteen hundreds was by all accounts a wild and wooly place.

"The whole thing was completely out of control," Earp said. "It was full of reprobates from the Civil War. All they knew was pillaging and murder."

The Federal Government wanted desperately to impose martial law. The last thing the outlaws wanted, however, was control by the very government that had kicked their butts in the Civil War.

Tensions were running hot on October 26, 1881, when the Earp brothers—Virgil, Wyatt and Morgan, plus Wyatt's lifelong pal, Doc Holliday—finally shot it out with the McLaury's and the Clantons on the streets of Tombstone. When the dust finally settled, the name Wyatt Earp was known in every household in America.

Now in its fifteenth season, the show has had 673 performances in eight countries and one cruise ship, averaging between 50 and 60 performances a year.

Wyatt Earp wants people—especially kids—to be aware of their history and of the value and importance of theatre in bringing that history to life.

"It's a legacy I can live and a legacy I can leave for the next generation," he said. "My goal is to bring Wyatt alive."

Miriam Hoffman finds herself at Jerusalem's Wailing Wall

It was the visit to Israel in 1974 that finally put Miriam Hoffman's identity crisis to rest. At the Wailing Wall, she saw a group of young Hassidic Jews praying fervently in a tight cluster with their rabbi. Following the ancient custom, she scribbled her own prayer on a slip of paper and lodged it in the wall. Then quite unexpectedly, she burst into tears and began kissing the stones and hugging the other women who had come there to worship.

"They thought I was a sabra," Hoffman remembers, "a native-born Israeli, though I spoke no Hebrew or Yiddish. But that didn't seem to matter. For the first time in my life, I was not being treated like a foreigner, which is how I always felt in the US. I came back to Colorado recharged and rejuvenated. I had discovered my Jewish identity."

Miriam Hoffman is a child of the Holocaust. Purely as a matter of survival, she was raised to deny the very heritage she would later reclaim at the Wall. In 1941, Italian troops invaded her native Greece, paving the way for German occupation and the annihilation of an estimated 89 percent of the country's Jewish population.

The Greeks, to their credit, were not of a mind to cooperate with their Nazi occupiers. Hoffman's grandfather was able to obtain false identity papers from the local chief of police. Everybody got a Christian name. Young Miriam was enrolled at a Christian school run by Orthodox nuns where she studied the catechism, said prayers to the icons, learned the names of the saints, and read the New Testament. At home, all Jewish observances were abandoned.

Fearful that the Nazis would discover their true identity, the family decided to split up into groups of two and to flee to Smokovu, a resistance stronghold in the mountains of central Greece. Miriam and her father traveled together in the back of a lorry carrying burlap sacks of potatoes and coal. On the way there, they encountered a road block. Everyone was ordered out of the truck.

"It was raining hard," Hoffman said. "We were hiding behind some sacks of coal, and we didn't move. I was sleeping under my father's coat. I heard machine guns shooting and the cries of people outside, but my father just held me tightly beneath his coat."

When a German soldier came back to search for stragglers, her father opened his coat and showed him the sleeping child. The soldier motioned for them to keep still. He jumped off the truck and left without saying anything to his superiors.

"My father always used to joke after that, that I had saved his life," Hoffman said.

She was ten years old when the war ended. In 1956, the family emigrated to Denver, where her father found work as a tailor. Although she learned English and married an American, she somehow felt like an outsider. Conditioned by her wartime experiences, she made no attempt to connect with the local Jewish community.

"But after I went to the Wailing Wall, I started to get more comfortable with my Jewishness," she said. "I'm not as afraid as I used to be to identify with my religion."

Her American family began, for the first time, to observe the Sabbath, lighting candles and saying prayers over the challah and wine every Friday evening. They joined the Hebrew Education Alliance and began sending their kids to Hebrew school. Hoffman connected with other Holocaust survivors and now gives lectures at area schools and churches.

"What I'm most proud of," she said, "is that our three kids all married Jewish and are raising *their* kids to carry on the tradition."

There's an old saying Hoffman remembers from her childhood: "To the Greeks, I am a Jew. To the Jews, I am a Greek."

"But after Israel," she said with a smile, "I now know who I really am."

John Rasko takes a bullet in the heart

Aurora resident John Rasko took a bullet in the heart and lived to tell about it. It happened in Vietnam on November 21, 1966. He was twenty-one years old and a fire team leader with the Eighth Army's Fourth Infantry Division.

"We were sent into Pleiku," he said. "Mountains. Hundred and thirty degrees. One hundred percent humidity. We were never dry, either from the rain or sweat. The clothes just rotted off our backs. They sent us in with nine meals apiece. After that, it was guavas and bananas—whatever we could find growing wild in the jungle."

The Vietcong had drawn the Americans into an L-shaped ambush, and for two days they were pinned down by sniper fire. Rasko's platoon was sent in to clean them out. They descended into a ravine, and when they got to the bottom, the enemy opened up on them with a .30-caliber machine gun. Bullets flew everywhere, and Rasko's men dove for cover.

Rasko turned to throw a grenade at the machine gun nest, and just as he let go, he was hit in the back by a stray bullet.

"It felt like I'd been kicked by a mule," he remembered. "It spun me around and I went down."

The bullet entered his back a half inch from the spine. On its way in, it broke a rib, punctured a lung, and lodged in his heart at the pulmonary artery. Oddly, when he retracted his arm from the grenade toss, a muscle slid over the wound so there was very little bleeding. So little, in fact, that the orderlies back at the battalion aid station didn't believe him when he told them he'd been shot. They took an X-ray anyway and showed it to the doctor who took one look at it and said, "So where's the corpse?"

"That's him there, sir," the orderly replied. "He's standing right behind you."

By now, Rasko was spitting up blood from the collapsed lung.

"Don't move," said the doctor. Turning to the orderly, he barked, "Get this man a litter."

He was strapped down, loaded onto a chopper, and airlifted out to a MASH unit.

"There was a chaplain on board," Rasko said. "All the color had drained out of my face, and he thought I was a goner. He started saying last rites for me."

The last thing he remembered as he passed into oblivion was a hail storm of rice. This was no hallucination. The Americans had confiscated it and were slitting the bags open and tossing them overboard.

At the MASH unit, he had a decision to make.

"We can leave the bullet in, and you'll have maybe two years to live" the surgeon informed him. "However, any movement could dislodge it, and if that happens, you'll bleed to death internally. If we do the surgery, there's only a fifty-fifty chance you'll survive. What do you want us to do?"

Rasko opted for surgery.

Waking up in the middle of the night, he heard a nurse say, "I can't get a pulse, Doctor. I think we've lost him." Rasko realized they were talking about him.

"That's when I took a deep breath and sat up fast," he said. "I wanted to show 'em I wasn't dead."

After four days at the MASH unit, the decision was made to send him to Japan for rehabilitation.

"Somehow, the army screwed up," he said, "and I got put on a plane to Honolulu instead. All I had when I got there were the PJs I was wearing and a set of X-rays. My baggage and records got sent to South Korea. I never saw 'em again."

The army kept him in Hawaii and trained him as an ambulance driver. He was awarded a Purple Heart and mustered out on November 4, 1967.

Did the experience change his life?

"Not really," he said. "I had bad dreams for a couple of months. Maybe if I'd been there longer . . . I was only in country forty-nine days. I think of it as a brief vacation in hell."

John Bell: go-to guy for the Buffalo Soldiers

Amateur historian John Bell is the go-to guy for all things Buffalo Soldier, but it was his dad who turned him on to them back in 1985.

"I was out at his house in Westminster watching a Bronco game," Bell said. "He walks into the room and says, 'What did they teach you in college about the Buffalo Soldiers?'

"I said, 'Nothing.'

"And he said 'Well then, I wasted my damned money.' Then he turned and walked out of the room. My dad was old school. He didn't say much, but when he did, you knew you'd better listen or you'd get your chops rocked. If it was that important to him, I figured I'd better look into it."

Given Bell's impressive academic credentials—he has a BA in history from Adam's State and a master's in education from CSU—it may seem surprising that he knew nothing about the Buffalo Soldiers. But then again, black history was not a fixture on college campuses in the late '50s and early '60s when he was going to school.

He also knew nothing about his father's World War II service. So like a good son and conscientious historian, he asked him about it. During the Depression, Bell learned, his father had worked as a mule skinner for the CCC (Civilian Conservation Corps). When the war broke out, he joined the Tenth Cavalry Regiment which, along with the Ninth, was one of two all-black cavalry units in the US Army.

"All-black" is not an entirely accurate designation, however, since only the enlisted men were black. The officers who commanded them were white to a man. Established by an act of Congress in 1866, the

Tenth Cavalry Regiment was a fighting unit intended to increase the size of a depleted Union Army after the Civil War.

"Their job was to protect the settlers who were moving westward," Bell explained. "They chased down cattle rustlers and provided cover for the crews building the transcontinental railroad. They built roads and forts, including Fort Garland in southern Colorado. Their most distasteful job was to move the Indians onto the reservations."

As it happens, it was the Native Americans who gave them the nickname Buffalo Soldiers.

"At first they called them *Wasichu Saba*, which means 'white man turned black,'" Bell said. "But seeing their curly hair, which resembled the hair between a buffalo's horns, and also the buffalo coats they wore in winter, the natives started calling them Buffalo Soldiers. The men liked the name. It was a term of respect and a whole lot nicer than some of the other names they were being called at the time."

Bell estimates that in the past twenty-five years, he's logged a million miles in search of accurate information about the unit. His house in Brighton is crammed with over three hundred pieces of memorabilia—McClelland saddles, swagger sticks, old photographs, uniforms, boots, and antique weapons—much of it donated by veterans determined to see the legacy of the Buffalo Soldiers passed on to future generations.

In 1992, Bell formed a historic reenactment troupe called the Buffalo Soldiers of the American West. It consists of twenty-five dedicated volunteers who wear reproductions of the regiment's original uniform. They also carry copies of powder weapons from the period, do horse drills, and give lectures and shows in schools, churches, universities, and businesses and, each October, at something called the Refuse Rendezvous at Rocky Mountain Arsenal.

"We're historians first and re-enactors second," Bell said. "Each man learns the story and takes on the role of an original Buffalo Soldier in the 1870s, '80s, and '90s, most of them Medal of Honor winners. Our guys come from all walks of life. There are two PhDs on our board. All the rest have master's degrees. A couple of them are Civil War historians. Our main purpose is to tell our stories, and it's definitely a story that needs to be told. For me it's a labor of love."

John H. Yee: original Flying Tiger

Lady Luck, it seems, has always been on the side of John Hua-ren Yee.

Yee, a retired social studies teacher in the Aurora Public School System, was born in 1921 in a small farming village about three hundred miles from Kunming, China. He remembers it as a primitive place—"worse than Wyoming"—where opium poppy and corn were the principle crops, and where the staple in the local diet was not rice, but cornmeal mush.

His family converted to Christianity, and as a result young Hua-ren was permitted to attend British missionary schools in Kunming, where he learned to speak and write proper English. He went on to university in Hong Kong. But his education came to an abrupt halt when the Japanese began bombing Kunming in 1937. He went home to a city under attack.

"They were bombing at will," he said. "We had no defenses, no anti-aircraft guns, and our planes were all World War I vintage. They would start at one end and bomb the entire length of the city. It would be like strafing Colfax all the way to Golden."

On one particularly horrific day, Yee's house came under fire. He dove for cover in a laundry shack in the backyard. When the raid was over, he emerged to a blackened sky, and there were corpses scattered all over the yard.

"It was a peasant family that lived next door: dad, mom, and two kids, all dead. There were guts hanging from the trees. That night, you could hear crying and moaning all across the city."

Kunming, it appeared, was headed for complete destruction. But the Japanese had not reckoned on China's secret weapon—one Claire Chennault, a retired US Army Air Corps officer and stunt pilot who had caught the attention of Generalissimo Chiang Kai-shek. Chiang recruited him in 1936 to bring his air force up to speed. Somehow, Chennault managed to wangle one hundred P-40 fighter planes out of the Roosevelt Administration, along with the pilots to fly them, plus a couple hundred maintenance and administrative staff.

The American Volunteer Group (AVG) as they were officially known, arrived in Kunming on December 21, 1941, twelve days after the attack on Pearl Harbor and one day before a planned raid on the city by the Japanese. Yee remembers the battle clearly.

"The Japanese sent in ten bombers from Hanoi," he said. "They had no idea the AVG were there. I heard machine guns in the sky and looked up to see three of their bombers go down. The Americans shot all the rest of them but one on the way back to Hanoi. It was the first time in the history of the Sino-Japanese War that there was resistance. The Flying Tigers (as the AVG came to be called) were never beaten. They downed fourteen Japanese planes for every P-40 lost."

In order to train Chinese pilots, Chennault needed interpreters. Yee volunteered and was commissioned as a second lieutenant in the Chinese Air Force, sometimes translating for Chennault himself.

In 1944, he was ordered to Biloxi, Mississippi to serve as a classroom interpreter at the aircraft mechanics school at Keesler Field. He came down with tuberculosis and was sent to Fitzsimons Army Hospital in Denver. Scheduled for return to China, Yee requested permission to stay in the US to complete his treatment. At the last possible moment, his request was granted.

"This changed the course of my life," he said. "If I'd have gone back to China, I'd have been forced to escape to Taiwan or been purged in the Cultural Revolution as an enemy of the people."

It was not the last time fortune would smile upon John Yee.

Cured of TB, he went to work in the shipping department at Samsonite Luggage, where he got to know the company's general manager. The GM was friends with the dean of academic affairs at Denver University, and as luck would have it, he just happened to be the brother of a missionary Yee had known in Kunming. The dean arranged a scholarship, and in 1955, nearly twenty years after quitting college to defend his native land, John Yee finally got his degree.

Postscript: In 1986, Kunming was named a Denver Sister City. John Yee is the honorary chair of the Kunming Sister City Association.

Arthur McFarlane keeps legacy of iconic civil rights leader alive

It's a moment that Arthur McFarlane, who is the maternal great-grandson of civil rights leader W.E.B. DuBois, describes as "heart stopping."

When he was twenty-one and still in college, he went to Baltimore to visit relatives. On Sunday, they took him to church where, after the service, a little old lady came up to him, took both his hands in hers, looked him straight in the eye, and said, "You are a prince of our people, and you need to carry that."

"She was squeezing my hands," he remembered. "It was clear to me how profound an impact my great-grandfather had had on her life and the choices she'd made. I didn't know how to respond, but I tried to take in the depth of the message she was delivering. I don't think I got it until later, after more people like her said how honored they were to meet me and told me of the impact Grandpa had had on their lives."

In 1895, W.E.B. DuBois became the first African American ever to earn a PhD from Harvard. He was an educator, writer, and researcher who conducted the first serious sociological studies of life in black America. He was also something of a firebrand, challenging the prevailing ideology within the black community of accommodation as a means of eliminating segregation. To end racism in America, he preached, blacks needed to mobilize and agitate. A founding member of the NAACP, many today consider him the father of the modern Civil Rights Movement.

McFarlane first met his famous forebear in 1958, when he was just three months old.

"It was at his ninetieth birthday party at the Roosevelt Hotel in New York City," he said. "He addressed his speech to me and offered words of advice to do work you enjoy and that the world needs to have done."

McFarlane didn't hear a lot about DuBois when he was growing up.

"It wasn't pushed on us," he said. "But in high school, it became a bigger deal. I started giving talks about him. My freshman year in college, I was invited to speak about him at a convention of the Congress of Racial Equality."

Born and educated in New York, McFarlane moved to Colorado in the 1980s to do graduate work at CU. Today he's an evaluator for the State Department of Public Health. But he also maintains a kind of second career, giving talks about DuBois once or twice a month, not only here in Colorado, but also all over the US and even in places as far away as Istanbul, Turkey.

"When I'm done talking about him, people always ask me what his words mean for us today. What would his advice be for people in our time?" McFarlane said. "DuBois believed that the problem of the twentieth century was the problem of the color line. I think the problem for the twentieth century is how we deal with our differences: religious, ethnic, racial, sexual orientation. You can see that every single day. That's what *we* wrestle with in our time. Our differences are important, and we have to respect them, not blow them up and use them to separate us from one another. So I think if he were alive today, he'd probably say, 'Talk to somebody who's different than you. Ask them to tell you their story. In that way we can learn our similarities and maybe make the world a better place.'"

Taking on the mantel of his iconic ancestor has not been without its difficulties.

"It's been a hard journey," McFarlane said. "DuBois cast such a great shadow. It was sometimes hard to see who *I* was apart from him. But to know that people are hearing his story and that there's still a place for his thoughts and example in our lives—keeping that alive has been honorable work."

Dr. Vincent Harding's mission of encouragement

If you ask Dr. Vincent Harding who he is, he won't mention that he's Professor Emeritus of Religion and Social Transformation at Iliff School of Theology. Nor will he volunteer that he was a close associate of Dr. Martin Luther King, or that he served as the first director of the King Memorial Center in Atlanta. He's not comfortable with titles, but if you push him on it, he will tell you that his job is "to encourage others to be their best selves and for the country to realize its best possibilities."

To that end, he and his late wife, Rosemarie, founded the Veterans of Hope Project at Iliff.

"Veterans of Hope invites people who've been working for human social change to tell the story of how they came to be engaged, their inspiration, and how they deal with discouragement," he said.

Although their stories are preserved on videotape, Harding doesn't see them merely as an historical record.

"We're putting these materials in the hands of younger people to help them see the possibilities," he said. "They're a source of encouragement to youth."

Harding's career as an advocate for peace and justice began while he was in the army in the early '50s. With time on his hands, he began a serious study of the New Testament, which in turn led him to question his role as a soldier.

"How do I reconcile killing with loving my enemies?" he asked himself. "To take Jesus Christ seriously, I had to be a conscientious objector. That realization drew me in the direction of the movement."

At the University of Chicago, where he went to study history after his stint in the military, Harding fell in with a group of Mennonites who wanted to establish an interracial church on the city's south side.

"We kept asking ourselves, 'Would we be doing this if we were in the Deep South?'" Harding said. "One day, somebody said, 'Why don't we head south and find out?'"

Which is how it came to pass that five young Mennonites—three whites and two blacks—crammed themselves into a station wagon and headed south on an odyssey that would take them from Little Rock, Arkansas, across Mississippi, to Montgomery, Alabama: a fairly dicey proposition considering that Dixie in '58 was still legally segregated.

Improbable as it may seem, the group located Martin Luther King's phone number in the Montgomery telephone directory and called him up. King's wife, Coretta, answered and invited them over. Dr. King welcomed them from his sickbed, where he was recuperating from a stab wound he'd received on a book tour in New York.

"We sat in chairs around the bed and talked," Harding recalled. "Martin was impressed that we'd made it through Mississippi alive. As we were leaving he said, 'You're Mennonites. You know about nonviolence. Why don't you come on down and help us out?'"

Two years later, Harding and his new bride took King up on his offer and moved to Atlanta, where they became the official Mennonite representatives to the Freedom Movement. The house they lived in was just around the corner from Dr. King's, and it wasn't long before a friendship developed.

"I saw him as an elder brother," Harding said. "We saw a lot of each other. Occasionally, he'd ask me to draft speeches and press releases for him. One significant piece was his speech calling for resistance to the Vietnam War. It was delivered at Riverside Church in New York on April 4, 1967, exactly one year before he was assassinated."

Harding feels that many teachers today are reluctant to talk about segregation, and as a result, students are coming away with a false impression of what it was really like back then.

"The story is much, much more than just Dr. King," Harding said. "Thousands of unnamed people took enormous risks by refusing to obey the laws of segregation. They need to be recognized and emulated."

Which brings us back round to Voices of Hope.

"Our mission," Harding said, "is to get the story out there. If we don't talk about it, tell the stories, times will continue to be difficult."

Denver mayoral candidate James Mejia:
"Sometimes losing is winning"

Former Denver mayoral candidate James Mejia said he couldn't quite grasp what Senator Mark Udall was trying to tell him during a campaign event back in 2011.

"Sometimes," Udall had said, "losing is winning."

Now he totally gets it. "Losing has opened some doors for me," he said.

After the election, job offers in both the public and private sectors started coming his way. But something told him that going back to work in some high-powered job might not be his most appropriate course of action. Instead, he decided to take time off for some personal reassessment and spiritual regeneration.

On election night, candidate Mejia was in North Denver, still knocking on doors and collecting mail-in ballots right up until the last minute. He got home twenty minutes after the polls closed and was greeted at the door by his seven-year-old daughter, who looked at him gravely and gave him the bad news.

"You've only got 25 percent, Dad."

Later, when they went to La Rumba to greet his supporters, they stepped into a maelstrom of flashbulbs and rapid-fire questions.

"How does it feel to lose the election?" the reporters had shouted, even though he and his advisors were thinking they might still have a shot.

"The kids were clinging to us," he said, "and I'm like, 'this is totally surreal.'"

But by the following morning, even he had to admit the game was up. He met with his staff to thank them for their hard work.

"They'd taken me from zero name recognition to 26 percent of the vote," he said. "We had a strong belief that we were the right people to run the city. So it was very difficult to say we didn't make it to those who had put everything on the line for me."

Later, he made his concession speech and that was that.

"My wife, Heather, took it pretty hard," he said. "There was a lot of second-guessing about what we could have done differently. My kids saw what had gone into it and knew after all that work we still lost."

Now what?

"Take some time," Heather said. "Don't rush into anything. Whatever you choose to do, make sure it's something you feel passionate about."

That would be long-distance running. Still revved from the campaign, Mejia entered his fifty-first marathon, only to find his body rebelling against the exertion.

"It wasn't from lack of training," he said. "It was from lack of sleep." So first thing on his agenda would be to get some rest.

And then there was the question of nutrition. "Your diet goes to hell in a campaign," Mejia said. "You're working long days with young staffers who have good metabolism, so you're munching on chips, cookies, and pizzas all day long."

And finally, there was that old saw about politicians quitting to spend more time with their families, a truism nonetheless true in Mejia's case.

"I reconnected with my kids and started looking at them with new eyes," he said. "I loved being able to drop them off at school, have ice cream, read books to them at night, and go to the park on weekends— all stuff I took for granted during the campaign since I was out of the house so much. During the campaign, none of this would have made sense. I'm grateful for what's happened to me since the election. In many ways, it's been an absolute reawakening. I feel a little wiser, more patient, and every bit as committed to making an impact on the city I love."

PART 6

Food, Shelter, and a Decent Education

Magda King gets a view from the highest peaks

Magda King began her climbing career in Spain in the 1960s. Back then, Spanish climbers were conquering one summit after another in the Andes and Himalayas. One problem, though: they were all men.

"No Spanish woman had ever summited an eight-thousand-meter peak," she said. "I began asking myself, 'If a man can do it, why not a woman? In fact, why not me?'"

Setting the conquest of an eight-thousand-meter peak as her life's goal, King began climbing higher and higher mountains in Europe, South America, Africa, and India. By 1987, she'd summited fifteen peaks, all of them over five thousand meters tall.

It was time for the next step. King assembled a team to scale Yalung Kang in Eastern Nepal, and she might very well have succeeded had the weather cooperated.

"We were caught for six days at twenty thousand feet in the worst storm in a century," she said. "There was so much snow that we had to come out of our tents every two hours to dig ourselves out. We survived on tea and soup."

Two years later, she tried again. This time, the goal was Mt. Cho Oyu on the Nepali-Tibetan border. King and another female climber, Monica Verge, literally raced up that mountain.

"It took us nineteen days from base camp to summit," King said, "and we did it on our first attempt."

Curiously, King felt no elation while standing on Cho Oyu's lofty summit. "There's no time for elation at eight thousand meters," she said. "You're just glad you have no farther to go. Mainly what you're thinking about is how to get back down safely."

The full impact of what they'd done did not strike them until they were safely back in Barcelona.

"Being the first women to conquer an eight-thousand-meter peak, we'd essentially rewritten the history of Spanish mountaineering," King said.

Even so, she was not prepared for the hero's welcome that awaited them when they returned.

"We became instant celebrities," she said. "The president of Spain called to congratulate us. Total strangers would come up to us on the streets to shake our hands. We were even the answer to a question on a quiz show on Spanish TV."

King went on to conquer seven of the fourteen highest peaks in the world. But by 1995, she was beginning to rethink her priorities.

"I'd always looked for ways to fulfill my own dreams," she said. "Now I wanted to gain meaning and purpose by helping others. It was a real paradigm shift for me."

She flew to Nepal to look for a project that might benefit the families of the Sherpas who'd accompanied her on her Himalayan expeditions. What they needed most, she decided, was an education for their kids.

Now married and living in Denver, Magda and her husband Hugh established Namlo International, a foundation dedicated to building schools in Nepal and, more recently, in Nicaragua. So far, they've built seven schools; and these days, King spends most of her time fund-raising out of a small office, which she called "A much bigger challenge than reaching a summit."

"We raise the money to get the projects off the ground," she said, "but the communities themselves pitch in to build the schools. We don't do welfare. The question we ask ourselves whenever we go into a village is, 'What do they need to become independent of Namlo?'"

Last year, the foundation weaned its first community, the Nepali village of Yarmasing.

"They now have a road, electricity, and telephones," King said. "Both the kids and their parents have received an education, and the standard of living has improved. We've learned that if you partner with people, miracles can and do happen."

Magda King's motto? "From the highest peaks you can see the furthest horizons."

Claude d'Estree: "old-time fiery abolitionist"

DU Professor Claude d'Estree calls himself an "old-time fiery abolitionist." Like a lot of folks in the antislavery movement, he came to it by way of his faith. Which is surprising, given the religious ambiguity of the household he grew up in. His Russian Orthodox grandparents were Jews forced to convert to Christianity. His dad, a Sorbonne-trained philosopher and strident ex-Catholic, nonetheless insisted that his son attend Catholic school.

"I was fascinated by religion," he said. "I was curious why people were even interested in it."

Not far from where he grew up in West Hollywood, California, there was a Japanese Zen garden where, at the age of ten, D'Estree would go and sit for hours in silent contemplation.

"I figured it out that the people who hung out there were Buddhists," he said. "I looked up Buddhism in the encyclopedia. Unlike the Western philosophy I got from my father, Buddhism seemed clear, practical, to the point, easy to understand. I started reading everything I could find on Asian spirituality: Thomas Merton, Alan Watts, T. Lobsang Rampa."

In 1979, His Holiness the Dalai Lama came to Harvard Divinity School, where D'Estree, now twenty-seven, was doing graduate work. As the "resident Buddhist" at Harvard Divinity, he was put in charge of the visit.

"His Holiness was friendly and informal," he recalled, "but I found myself trying on different personalities to impress him. He just chuckled at all of them. There were two of us in the room but only one ego. Mine. Finally, I let go of the effort, at which point he gave me a big hug and a head bump and said, 'It's so good to see my old friend Claude again.' It was a moment that stood still for me, a moment of clarity in which I saw that I wasn't all these personae. For the first time in my life, I was who I really was."

On the spot, the Dalai Lama authorized him to begin teaching.

"There was no ceremony or initiation or anything," D'Estree said. "I made a decision to teach only what I myself was able to practice."

Over the next twenty-six years, he co-taught with His Holiness whenever the latter was in the States.

D'Estree came to DU as a law professor in 2002, and that year he attended a talk in Boulder by a woman named Jolene Smith. Speaking in behalf of a human trafficking awareness group called Free the Slaves, Smith didn't pull any punches. There were, she said, more slaves now than at any other time in human history, an estimated twenty-three to twenty-seven million worldwide. Upward of seventeen thousand were being trafficked into the US every year.

"She told us that fifty to one hundred thousand human beings in this country are doing hard labor or working in the commercial sex trade without pay and against their will," D'Estree said. "Human trafficking is second only to drugs in terms of illicit profitability. I realized I had to do something about it."

Back at DU, he established the Task Force on Modern Slavery and Human Trafficking, which brings together people from different disciplines to work on the issue. Then in 2008, he set up the only two-year graduate training program on human trafficking in the US.

"Data and research in this area are piss-poor," he said. "Our task is to provide sound research so we can come up with good policy decisions. I'm training a whole new generation of abolitionists."

And his dharma practice?

"This *is* my dharma practice. This *is* my meditation," he said. "This is where the rubber meets the road. My whole teaching area is about some of the darkest aspects of human behavior. I put everything I learned as a dharma student and teacher into it. All those twenty-six years of teaching and practice. That's what laid the foundation stones to be able to do this work with equanimity and compassion."

City planner George Nez: "Nobody should be without a roof over his head"

"Nobody should be without a roof over his head." That, in a nutshell, is the philosophy of city planner George Nez who, for the past fifty years, has been providing basic shelter for the dispossessed in some of the world's poorest places.

During the 1950s, Nez headed Denver's Department of City Planning. But when the UN offered him the opportunity to create an infrastructure plan for the Nation of Ghana in 1961, he jumped at the chance. A former British colony, Ghana was a country without ports, bridges, or electricity. "A stone-age culture," Nez remembered, "with lions roaring outside the villages at night."

What Ghana did have, though, were huge deposits of bauxite which Kaiser Aluminum had agreed to buy if the government could provide the electricity necessary to mine it—which meant building a dam that would wipe out six hundred villages and displace one hundred thousand people. Nez was appointed project manager for the UN team charged with the task of resettling them.

The plan he devised was dead simple: build the roofs first, move the occupants in, and let them fill in the walls at their leisure with adobe block. He trained small crews to go from site to site, planting concrete posts to which were attached ready-made metal trusses, and covering them with corrugated aluminum roofing. His strategy worked; in just two years, Nez and his team built an astounding fourteen thousand houses in twenty new towns and villages.

He went on to do city planning in earthquake devastated municipalities such as Skopje, Macedonia, and Managua, Nicaragua. It was in Managua that he began thinking about alternatives to traditional materials.

"The old-style roofs needed a forest of rafters," he said, "and in many third-world countries they were running out of forests because they'd used all their wood for cooking. So I was thinking, 'What else can we use?'"

One promising alternative was something called a hyperbolic paraboloid (hypar) arch. Visualize a square frame with one raised corner. That's a hypar arch. Put two of those raised corners together and you get a square base that ascends to a tentlike point in the center. That's a double hypar arch and the basic shape for the roof system Nez had in mind.

"In the old days, hypars were built over wooden forms and reinforced with finger-thick steel mesh," he explained. Cement was then poured over the entire structure. When it cured, the wooden form was removed and—hey, presto—you had a very strong, freestanding concrete roof.

One obvious advantage: hypars needed no rafters. The downside: traditional construction methods were expensive and time consuming. The problem for Nez was how to make the technology accessible and cost effective in a third-world setting.

In 1977, he approached the National Parks Service with the idea of building hypar shelters in the parks.

"I wanted to build the lightest (and cheapest) possible structure," he said. "At the time, the Parks Service was spending $70 a square foot. I told them I could do it for a tenth of the price."

Instead of finger-thick steel mesh, he stretched fly screen over a basic wooden frame to form a double hypar arch. Then he painted it with a slurry of sand, Portland cement, and liquid latex. Only a centimeter thick, Nez' structures turned out to be lightweight, resilient, and incredibly strong.

"A half-inch thick hypar can hold up to twenty-one feet of wet snow," he said, "and you can build them on the ground and lift them up without cracking them."

They're also simple to construct, making them ideal for third-world applications.

Not surprisingly, Nez' ideas have caught on, and today his roofs are being built from Afghanistan to South Sudan, Bangladesh to Rwanda, Kenya to earthquake-ravaged Haiti.

At ninety, he still travels the globe, supervising construction and advising local governments on his methods.

What makes George Nez run? "I've had so much luck in my life," he said. "I survived malaria in Africa, and walked away from burning planes during the war. I feel like I owe it to my country for the GI Bill that gave me an education and got me started."

Heather Forbes finds a new way to work with troubled adoptees

It's a story we're hearing a lot these days. A young couple adopts a child, only to discover that he's combative, hostile, and impossible to live with. Keeping him is intolerable. Sending him back is out of the question. What's a mother to do?

In 1996, Heather Forbes and her former husband adopted a two-and-a-half-year-old boy from Russia.

"Right from the start, he was coming after me with scissors, pulling my hair, punching me in the mouth, and breaking windows," said Forbes, a licensed clinical social worker who lives in Boulder. "That puts a lot of fear in a mom. What's he gonna be like at fifteen?"

Thinking it might help if they adopted a second child, the couple took in a four-year-old girl—also from Russia—who turned out to be emotionally withdrawn and totally uncommunicative.

"I couldn't connect with her," Forbes said. "I was feeling helpless, ineffective, and alone. It was a real dark night of the soul."

She sought the advice of child psychologists.

"The standard approach in the mid-to-late '90s was all about control," she said. "If I told my son to put on his shoes so we could go to the park, three hours later, still no shoes. The experts told me to 'keep insisting 'til the child obeys.' Not only did that not work, it made things worse. It also went against all my maternal instincts. There was no empathy, no nurturing in that approach."

Forbes quit her job and went back to graduate school to train with professionals in the field of trauma and attachment: a new discipline that had arisen in response to the problems parents were having from international adoptions.

In grad school, Forbes had a lightbulb moment: "This is not a defiant child," she realized. "This is a scared child. He's just lost everything—parents, home, culture, climate—and he's thinking, 'I'm not safe.' A fearful child does not need more control. What he needs is love. I finally started asking the right questions: not, 'How can I change him?' but, 'What's driving this behavior?'"

Her task, as she saw it, was to somehow lessen the fear, stress, and overwhelm her kids were feeling.

"I took away the environmental factors that were contributing to their distress," she said, "and made a very small world for them. No more soccer practice. No more outside family members. No more *Chuck E. Cheese.* I homeschooled them and little by little added elements of the world back in."

She also worked to acknowledge their feelings.

"You don't stuff the behavior," she said. "You let it out. You ask for feedback and join them in their emotional distress. It's when they're acting out that you create the deepest level of love and relationship. In relationship, the child learns self-regulation, how to calm him*self* down. That's the reason kids live with us for eighteen years. It takes that long."

Six months into the new regime, and the frequency, intensity, and duration of the behaviors had decreased dramatically, and Forbes was no longer feeling hopeless and helpless.

"I understood my children," she said. "Their behaviors were not about me. They weren't rejecting *me*. They were just in self-preservation mode."

Her method worked so well that when her son went back to school, he was able to skip the seventh grade. He's now a freshman at CU. Her daughter emerged more slowly from *her* protective cocoon.

"She's still subject to anxiety in over-stimulating environments," Forbes said, "but she's blossoming as a junior at a small private high school in Boulder."

Forbes's two books on working with problem kids, *Beyond Consequences, Logic and Control, Parts 1 and 2,* recently hit the top of the charts in her category on Amazon.com. Today she gives seminars and trainings to parents with problem kids.

"There's a huge market," she said. "People all over the world are interested. What my experience proves is that love works, love heals, and love never fails. Don't give up on your kids. Healing is always possible."

Rev. Diana Flahive addresses the plight of Denver's homeless women

"On any given night in Denver, there are eight hundred women on the streets, many of whom have no place to sleep at night," said the Rev. Diana Flahive.

Flahive is coordinator of the Women's Homelessness Initiative, a project established by Capitol Hill United Ministries (CHUM) to address the plight of homeless women in Denver.

"They're vulnerable to violence and abuse," she said. "Our purpose is to provide sanctuary for twenty of those women every night, year round. We offer them dignity, care, compassion, presence, and respect."

Participating churches provide a cot and a hot meal. Usually by eight thirty, everybody's bedded down. A couple of volunteers stay the night, and the following morning, each guest is given a breakfast bag containing soft granola, a hardboiled egg, a carton of juice, some yoghurt, sometimes a peanut butter sandwich.

Who are these homeless women?

"They could be any one of us if our lives took a different turn," Flahive said. "We've had elderly women with dementia, a woman with cerebral palsy in a wheelchair, a forty-five-year-old who's pregnant with twins. We even had one who'd been a teacher for twenty years. She made some bad financial decisions and lost everything."

The homeless issue "just kind of dropped in my lap," she said. In October of 2011, a group of ministers got together to discuss the situation at the invitation of Rebecca Crummey, a former priest at St. John's Episcopal Church. They established three goals for themselves:

to offer sanctuary, to educate others about the issues, and to advocate for better solutions.

"Out of that, we devised a concept where seven churches would each host twenty homeless women once a week," Flahive said. "We also partnered with St. Francis Center, a day shelter for the homeless. Every morning at eight thirty, they conduct a lottery to select the twenty who will get a place for the night."

The Women's Homeless Initiative is run totally by volunteers who take turns setting up the space, cooking a meal, spending the night, and handing out the breakfast bags in the mornings. In their first year, they put in twenty thousand volunteer hours, providing over $35,000 worth of in-kind services.

At the heart of the program sits Diana Flahive, connecting resources and people, meeting challenges, and solving logistical problems as they arise.

"I'm on the phone a lot," she said, "making sure our volunteers have what they need, looking for partner churches, and recruiting volunteers."

For Flahive, though, it's about more than just bricks and mortar.

"It's about opening up another part of yourself," she said. "Just like the rest of us, people who are homeless want to be seen, heard, and known. So when I see somebody standing on a corner holding a sign, I don't give them money. I talk to them: 'How are you today? Did you have a place to sleep last night? My name is Diana. What's your name?'"

Is there a solution to the problem of homelessness in Denver?

"Serve. Educate. Advocate," she said. "If we're a civil society, where should our money be going? There are lots of people out there doing good things, but we need resources and a change of heart. Where I'm at right now, I don't understand all the suffering in the world. I hope there is justice. I used to think I could change the world. Now I know I can only do what's right in front of me. But still it pains me to see so much suffering out there."

Douglas Eichelberger recycles plastic to house the world's poor

The third world is awash in plastic. Some rivers in Indonesia, for example, are so clogged with the stuff that you can no longer see the water. There's no system for recycling it and no market for it, so it just keeps accumulating year after year, wreaking environmental havoc and threatening the health and safety of those forced to live with it.

But Denver architect Douglas Eichelberger thinks he may have a solution, not only to the third world's plastic disposal problem, but also to its shelter problem. He's come up with a scheme to use old plastic bottles, compressed into manageable forty-pound bales and contained in wire-mesh baskets, to build low-cost housing for the poor.

The idea came to him after he left his job at RNL Architects and opened his own firm in the 1400 block of Wewatta Street. Back in 1989, the neighborhood had two defining characteristics. It was the center of Denver's burgeoning recycling industry, and it was full of homeless people sleeping under viaducts.

"I wasn't bustin'-my-ass busy," Eichelberger said. "I had lots of time to think and be creative. One day, I'm sitting at my drafting table, and this homeless guy knocks on my door and asks if he can borrow a hose. Pretty soon, I'm smelling soap and shampoo, and I realize that he's using my hose to take a shower. I used to see stuff like that every day down there."

He was also driving by the recycling plants on his way to and from work.

"I kept seeing these big bales of plastic," he said. "To me they were beautiful. Gradually, it dawned on me that there was a connection between waste and poverty."

Given his upbringing, that conceptual leap was not surprising. Eichelberger was raised a Mennonite, a denomination renowned for its concern for the poor and for its husbanding of resources and materials. He also hales from a family of builders. His grandfather was a contractor, his dad a structural engineer. His uncle owned Eichelberger Construction, where young Douglas worked on weekends all through architecture school at CU Denver.

"My uncle grew up during the Depression and was a steward of resources," he said. "He took extra care and responsibility with his building materials like straightening out bent nails and reusing old two-by-fours. Nothing was ever wasted. What I brought to architecture was my fine arts background (he has an undergraduate degree in sculpture from UNC-Greeley), my sensibility regarding the husbanding of materials, and a sense of responsibility to the poor."

Eichelberger contacted Tri-R Recycling and told them his idea of using plastic bales as a building material.

"Tri-R was 100 percent supportive," he said. "They offered me materials and a place to work."

With the help of contractor buddy Charley Gyden, he built a twelve-by-twelve test structure on the Tri-R lot.

"The premise of that building was to use plastic bales as the foundation, paper bales for the walls, and then to cover the whole thing with stucco. The workers at Tri-R called it the Piñata House because of the bright colors."

In the eighteen years since Eichelberger built that first structure, the recycling industry has come of age, and today there's a huge market for recycled paper. Used plastic, on the other hand, has no takers. Which is what makes Eichleberger's idea so compelling in a third-world setting.

"I'm looking for an NGO to pick up on this," he said. "All they'd have to provide are the wire-mesh baskets, which can be filled with rubble, trash, whatever, and covered with indigenous, site-specific materials like stucco or adobe. It's simple, cheap, and uses sweat equity. What gets to me conceptually is that we as Westerners complicate everything. We make it as refined and specialized as possible. That's where our culture has taken us. But I think the true sustainable answer is to go the other way, to make it as simple and universal as possible."

Karen Stewart: at home in the world's most dangerous places

In the eight years since she began working as a mental health coach for Doctors Without Borders, Karen Stewart has learned to make herself at home in some of the world's most dangerous places.

For Stewart, the idea of working abroad had always been a dream deferred. But then in 2002, a series of personal tragedies—the suicide deaths of her sister and a cousin, the end of a ten-year love affair, the death of her dog, the loss of her job—got her to thinking.

"Am I happy? Am I doing what I really want with my life? If my life ended tomorrow, would I have done what I wanted to do? What popped up immediately," she said, "was *no!*"

She considered the Peace Corps but then thought better of it. What attracted her to Doctors Without Borders was their stated policy of not accepting funding from any government.

"They wanted to do what was truly needed," she said, "not something on someone else's agenda. The Peace Corps has an agenda, plus you're all alone out there. With Doctors, you go with a team: a driver, a cook, a cleaner, a translator. Their idea is that you be able to spend twelve hours a day doing what you've come to do."

Stewart sold her car and motorcycle, put everything else in storage, and took a one-year contract with Doctors to work on an HIV/AIDS project in Lagos, Nigeria.

"People in Lagos are loud, open, honest, and have a great sense of humor," she said, "but there's always a high potential for violence whenever a crowd gathers. One time, my driver was backing up and, for some reason, a group of guys just pulled him out the car and beat him up."

Lagos was hot, crowded, and awash in garbage, just the place to start a new life. When Stewart showed up there in 2004, very few of the locals were coming forward for HIV/AIDS treatment despite the fact that it was readily available through Doctors Without Borders. A huge stigma had attached itself to the disease, and the air was rife with myth and misinformation. Rumor had it, to give but one glaring example, that HIV was nothing more than a hoax fabricated by the Americans to discourage sexual activity.

"Our goal was to educate the people," Stewart said, "and to go from under one hundred on treatment to over one thousand on treatment in one year. My job was to train a staff of twelve locals to see patients and teach them to adhere to the program. It was intense, very hard work. But we met our target. I was super-proud of the team for what we were able to accomplish."

Stewart has gone on to do missions in Zimbabwe, Papua New Guinea, Indonesia, Sri Lanka, Democratic Republic of the Congo, India, and Uzbekistan. Along the way, she's learned to take care of herself.

"I read, take time off, get my rest, de-stress. When I come home to Denver, I go back to simplicity: play tennis, hang out with my friends."

Despite the hardships, the work has been deeply rewarding.

"It's an amazing job," she said. "When I work in Denver, I use only 20 to 30 percent of my skills. Over there, I use everything I've got."

And while the job has given her an appreciation for the opportunities, freedoms, and safety enjoyed by women in this country, she's also come to respect the resilience of the women she's met overseas.

"They've witnessed torture. Their families have been killed, and yet they still have hope. They still keep going. I look upon every mission as an honor."

Judy Beggs: educating the girls of Guéoul

In 2005, Denver attorney Judy Beggs organized a tour of Guéoul (pronounced *gay-ool*), Senegal, for a group of friends and fellow lawyers. She had an intimate knowledge of the West African nation, having served there with the Peace Corps in the early '90s.

"I was doing rural health education at a time when the mortality rate for kids aged five and under was something on the order of 25 percent," she said. "Three-quarters of those deaths could have been prevented with knowledge of basic hygiene."

As a volunteer, she'd lived with a Senegalese grandmother and her five grandchildren; and after her stint with the Peace Corps, she'd kept in touch and sent money. The news from Guéoul, however, was never really good. Two of the girls dropped out of school, then one of the boys. The youngest girl, Astou, who was two when Beggs left, was now ready to enter middle school, and Beggs was determined to see her succeed.

Along with her on the tour was her friend John Montaña who, upon meeting Astou, said "Y'know, Judy, we could be keeping a lot of these girls in school."

That modest assertion would become the inspiration for Friends of Guéoul, a Denver-based 501(c)(3) whose mission it is to educate some of Senegal's most impoverished young women.

"Every year we find the twelve poorest girls in Guéoul and enroll them in first grade," Beggs said. "We promise to pay their parents $100 per year (a substantial sum for a family whose annual income might just barely top that figure) as long as the child remains in school."

Beggs goes to Senegal once a year to verify participation. To help keep her charges up to standard, she's established an after-school tutoring program and an arts-and-crafts club.

"We've reached ninety-eight girls so far," she said. "Fourteen of them have finished school. Of those, three are now in university where they continue to get support from Friends of Guéoul."

Although attitudes are starting to shift, the fundamental belief in Senegal is still that women are valueless and that educating girls is a waste of time. It's an ethos against which Beggs has been struggling for much of her personal and professional life, not only in Senegal, but here in the US as well. Back in the early '60s, armed with a degree in biz ad, she found herself applying for corporate jobs at a time when sexism in the workplace was still blatant, unapologetic, and pretty much sanctioned by law.

"I didn't know that climbing the corporate ladder meant boys only," she said. At IBM, to give but one egregious example, her application was rejected on the grounds that "girls are secretaries, boys are technicians." Unable to find meaningful work, she grew despondent, at which point her husband suggested she go to law school and open her own practice. She was pregnant at the time, but she went ahead and enrolled at DU, got her law degree, and began working out of her house as both a lawyer and a stay-at-home mom.

"When women are educated and have income, they bring it back to the community," she said of her experience in Senegal. "Their children are statistically healthier, and they too will be better educated. They're not going to be married off at age twelve. The maternal death rate drops. In Senegal, a good percentage of the men go off to work in the city, leaving the women and children behind. So women are the backbone of the community, and really, they're the hope of the future."

In October 2011, the City Council of Guéoul named Judy Beggs an honorary citizen. Astou, the two-year-old whom she'd helped put through school twenty years ago, is now at university.

"She's the only one in her family to go to college," Beggs said proudly. "She's really respected. She's the one they turn to for advice."

John Moorhead: caring for Denver's "hurt and broken"

Every Friday morning, a group of volunteers gets together to cook and serve a breakfast of pancakes and sausages at Christ's Body Ministries (CBM), a center for the homeless in a former office building at 850 Lincoln Street.

CBM serves upward of a thousand meals a week, distributes donated clothing, provides free showers and laundry, offers intensive case management, and maintains five respite care beds for homeless guys recovering from surgery.

"Our mission is to feed, clothe, and share the Gospel 365 days a year," said Pastor John Moorhead, who's been presiding over the festivities at CBM for the past twelve years. Before that, he was a business executive running a printing company called Denver Forms.

In 1997, he and his partners sold the business. He worked for the new owners for another three years, wrestling with the question of what to do with his life. One day, he came home and told his wife, Kathy, "Honey, I'm thinking of going into full-time inner-city ministry."

To which she replied, "Are you outta your mind?"

Not an unreasonable response, given who her husband was and where he'd come from.

"I grew up in rebellion and anger at God and religion," he said. "To me it was phony and hypocritical and part of the system. I was at Woodstock in the '60s. Dropped acid, marched on the Pentagon, got tear-gassed at the White House."

He'd worked hard at his job, made good money; but all through his career, something inside had gnawed at him.

"I kept asking myself, 'What's the point?' My life had no meaning. I'd tried to find it in sex, drugs, rock 'n' roll, money, success, power, but none of it was able to fill the God-shaped hole within me. That's when I started looking."

He and Kathy kicked around the idea of joining a church, if for no other reason than to connect with a community of friends. Their search led them to Grace Chapel in Englewood, where their initial reaction was less than positive.

"Kathy said, 'Oh my God, they're all carrying Bibles,'" Moorhead remembered. "We almost turned around."

But something about this particular church appealed to them. Maybe it was its thirty-five-year-old minister, Rev. Paul Barnes, who read scripture from a modern English translation and spoke in his sermons about everyday matters. Or maybe it was its youthful congregation, who seemed eager to connect and make them feel welcome.

"I asked a lot of questions," Moorhead said. "I had an education in science. I thought, and still think, that the anti-science, anti-evolutionary bias is nonsense. Eventually, I became comfortable with the idea that the major issue was 'What does it mean to follow Jesus?'"

Following Jesus, he realized, would mean caring for the poor and downtrodden, an ambition he'd secretly harbored since his activist days in the '60s.

"That those who are hurt and broken ought to be cared for was part of the sensibility of the times," he explained.

Somebody suggested he talk to a guy named Bruce McBogg, who was running a homeless operation out of a run-down building on Lincoln Street called Christ's Body Ministries.

"The bookkeeper had stolen some money, and the place was in big financial trouble," Moorhead remembered. "Bruce saw me as somebody who could bring business skills to the ministry. So I started raising money. Within three months, we'd raised enough for our personal support, plus adequate funds to keep CBM afloat for another year. I learned a lot from Bruce. A year before he died, he ordained me as a pastor, which means shepherd, which is what I am."

Moorhead said that he's happier and more satisfied now than at any other time in his life.

"I love what I do and can't believe I get paid to do it. It's such an honor and a joy to be trusted by people who generally don't trust *anybody*. I've had various goals in my life: to change society, to become a successful businessman, to raise two godly sons. But for the past fifteen years, my goal has been to love people as Jesus loved them. That's a very different goal. I fall short often. The world needs more Jesus and less John Moorhead."

Bill Huggins's biked-based solution feeds the hungry

Like a lot of off-the-wall ideas, this one got its start in Boulder.

Donated fresh food with an extremely limited shelf life—dairy, fruit, veggies—is picked up at area markets and trundled by bicycle directly to kitchens in North Denver that are operated by a punk/activist group called Food-Not-Bombs. The fresh produce is cooked immediately and dished up the same day at a couple of local parks, mainly to the homeless.

"We did some research on how much food was actually being tossed in Boulder County," said Bill Huggins, a twenty-two-year-old CU graduate with a degree in mathematics. "It was probably enough to feed every homeless person in the county. The problem is that fresh produce goes bad easily. Some food banks were picking it up, but by the time they were ready to use it, it had already gone bad. Our idea was to pick it up and use it within a day."

To do that, Huggins and some activist friends formed a nonprofit called Boulder Food Rescue and made an arrangement with Ideal Market to collect their discards. But what really gives the scheme its edge is how the food is transported.

"We use bikes, mainly to reduce the environmental impact, but also because it's a cool, radical way to do it," Huggins said. "You're making a statement when you strap two hundred pounds of food to a bike (actually a converted kiddy cart attached to the bike). 'If we can haul groceries on a bike, you can do your grocery shopping on a bike.' It's kind of a thumb in the nose of consumer culture."

After nearly a year working with the Boulder group, Huggins decided it was time to transplant the idea to Denver, where he grew up.

"I saw it as a way of giving back," he said. "Plus this is a bike-friendly city, so hauling food on a bike doesn't feel like a chore. It's more like a great adventure."

Accompanying him on this great adventure are a dozen volunteers who gather Tuesdays, Saturdays, and Sundays at 1:00 p.m. at the Capitol Hill Whole Foods. There they load boxes of produce and even crates of ready-made foods such as guacamole, into the kiddie carts, which are kept at the store. Volunteers provide their own bikes. Each bike takes between one hundred and two hundred pounds, and food is weighed on a bathroom scale before loading to provide accurate tax receipts to the donor. Once loaded, the group pedals to the two houses used by Food-Not-Bombs, one at 37th and Franklin, the other at 7th and Lipan.

"It's a couple-mile trek," Huggins said, "but we go in a caravan, which makes it more fun. Do it once and you're hooked."

Getting a nonprofit organization up and running in Denver has been frustrating at times for the young activist/entrepreneur.

"In Boulder, we have a dozen people who commit to twenty hours a week plus one paid employee," he said. "In Denver, not so much, mainly because there's not a tight-knit community of activists here like there is in Boulder. People are already overcommitted."

On the other hand, it's the folks who *do* volunteer that keep him interested and involved.

"I've met some wonderful people doing this," he said. "It tends to draw in some off-the-beaten-track types, people willing to take risks and do something crazy. I've always been drawn to that counter-authority strain."

Huggins plans to go back to graduate school to learn more useful skills. "This experience has shown me that to make a significant impact, you need all the skills you can get," he said. "I want to study computer science and use that math to do something really cool."

AIDS activist Penny DeNoble: "Doing what I was preserved to do"

Billy DeNoble died of AIDS on July 14, 1986, three days after his thirty-sixth birthday. He and his wife Penny, twenty-three, had been together three years, living in Greeley and working on graduate degrees—hers in education, his in health and human services.

"Billy was my best friend and teacher," Penny said. "We were in a monogamous relationship. It wasn't on our radar screen to use condoms. He never mentioned his drug use."

In the mid-1980s, AIDS was still thought of as a gay disease. So it came as a shock when a lot of Billy's pals, guys he'd grown up with in Jersey City, started coming down with it. None of them were gay, so it never occurred to him to tell his wife that in his teens, he and his crew were shooting up and sharing dirty needles. Besides, he'd been clean for decades, and by all appearances, he was healthy.

But in 1985, Billy came down with a strange illness.

"His testicles were raw, red, tender, and swollen to the size of grapefruits," his wife remembers. "He was in a lot of pain. He couldn't walk, and he was flat on his back for weeks at a time."

Despite the pain, he refused to see a doctor. The symptoms subsided, and that spring, he graduated and began commuting to a job in Denver.

"One night, he didn't come home," DeNoble said. "I was frantic. He finally called from a hospital and said, 'I blacked out behind the wheel. I totaled the car.'"

By now, not even Billy could deny that something was seriously wrong with him. He flew to New Jersey to be examined by his family doctor and came back with the news that he had AIDS. In 1986, the diagnosis was a virtual death sentence.

"Billy gave up all hope," DeNoble said. "He stopped working. He started doing methadone to anesthetize himself. That spring, he went blind."

He decided to go East to be cared for by his parents, and he asked Penny to quit her teaching job and go with him.

"That was the breaking point for me," she said. "I just couldn't do it. I had to live my life."

Subsequent testing revealed that she too was HIV positive.

"I was floored and stunned," she said. "When I called Billy, he absolutely wept, knowing he'd passed it on to me. I tried to console and comfort him. I told him I loved him and had no regrets. He said he was sorry and told me to go on living."

DeNoble continued her teaching career and kept her diagnosis to herself.

"I was living in denial," she said. "Basically, I navigated my way by myself."

When AZT became available three years later, she started taking a fifteen-pill cocktail twice a day to keep the virus at bay. But in 2005, tired of ingesting so many chemicals, she stopped taking her meds altogether. It turned out to be a costly mistake. She woke up one morning with excruciating pain in her legs, and when she tried to get out of bed, she found she couldn't move.

"My immune system had turned on itself and was destroying my nerves," she said.

In the two years it took her to recover, DeNoble sat alone in her living room, praying.

"I promised God that if I ever regained the use of my legs, I'd be a voice for the voiceless in the HIV community, particularly women and especially women of color."

As it turned out, her prayers were answered, and true to her word, Penny DeNoble has become a mentor and advocate for women living with HIV/AIDS.

"I do prevention, awareness, and education," she said. "I try to help women get past their shame and stigma by encouraging them to tell their stories. Twenty-five years after Billy's death, I'm still here. It's been a painful journey, living with fear, isolation, stigma, self-hatred, pain, lies, and loneliness. If I can help women know they don't have to cower in silence, I will have fulfilled what I was preserved to do."

Jacqueline St. Joan: fighting the injustice of honor killing

Honor killing.

It's a concept so alien, inhumane, and stupifyingly unjust that it's almost impossible to grasp. So quite naturally, when the issue first came to her attention, Jacqueline St. Joan felt compelled to do something about it.

"It's a cultural practice rooted in tribalism, patriarchy, and economics," she explained. "If a woman violates the sexual mores of the culture, her family becomes dishonored."

A girl may be said to have violated her clan's sexual mores by dressing inappropriately or resisting an arranged marriage or, in one particularly egregious example, for chatting with a boy on Facebook.

"To restore their honor, the family—usually a brother or the father—has to kill her."

St. Joan got involved in the issue almost by accident when, in December of 2002, she was invited to a party where the guest of honor was a forty-one-year-old Pakistani woman whom she calls Aisha. For the past twenty-five years, Aisha had been teaching girls to read—itself a revolutionary act in a country where more than half the women are illiterate.

At the party, Aisha showed a video about honor crimes, which she said accounted for an estimated 20 percent of all homicides in Pakistan. The practice, however, is not limited to Pakistan, nor is it exclusively Muslim. Christians and Hindus are also guilty, and in most Middle Eastern countries, perpetrators are seldom brought to justice.

Deep in conversation for the rest of that evening, the two women found they had much in common. Like Aisha, St. Joan had spent her entire life fighting for the rights of women and children. As a Denver County Court judge, 80 percent of the cases she heard had involved domestic abuse. As a DU law professor, she was able to secure a federal grant to allow her students, with the help of some mental health professionals, to represent victims of spousal abuse in court.

Like Aisha, St. Joan had a personal stake in the issue.

"When I was twenty-one," she said, "I married a black man. My parents didn't speak to me or meet their grandkids for fifteen years. I had been punished for breaching the social mores."

Of her encounter with Aisha, she said, "There was a heart connection. We spoke the same language. We understood each other. We didn't have to explain. When she told me that she'd helped a number of her students escape, I realized that here was the Harriet Tubman of Pakistan. I knew then that I had to write her story."

Aisha agreed, and St. Joan immediately began working on a book about her friend.

"I'd never written a novel before (to protect Aisha from reprisals back home, St. Joan fictionalized the story). So I broke it down into manageable segments. I'd write twenty pages, and every two weeks we'd meet to go over the manuscript."

In January of 2004, she went to Pakistan to gain some firsthand knowledge of the country.

"I called it my human rights tour," she said. "I visited schools, human rights offices, and bonded labor camps. I interviewed a couple in hiding and talked with women who'd escaped families bent on killing them. I came away with a lot of stories and an enormous respect for the people there willing to risk their lives to stand up for their rights."

She also emerged with a more nuanced picture of the country.

"There's something very beautiful about a culture where people stop to pray five times a day," she said. "I found them to be gentle and soft spoken. I wanted to do justice to that in my book."

Finished in 2006, *My Sisters Made of Light* was finally published in 2010. Since then, St. Joan has been touring the country both to promote the book and to raise awareness of the plight of women and children in the Middle East.

"The book is really an extension of what I've been doing for a long time," she said. "I have a strong sense of injustice and a deep need to cure it."

Foster Brashear: saving Colorado's wild horses and burros

The kid's question stopped him cold.

Foster Brashear had been invited to talk to a marketing class at Worcester Polytechnic Institute about a successful ad campaign he'd run for the Charles Bank and Trust Company of Boston. He'd moved to Boston from Denver in '68 to launch Adastra Advertising.

"That first year we billed a million bucks," he said, "which, of course, did not escape the attention of the bank. They hired us to promote their new line of free checking accounts."

For the campaign, Brashear came up with a brilliant scheme. He wrote what appeared to be a personal letter from the bank's president addressed to each customer by name, inviting them to stop by and say hello.

"We had this machine that could replicate the president's signature in water soluble ink, so it looked like he'd signed each letter personally. It was an intentional deception, but I didn't think of it that way. I was just doing my job."

As it happened, the ploy worked. Customers, flattered by the seeming personal attention, came to the bank in droves to meet the president and open a free checking account.

It was during the Q and A that followed his talk that the kid had raised his hand and asked the question that was to change Brashear's life.

"Do you think advertising is a moral phenomenon?"

"Basically, he was calling me on my deception," Brashear said. "Up until then, it had never occurred to me to question the morality of what I was doing."

Brashear went home to ponder the question. "I remembered a truism from the industry," he said. "'The purpose of advertising is to create dissatisfaction.' Was that what I was about? Creating dissatisfaction?"

At age thirty-two, Brashear was at the top of his game. "I wore flashy suits," he said, "got my hair cut every ten days, drove a red Jaguar XKE to work, but deep down inside, I was desperately unhappy."

Eventually, he sold the agency and came back to Colorado, where he moved into his family's cabin above Idaho Springs and spent his days reading Proust, playing the guitar, and thinking about where he was heading. It was during this time that he met and married his wife, Jill, and together they moved to Conifer to start a family. One day, his mother called to tell him of an article she'd read about a movement to save America's wild horses and burros.

"Now that you've got some land, why don't you adopt a wild burro?" she said.

Brashear got interested in the project; so interested, in fact, that he became president of the National Organization for Wild American Horses (NOWAH). "We leased four thousand acres in South Park and cared for six hundred wild burros and horses out there," he said.

Together with a group of volunteer cowboys, the former ad man found himself out on the trail every day, rounding up wild horses and learning how to brand, geld, and gentle them. Then one day, he got a call from his pal Ron Zaidlicz, NOWAH's founder.

"Ya know," Zaidlicz said, "we really ought to be doing this in the prisons."

Together they approached the Colorado Bureau of Prisons and argued that getting the inmates involved in taming wild horses would not only teach them a trade, it would reduce recidivism. "That argument fell on deaf ears," Brashear said. "They had zero interest in rehab. What got it to happen was one guy turned to another and said, 'We might get some good PR out of this.'"

The program, begun in 1985, is still going strong.

"It's made a huge difference in their lives. These are guys who've made it through life by deception and trickery. But you can't BS a wild horse. You have to come to them on their own terms. You have to change your stance and learn how to relate in a different way.

We often do things without thinking of the consequences," he said, reflecting on the long trail that has taken him from the boardrooms of Boston to bronc busting in Colorado. "I'm more aware these days of how what I do fits into the larger scheme of things. I think a lot about morality."

Tanya Diabagate: homeless experience leads to founding of Femicare Project

Any woman, regardless of her station in life, wants to feel feminine, pretty, and above all, clean.

Tanya Diabagate came to understand this in a visceral way when she was casting about for a topic for her senior capstone at Regis University. The capstone requires that students come up with a service project and then write about it. To get some ideas, her instructor suggested she go to St. Barnabas Church and volunteer for the Women's Homelessness Initiative.

"One of the women came out of the restroom and asked, 'Where's the toothbrush?'" Diabagate said. "Not *a* toothbrush, *the* toothbrush. That's when I realized they were actually *sharing* toothbrushes and that there was a limited supply of toiletries at St. Barnabas."

Two ideas came to her in that moment. First, she could do her capstone on the Women's Homelessness Initiative; and second, she could initiate a project to provide toiletry bags for homeless women.

Such a program would of course cost money—she figured $400 for 40 bags—and she had no idea how to go about raising it. So she called a guy named Dwayne Taylor at Dwayne Taylor Productions, who picked up the phone and said, "You got ten minutes. Go!"

Those ten minutes turned into an hour-long conversation in which Taylor came up with the idea of doing a happy-hour fund-raiser at the Cherry Lounge in Cherry Creek, with a $10 cover charge to be donated to the project. The Lounge kicked in free drinks, and Taylor threw in forty nylon backpacks and one hundred T-shirts from another event.

"We raised $950 plus the T-shirts and backpacks," Diabagate said. "The *Femicare Project* was off and running."

She went on a shopping spree at Wal-Mart and the Dollar Store and bought soap, baby wipes, tooth brushes, toothpaste, sanitary products, Chapstick, suntan lotion, hairbrushes, hand sanitizer, and some adult diapers for seniors suffering from incontinence.

"I also wanted the women to have something to make them feel a little more feminine," she said, "so I threw in manicure kits and face cream."

Having been homeless herself, Diabagate knows a thing or two about the needs of women in transition. In March 2012, she lost her job as a wealth management service rep, a position she'd held for ten years. She went on unemployment and started sending out résumés.

But with an unpaid bill of $2,000, X-cel finally turned off her electricity, and then the mortgage company padlocked her three-bedroom Aurora home. When she was able to get back in, she discovered that her clothes and personal possessions had been carted off.

She and her nineteen-year-old son moved in with her older son and his family in their two-bedroom, nine-hundred-square-foot apartment.

"We slept on the floor for three months on air mattresses," she said. "After living on my own and supporting myself, it was so bad I sank into the lowest depression of my life. I thought I was being punished by God. It made me realize that many of us are just one paycheck away from disaster. The experience totally changed the way I look at homeless and disenfranchised people. Nobody wants to be there. People think you're homeless because you're financially irresponsible or you drink or drug it up or that you wanna be that way. I was none of that."

A job finally came through as a resource coordinator at Mercy Housing, a nonprofit affordable housing organization under the auspices of the Catholic Archdiocese. The job enabled her to get back on her feet, get an apartment, and begin taking classes at Regis.

Diabagate has one more course to go before she graduates. She plans to pursue a master's in organizational leadership next fall. She's also filed for 501(c)(3) status for Femicare.

"It's amazing to be able to give back," she said. "I'd rather give than receive any day."

Launcelot Hawk takes the hot seat to help abused kids

Launcelot Hawk put himself in the hot seat to help stamp out child abuse. Literally.

A couple of summers ago, he made up his mind to sit in every one of the fifty thousand seats at CU's Folsom Field to raise money for the Kempe Center for the Prevention and Treatment of Child Abuse and Neglect, a Colorado-based charity with global reach. Kempe's mission resonated with Hawk, who was himself a victim of child abuse.

"My mother abused all of us," he said, "but me in particular. One day, I mouthed off to her, and she punched me in the face. I must've been eight or nine. My sister found me with blood all over my face and took me into the bathroom and locked the door. I know what abused kids are going through, so Kempe was a natural fit."

The idea for the butt-busting fund-raiser came to him when he heard of a similar feat that KNUS talk show host Steve Kelly did at INVESCO Field back in the year 2000.

"I heard about it on the radio, and a lightbulb went off in my head," Hawk said. "Kelly used to do stunts like crawling the Boulder Mall or winning the record for the longest time on a Pogo Stick, but nobody was doing stuff like that anymore."

He began pitching the idea to management at stadiums throughout the region, all of whom loved it but for one reason or another couldn't—or wouldn't—allow him access to their facilities.

"Finally, I got in touch with Folsom Field," Hawk said. "They agreed to it, but I had to jump through a lot of hoops. They wanted to charge a rental fee of $500 per hour, but I was able to negotiate them down to $100 a day. I also had to get insurance, which cost another $100 per day, so my overall cost was around $400 bucks."

What Hawk had not figured on, though, were the record temperatures on those two days in June 2012.

"The mean temperature was around ninety-eight degrees," he said, "but way hotter in the stadium due to the metal bench seats. I slid from one seat to the next, but it was so hot I got second-degree burns on my hands. And that was just on the first day in the first section. I had to borrow gloves from the maintenance man to keep on going."

He started at eight in the morning and went 'til five that evening, taking ten-minute breaks every hour and drinking gallons of Gatorade to fend off heat exhaustion.

"There was nobody there to cheer me on," he said, "so I was getting depressed. On day two, Angie Austin (AM 670, KLTT) did an interview with me over the phone. That boosted my spirits."

In the end, Hawk was able to sit in approximately half of the stadium's fifty thousand seats. He has no idea how much money he raised and said that for his next fund-raiser—stair running for the Denver Dumb Friends League—he plans to recruit an assistant to keep track of the donations. He's also looking for a media sponsor and has begun training for the event, working out on a Stair Master, and taking the stairs instead of the elevator whenever possible.

Looking back on his bun-broiling escapade at Folsom Field, Hawk said, "The stunt garnered attention for the cause and the issue. I looked at it like every seat in the stadium represented a child I could help. I felt really good about giving myself completely for the benefit of others, and even though it totally kicked my butt, I got some idea of what I'm capable of physically."

Nico Novelli: "no such thing as a disposable animal"

When animal advocate Nico Novelli moved to Colorado in 1992, he brought his entire menagerie—four iguanas, eight snakes, two turtles, and five lizards—with him in the back of his van. Today his personal zoo has grown to some fifty-four animals, mostly reptiles, many rescued from people who had no idea what they were getting into when they bought them.

"I do my best to talk people out of owning exotic pets," he said, "or at least to alert them to the realities. Sixty to eighty percent of pet reptiles die in their first year because people don't know how to care for them properly."

Novelli has been rescuing animals since he was a kid. At age nine, he nursed an injured bird back to health with an eyedropper. As an adult, he worked for outfits such as Animal Actors and Reptile Rentals in Hollywood, wrangling spiders in the film *Arachnophobia* and snakes in *Indiana Jones*.

He also worked as an animal control officer for the LA County Animal Shelter, a job which put him at odds with official policy regarding euthanasia.

"Generally, animal shelters won't hold strays for longer than a week," he said. "In LA, they were putting them down at the rate of three hundred a day. I refused to euthanize them unless they were half dead or it was court ordered."

He started taking animals home with him and trying to find people to adopt them. It was a friend of his landlady in Boulder who suggested that he bring his iguana to a local elementary school and talk to the kids about it. The kids, of course, ate it up.

For Novelli, however, the experience was a eureka moment. By bringing his animals into the schools, he realized, he could finance his rescue operations. At the same time, he'd be reducing the number of abandoned pets by educating young people about the realities of pet ownership. He started his company, Canyon Critters, and began doing live animal shows at libraries, schools, summer camps, and birthday parties. Today he averages twenty shows a month at $185 a pop.

Most of what he earns goes toward basic maintenance.

"I'll buy five to six thousand crickets, eight hundred frozen rodents, and between one and two thousand worms a month," he said. "Then there are the beef ribs for my dog, Patch, and my two hybrid wolves, Harper and Lupa. Pet shop owners want you to think you can get away with feeding an iguana nothing but crickets, but lizards need veggies too. Tons of them."

If you're thinking of acquiring an exotic pet, here are some things Novelli would like you to think about:

Are you prepared to care for your pet long term? Reptiles live longer than dogs and cats. A lizard can live up to twenty years. A snapping turtle might survive to two hundred. Long after you leave home, your Bearded Dragon, "Spike," will still be there.

Can you afford it? Here's the deal: An iguana will cost you three times what you initially paid for it just to feed it for one month. They grow quickly, which means bigger and bigger enclosures to house them. Then there are the vet bills, which can cost you a pant load; that is, if you can even find one in your area who specializes in exotics.

Are you prepared to work your ass off? Unlike dogs and cats, caged reptiles can't fend for themselves. Enclosures need to be cleaned twice daily. Water for drinking and bathing gets changed several times a day. Novelli spends his first hour every morning making salads for his reptilian roommates.

Forget about vacations. While it might be easy to find somebody to feed and walk your Chihuahua while you waltz off to St. Thomas, good luck finding a neighbor willing to cuddle your three-hundred-pound albino Burmese python.

For all the work and expense, Nico Novelli wouldn't have it any other way.

"Animals provide companionship, happiness, and fulfillment," he said. "I get a lot of satisfaction from the relationship I have with my pets. There's no such thing as a disposable animal."

Vicki Munroe aims to save the bees

Vicki Munroe has a bee in her bonnet. What put it there was an article she read in 2008 about the mysterious disappearance of bees—both honey and bumble—that seems to be taking place all over the planet these days. Scientists call it "Colony Collapse Disorder."

"You open a hive, there's honey, food, but no bees," Munroe said. "Nobody knows what's causing it. Lots of things may be contributing to it. We had big losses last winter due to drought. Varroa mites are another factor. These are insects the size of a head of a pin. They attach themselves to the bees and suck out their bodily fluids. This weakens them and makes them susceptible to disease. Then there're the pesticides. When they do autopsies on bees, they'll find 20 different pesticides in their bodies."

Why is this a big deal? To put it starkly, civilization as we know it may not be possible without them. Bees pollinate an estimated $15 billion worth of produce each year in this country alone.

"That's about a third of what we eat in fruits, nuts, and vegetables," she said. "If the bees die off we won't have any food. They also give us honey, wax, and *propolis.*"

Propolis? That's a resinous mixture the bees collect from tree buds, sap flows, and other botanical sources, which they use as a sealant for unwanted open spaces in their hives. Propolis may have potentially beneficial uses for human beings, ranging from the treatment of skin burns to the prevention of cancer.

Once she understood the situation, Munroe decided to get involved. She started by installing three beehives in her backyard.

"My goal was just to take care of them," she said. "I'm passionate about it. The honey was secondary."

She also wanted to do something to alert the general public about the dangers bees—and humans—are facing. One thing led to another, and on St. Patrick's Day, 2009, she opened *To Bee or Not to Bee,* a shop catering to the backyard beekeeper. It's located in a Quonset hut behind the family equipment rental business at 39th and Fox.

"This used to be the paint booth where we painted all our construction equipment," she said. "We sell beekeeping supplies. In the spring we sell bee packages, a small box containing 30,000 bees, a can of food (sugar syrup), and a smaller cage with a queen bee in it."

The shop also serves a larger purpose. "I see it as an information highway for everything bee related," she said. "Education is my main focus. We try to be a clearinghouse for speakers, mentors, and clubs along the Front Range. My objective is to keep the bees alive."

Even if you don't keep a hive in your back yard, Munroe thinks there are things you can do to help the bees survive.

"Plant flowers in your yard that the bees like; dandelions, thistle, lavender, Russian sage," she said. "We should be planting flowers along the highways to support the pollinators instead of spraying pesticides to control the weeds. Don't use pesticides of any kind, and don't ever spray a swarm. If you've got bees, call us and we'll come get them. You don't need to be afraid of bees. If you don't threaten them, they'll leave you alone."

It may be a niche business with a limited clientele, but five years into it, *To Bee or Not To Bee* is managing to stay afloat. "I'm not into it for the profit," Munroe said. "I'd rather spend my life on earth doing something like this. Each one should try to do a little bit."

PART 7

Hierophants, Healers, and Tap Dance Preachers

Alex Augustine sees dead people—seriously

If you've ever undergone psychotherapy, you know that it's not a hands-on kind of a deal. You sit on *your* side of the room, the therapist on his or hers, and you *talk* about your issues. Alex Augustine pretty much followed this approach until the day when she heard a still small voice say "touch them."

Problem is, there are some ethical and legal issues around therapists touching their patients. So Augustine began experimenting by laying hands on friends and family members and found, much to her amazement, that she could understand them in ways she hadn't been able to before.

"It was like a kundalini opening for me," she said. "I could literally hear their childhood issues." The therapeutic value of such a skill was enormous, she realized. "I could harness this energy to discover exactly where my patients needed to work."

Frustrated by the limitations imposed by traditional psychotherapy, Augustine developed a new mode of treatment she calls "body-centered energy work," an approach that allowed her to touch her patients and "read their souls."

This is where the story takes an unexpected turn, because it was while doing the body work that the dead people started showing up.

"I was actually seeing them," Augustine said. "They were kind of hazy, but I could make out distinctive characteristics like size, hair color, a cowlick." She would then describe what she was seeing to her patients, who immediately recognized their loved ones in her descriptions.

Communicating with the dead is only one of a whole range of paranormal skills Augustine has uncovered over the course of her twenty-five years as a practicing psychotherapist. She is able, for example, to communicate with beings still on the top side of the turf who, for whatever reason, are unable to speak for themselves. She discovered this ability one day in 2005 when she went to visit a woman who was lying in hospice, unconscious and near death. The woman, who was the mother of a friend, had suffered from Alzheimer's disease.

"I could feel that she was having a hard time letting go," Augustine said. "It was as though she was regretting in advance all of the things she would have to leave behind in this world. Then I touched her, and suddenly, her whole life just opened up for me. I started seeing all of her relationships—with her daughter, her son, her ex-husband, and with a man she had fallen in love with in the Alzheimer's unit."

After her death, Augustine and the daughter stood watching as the hospice workers went about removing the body. In that moment, Augustine said, she and the mother merged.

"I sat down, grounded, released her, and experienced what it was like to leave the world."

That encounter showed Augustine that she could understand and be of service not only to Alzheimer's patients, but also to stroke victims, people in comas, animals, kids, and those on the brink of death.

"I could feel their feelings and translate what their needs were or what they were working on in order to let go. I could read their souls."

Augustine retired from psychotherapy and has since become an active spiritual teacher. She does medium work, communicating with the dead in behalf of their living relatives and friends. She also leads a group for those who want to touch in with the departed in their own behalf.

"I think people can learn to pick up cues from their loved ones," Augustine said. "All it takes is mindfulness, groundedness, and presence."

Imam Ibrahim Kazerooni: tested by torture

Imam Ibrahim Kazerooni speaks in a monotone when he describes the torture he endured at the hands of the Iraqi State Security Agency. In the early 1970s, Saddam Hussein was making a concerted effort to weaken the influence of the Shias through a campaign of exile and intimidation. A prime target for his wrath was the Shi'ite theological seminary in Al-Najaf, where Kazerooni was a student and an outspoken critic of the Baathist regime

A past director of the Abrahamic Initiative at Denver's St. John's Episcopal Cathedral, and a member of the Rocky Mountain Peace and Justice Center in Boulder, Kazerooni is currently at work on a PhD at Iliff School of Theology.

In June 1974, a black limousine pulled up outside the seminary gates at Al-Najaf, and Kazerooni was nabbed. He was taken to a detention center in Baghdad, where his abductors tied him to a chair and beat the bottoms of his feet with truncheons in an effort to get him to sign a document admitting that he was an Iranian spy. He refused.

"I was only fifteen years old," he said. "I knew nothing."

He was dragged to a dungeon and thrown in for the night.

"When my eyes adjusted, I saw that it was filled with men who had also been tortured. I was confused and completely paralyzed with fear."

An old man crawled over to him and said, "Whatever they do to you, do not sign anything. If you do, they will kill you."

For the next two weeks, Kazerooni was subjected to savage beatings and interminable interrogations. He was starved, electrocuted, chained to a wall, and hanged from a ceiling fan. After each session, his tormentors would place a document in front of him and demand that he sign. Each time, he refused. Unable to break him, they sent him to the Last Palace, a detention center where the torture was primarily psychological.

"I was put into a tiny concrete cell with a dirt floor," he said. "Either you could have your head up, or your feet up, but you could never lie down."

At the Last Palace, he was subjected to Chinese Water Torture, one drop at a time falling onto his shaven head.

"After about ten minutes, each drop felt like a stone," he said, "and after a half hour, I couldn't take it anymore. I just passed out."

During a subsequent interrogation, his jaws were pried open and boiling water thrown into his mouth. "When I awoke, my mouth was full of blisters, and I couldn't stop screaming," he said.

Several times, he was forced to witness executions. "After each one, somebody would hand me a towel and say, 'Clean up the blood, Kazerooni. You're next.'"

His captors made a daily ritual of standing him up against a wall, aiming their guns, and then calling it off at the last second. One day he was handed a bag containing his clothes and some money, put aboard a truck, driven around for an hour, and dumped onto a backstreet near the Baghdad bus terminal.

A month later, the father of a classmate arranged to have him smuggled out of the country in a box on the back of a donkey. He made his way to Britain and eventually to the US. Because of their association with him, his brother, cousin, an uncle, and several close friends in Al-Najaf were killed.

The psychological scars from his ordeal have not healed.

"People say 'forgive and forget,' but I've always struggled with that idea," he said. "Forgetting is not possible. I would like someday to confront the people who did this to me to see what moved them to such viciousness. I saw no remorse in them, no hesitation, no regret. They actually enjoyed it, and in the end, they got away with it. If I could confront them, maybe I could forgive them. But not yet."

Lisa Jones hears the voice in the whirlwind

Freelance writer Lisa Jones figured it'd be a simple assignment: drive up to the Wind River Indian Reservation near Lander, Wyoming, and interview a Native American healer and horse gentler named Stanford Addison for *Smithsonian Magazine*.

"I wasn't going there as a seeker or anything," Jones said, "though I'd heard he had magical powers."

Paralyzed in a car accident at the age of twenty, Addison is said to have the power to cure everything from cancer to bipolar disorder. He also has a knack for making wild horses rideable without traumatizing them or breaking their spirits.

"I watched him come out of the house in his electric wheelchair," Jones said of their first encounter. "His legs were so atrophied and his body so broken I had to look away. There was so much misfortune on that body."

What happened next, she said, would change her life forever.

"I was hit by a jolt of energy so strong that it literally knocked me back. I'd been around some pretty powerful Tibetan lamas and had never experienced anything like this. It was like news being delivered to me from another place. I knew his guy was not going to buy any of my BS."

Jones went home to Paonia, Colorado, wrote the article, and sent it off. But she knew somehow that she was not yet done with Stanford Addison. She called him and asked if she could write a book about him.

"Sure, come on up," he said.

"I intended to go for a week, interview him, and come right back," she said. "But I stayed six weeks and felt more at home there than anywhere else I'd been since childhood."

Addison invited her to join him for a trip to the Meskwaki Settlement in Iowa, where a controversy was brewing over the distribution of the tribe's casino revenues. A respected elder in the Native American Community, he'd been asked to come and help resolve the situation. He told Jones he was planning to invoke Little Whirlwind, a spirit said to be able to heal grudges.

"I remember thinking, 'Yeah, right. That's an Indian thing, not something that works for blonde-haired, blue-eyed Presbyterian Buddhists like me," she said.

But then a couple of days later, she was out jogging and saw a forty-foot-tall whirlwind moving erratically across the prairie in her direction.

"It kind of freaked me out," she said. "It was right there in my face. Later, I mentioned it to Stan, and all he said was, 'Got any grudges?'"

That night she called home, and her live-in boyfriend told her he might be falling for another woman. Distraught, Jones drove back to Paonia to deal with the situation.

"Normally, I'm something of a drama queen," she said, "but over the next four days, it felt like I was channeling Mother Theresa. I'm totally equanimous, not taking anything personally, dealing with it like an adult."

Then Addison telephoned. "How ya doing?" he asked.

"Did you put a spell on me or something?" she said. "'Cause I'm a way better person than normal."

"I didn't put no spell on you," he replied. "I just gave you some protection."

"That experience broadened my definition of reality," Jones said. "Up until then, I was very attached to a scientific-rationalist worldview. You know, 'We're in control, and if we're not in control, we can at least figure out how things work. But Little Whirlwind turned that notion on its head. The world is so much bigger than we imagine."

Jones believes that her relationship with Addison cured her of a longstanding mistrust of men.

"I came to trust him completely, and from that platform, I learned I could trust other men too." (Like for instance, the aforementioned boyfriend, whom she wed in 2006). "Without Stan, I'd never have gotten married," she said.

Jones spent five years travelling between her home in Paonia and Addison's place in Wyoming, researching her book and soaking up the vibe.

"Just being with him, I'd get this hit of divinity. A stream of divinity flows through the man. There's nothing like it," she said. "It's the best feeling in the world."

Amma Thanasanti survives a bear attack

Amma Thanasanti Bhikkhuni (the name means "foundation of peace") is an American Buddhist nun who lives in Colorado Springs and teaches meditation worldwide. Her meditation career began when, as a student in the late 1970s, she took a course on the religions of India at UC Santa Cruz.

"It felt like somebody had thrown a match on a bonfire and doused it with kerosene," she said. "I was on fire with the possibility of dedicating my life to ending suffering."

It was during that course that she resolved (a) to learn to meditate and (b) to someday take a pilgrimage to India. She began attending retreats where she learned mindfulness meditation, an awareness technique in which thoughts, feelings, and bodily sensations are noted with precision and care. After graduation, she moved in with her high school sweetheart and went to work as an analytical chemist. Seven years later, she was ready to take the pilgrimage.

She quit her job, bought a one-way ticket to India, and said goodbye to her boyfriend. But after a couple of months in India, during which time she'd continued her mindfulness training with some of the country's more illustrious teachers, she started feeling homesick.

"This was my first time out of the US and my first time travelling alone," she said. "I was feeling disoriented, and I missed my boyfriend."

Hoping to ground herself by spending time in the outdoors, she headed for the mountains of North India. At the Tibetan guesthouse in Dharamsala, she met a Brit named Bryan whom she asked to join her for a spot of hiking and camping. They walked into the hills and camped out under a full moon. The next morning, Bryan climbed to the top of a large rock while she remained below, looking into the mouth of a cave.

And that's when her world turned upside down. She heard "a roar, a growl, and a snort," and out of the cave stalked a very large, very angry Himalayan black bear.

"It took him a split second to reach me," she said. "I screamed, jumped backward, landed facedown on a low-lying tree branch, and blacked-out from sheer terror."

When she came to, the bear was straddling her and had her head in his mouth.

"I could feel his teeth in my scalp," she said. "He could have cracked my skull like an egg."

But then something quite remarkable happened. Her years of meditation training kicked in. There was terror, and the "knowing of terror," and then a total surrender of body and mind, which in turn gave rise to "a state of joy and rapture and interest and curiosity at how this whole dying process was going to occur."

Inexplicably, the sound of *Om* arose in her mind, and at that very instant, the bear jumped off and ran headlong down the mountainside.

"Bryan was in a state of shock," she said. "For him it was a total nightmare. But I was in a state of bliss. I had deep gashes on my head and neck but, for some reason, not a lot of blood."

Bryan patched her up and helped her negotiate the four-hour walk back to civilization. Later that day, the bliss wore off and the pain set in.

"There was no place on my body that didn't hurt," she said, "and the tears were streaming down my face."

The experience marked a turning point in her life.

"Before the incident, I would not have been able to tell you why I was able to survive," she said. "Afterward, I knew quite clearly that the reason I was still alive was directly due to the mindfulness training I had done. For me, the blessing was not that I lived, but that at the moment of the attack, I was totally at peace."

Leonard Barrett cures multiple sclerosis with meditation

Ever since he was a kid, vocalist Leonard Barrett has been having what he calls "light bursts."

"It happens right here," he said, holding his hand in front of his heart. "And it always coincides with some outward event. Like one night, I got home from a gig and realized I'd forgotten to pack the microphones. Mics are expensive, and they're usually the first thing to disappear. I was beginning to get really uptight, and then I got a light burst. It said, 'Breathe . . . Hold . . . Observe.' I said, 'Ok-a-a-a-y.' Next night we're setting up, and literally ten seconds before show time, this guy comes up and hands me the mics. This was all the proof I needed that the *Spirit* was watching out for me."

The son of a Methodist minister, Barrett grew up singing in church. In his early twenties, he and his wife put together a band called Barrett and Barrett and did a lounge act in Atlantic City that lasted thirteen years. It was during this time that his interest in spirituality, dormant since his teens, was rekindled.

"I'd hit a wall," he said. "The world made no sense to me. None!"

He began experimenting with meditation and eventually found his way to the Self-Realization Fellowship, where they teach an arduous form of breath practice. "The basic idea is to observe the ego fighting you while you just sit there watching the breath," he said.

In 1993, Barrett's marriage broke up and so did his band. He stopped singing, moved to Boston, and got a job as a temp secretary. One morning on his way to work, something happened that was to alter his life forever.

"My girlfriend was driving," he recalled. "I'm sitting in the passenger seat, and suddenly, my eyesight started to fade. My speech slurred, and my body felt numb all over. I thought I was having a stroke."

An MRI revealed degeneration of the myelin sheath surrounding the nerves, a clear indication that Barrett had multiple sclerosis.

"After a week, my sight returned," he said. "After a month, I could walk again. I thought maybe I was okay."

Then the *exacerbations* began.

"I was standing in front of the stove, reading a magazine, waiting for some water to boil. My girlfriend screamed, and I looked down and saw that my hand was in the water. I never felt a thing. I just laughed. It was like I was Superman."

The doctors assured him that with proper medication, they could cure the exacerbations, but "crazy Leonard" wanted nothing to do with pharmaceutical dependence. "They gave me two bottles of prednisone, which I tossed into the trash on my way out the door," he said.

Barrett moved to Colorado and got a job teaching computer software at CU. Meanwhile, the exacerbations kept coming, on average once every three months. One day, it occurred to him that meditation might help. "I'd pretty much given up on it after my divorce," he said. But now, desperate for a cure, he resumed the practice with a vengeance. When he was able to sit for three hours, he started feeling better. Encouraged, he added another three-hour session in the evenings. At six hours, the exacerbations stopped.

Barrett hasn't had a flare-up in four years. And he's back doing what he loves best. Last summer, he sang the lead in *Man of La Mancha* at the Denver Center. In January, he will open a two-month engagement at Lanny Garrett's called *Loved in Return: a Tribute to Nat King Cole*.

"Meditation is a powerful tool for navigating through this monstrosity," he said. "My focus on being centered is what healed me. It's made the journey easier."

Santidevi: Mother Mary comes to me

"As a child of five or six, I could hear other people's thoughts and literally see the sickness in their bodies," said medical intuitive, healer, and spiritual teacher Santidevi. "I knew why they were suffering and what was troubling them."

Her intuitive gifts seemed so natural and effortless that she assumed everyone had them.

"I'd blurt out something somebody was thinking, and I'd see this look of alarm come over their face. So I learned very quickly to keep it to myself."

This led, she said, to feelings of loneliness and alienation. "I felt like I lived in a very beautiful world that others couldn't share in. It was as if I had to separate out these two parts of my being, the sacred and the profane. I couldn't be who I was. It was very painful."

One of four sibs raised by a single mom in the '60s and '70s, Santidevi grew up in Denver's North Capitol Hill. One day when she was ten, her mom asked her to stay home and take care of her little sister. Later that morning, she heard a knock at the door. She opened it to a man brandishing a machete who pushed his way in, grabbed her, and raped her. At that moment, Santidevi entered "a state of grace."

"I had a vision of a white light—gentle, soft, and safe," she said. "It coalesced into the form of Mother Mary who said, 'Do not be afraid. This man is suffering. He has never known love or compassion.' I realized that the divine actually manifests in the world and that the sacred and the profane are one. There was the terrified little girl, totally aware of what was happening to her. But there was also a sense of myself as infinite, boundless, an ocean of compassion. What enabled me to survive this ordeal was the realization that I could not be separated from the divine."

Her assailant, a nineteen-year-old heroin addict, burglar, and serial rapist named Joseph Michael Ervin, was later acquitted by reason of insanity and sent to the Colorado State Mental Hospital in Pueblo. But for Santidevi, the experience marked a turning point in her spiritual life.

"A channel was opened in me that would never close again," she said. "It was the pivotal experience that revealed my true self to me. No matter what happens to me in this lifetime, I remain pure. Nothing can touch that."

What's more, from that day forward, she no longer felt the need to keep her psychic gifts under wraps. The inner schism had been healed.

There's an addendum to this story: On July 17, 2006, Santidevi was participating in a guided yoga session when she happened to glance down at the silver *mala* she wore on her wrist.

"Each of the *mala's* 108 seeds appeared as one of my past lifetimes," she said. "All of a sudden, I heard this *whoosh*, and I saw the seeds igniting. My past lives—gone. Everything—gone. In that moment, the sense of a separate self was extinguished. It was very much like what happened to me when I was ten. Peace. Spaciousness. I exist everywhere, but I am nothing. Just this vastness."

The experience, she said, brought about a fundamental transformation in her personality.

"I'm no longer incessantly thinking," she said, "and my intuitive abilities have been heightened. These days, when I work with my patients, there's no longer a gap. It's like I know instantly what the problem is and how to heal it. Now all I want to do is to be of service."

Sadananda: chaos has its own way

This story is about the convoluted workings of karma and of how Frank Reck became a devotee of Indian spirituality who now goes by the name Sadananda.

"I was always spiritually inclined," Sadananda said, "but it was my baptismal ceremony at the age of thirteen that led me to take the spiritual path. When the priest poured the water on my head, I felt a flood of Christ energy. It was my first taste of desirelessness, of no craving."

In 1980, Reck spent some time at Christapremseva, a Christian ashram in Pune, India. There he met a yoga teacher named Mrs. Patwardin who invited him to come stay with her and her family in a village in the mountains between Pune and Bombay.

On the train ride to Mrs. Patwardin's village, he came down with what he thinks may have been typhoid fever. She and her family took him in and, for the next forty days, nursed him back to health.

"If they hadn't," he said, "I'd have died."

By now his visa had expired, he had $300 left in his pockets, and he decided to use the money to go to Sri Lanka and become a monk. But Mrs. Patwardin had other ideas. She asked if she could borrow the money in exchange for which she would go to Bombay and renew his visa.

"She had some disciples in the Bombay police department," Sadananda said, "and for the next eight months, she went back and forth to work on it. Then one day she said, 'The police say they can't renew your visa. You are here illegally, so I must ask you to leave.'"

"And my $300?" he asked.

She handed him a list of every glass of tea, bar of soap, and morsel of food he had consumed over the previous eight months. The sum total far exceeded his $300.

"Up until then, I was trying to be legal and stay in India," he said. "But now as an illegal, if I tried to leave, I'd get arrested. I saw this as a golden opportunity. I could just stay on illegally and renounce the world. The universe made the decision for me."

He had a few rupees, his passport, a blanket, a sleeping bag, a piece of cloth to wrap around his waist, another to wear over his shoulders, and with these few possessions he became a sadhu, a wandering holy man.

He took a train to Goa—"It's an unwritten rule in India," he said, "sadhus go free"—and camped out in a forest where he lived on wild leaves, rice, and the occasional fish given to him by Goan fishermen for helping them haul in their nets.

Eventually, he made his way to a Catholic ashram in Tamil Nadu State, where he met a young British woman, a former nun and medical doctor who went by the name of Alakananda. For the next four and a half years, they tramped the roads of India together as "guru brother and sister," visiting ashrams and surviving on whatever food, shelter, and clothing were offered them.

"If you're on a spiritual path," he said, "people can be very generous."

By the mid-'80s Sadananda (he was given the name by a female guru named Godarvi Mataji) was ready to return to Denver. He wrote to his parents who sent him $250, a portion of which he used to bribe a cop in Gaya who made the necessary arrangements and got him across the border into Nepal.

In Katmandu, he caught a plane to London, where he reunited with Alakananda. Back in the States, the two opened a center in Boulder called Alandie Ashram, where today they teach ayurvedic medicine and insight meditation.

"I got the sense that God was running the universe," Sadananda said of his travels. "When I tried to run the show, nothing worked. When I let go, everything fell into place. All that adversity—the visa problems, my illegal status, not having any money—that's what led to the blessings. Chaos has its own way."

Carol "Gansho" O'Dowd discovers the mysterious workings of karma

This is a tale of the mysterious workings of Karma and of how one reluctant American woman found her calling as a Jodo Shinshu Buddhist priest.

Like a lot of baby boomers, Carol "Gansho" O'Dowd was curious about the meditative traditions of the East. One day in 1983, she was driving down a street in Arvada when she noticed a house that was doing double duty as a Vietnamese Buddhist temple. She phoned the temple and was invited to come for a visit. The following Sunday, she wrote some questions on a sheet of paper, stuffed it into her back pocket, and went on over.

"I sat in back by the door and listened to a talk that was given entirely in Vietnamese," she said "I didn't want to be rude, so I just sat through it."

After the service, she noticed some Westerners standing in front of the place and learned that they were a group of Gnostics in the process of buying the temple. They invited her to join them in their negotiations with an English-speaking monk named Thich Thom Won. Feeling very out of place, O'Dowd sat against a wall and tried to make herself inconspicuous. But then a very strange thing happened. Thom Won entered the room, sat down, turned to her, and said, "So what are your questions?"

"Maybe after the meeting?" she offered.

"You will find the answers you seek," he said, "when you let go of everything."

Later, completely oblivious to the fact that Buddhist monks are enjoined from any physical contact with women, she tried to shake his hand. Master Thom Won did not stand on ceremony. He took her hand and shook it warmly.

"It was like shaking hands with a living rock," she remembered. "Later, as I was driving home, light was pouring out of everything: trees, rocks, people, cars. I said, 'Wow, *that* was something.' Then I forgot the whole thing and got on with my career."

For the rest of the decade, O'Dowd served as town manager for a number of Colorado communities including Morrison, Snow Mass, and Aspen. In 1990, she left government service and moved back to Arvada, where she launched a consulting business and got more involved in raising her son, Scotty.

One day, Scotty's second-grade class took a field trip to Denver's Tri-State Buddhist Temple, and O'Dowd went along to chaperone. In the middle of a talk on Buddhism, Scotty looked up at her and said he wanted to join the church.

"I'd been thinking that he needed some religious education, and I'd made a deal with him that he had to go to church but that he could choose whatever church he wanted to belong to," O'Dowd said. "Actually, what he said was 'you said I could choose my church, but you didn't say which religion.'"

O'Dowd realized she felt completely at home at Tri-State, despite the fact that she was Caucasian and the church was 85 percent Japanese American.

One Sunday morning, she was standing next to an elderly Japanese man named Henry, waiting to enter the shrine hall, when he turned to her and said, "Have you ever thought of becoming a minister?"

"Never crossed my mind," she said and waited for him to enter the shrine hall so that she could go in, temple protocol requiring that a junior member wait for a senior member to enter first. But Henry didn't budge. "Well," he said, "would you at least *think* about becoming a minister?"

"To shut him up and get the line moving, I said, 'Okay, Henry. I'll think about it.' He got this big grin on his face and stepped into the shrine room. I put the whole thing out of my mind."

But then other temple members, many of them in leadership positions, began urging her to consider it. Once she made up her mind, O'Dowd jumped in with both feet.

"It was like I'd been getting little sips of water, and now I wanted to swallow the whole ocean," she said.

She enrolled at Naropa University and earned a master's in divinity. She took courses online from the Institute of Buddhist Studies in Berkeley and ordained as a full-fledged Jodo Shinshu priest. Today O'Dowd serves as minister at Longmont Buddhist Temple.

"We offer a meditation service twice a month where people are free to practice in any way they choose," she said. "I call it come-as-you-are Buddhism."

Of her own spiritual journey, she said, "I'm getting better at being open to both the seen and unseen blessings of life. When I reach out to others, I'm touched by light and life from all directions."

Rev. David Sharp: tap dancing on the stairway to heaven

Unlike conventional preachers who stand behind a pulpit when they preach, the Reverend Dr. David Sharp taps out his message of hope and personal transformation on a portable dance floor.

"Are you dancing around your problems?" he'll ask the congregation as he shuffles in a desultory circle. Then hopping in, he'll set up a riff and shout, "Jump to the center and work it out."

Or dropping down into the splits, he'll say, "Sometimes you might make a mistake," before rising smoothly to a standing position and exhorting his audience to "Pick yourself right back up again."

Sharp credits his parents for his spirituality, his love of the arts, and his desire to be of service to humanity. His dad was a jazz saxophonist and comedian, his mother a singer in the church choir. They met at Denver's Manual High, got married, and moved to Atlanta where Sharp Sr. studied for the Presbyterian ministry. Young David grew up there during the heady days of the Civil Rights movement.

"My dad was pals with Martin Luther King, Ralph Abernathy, and Andrew Young," he said.

He picked up tap dancing from his mother.

"Tap was a way to create joy out of pain," he said. "She'd go into the kitchen when she was down, and we'd watch her demeanor change as she tap danced on the kitchen floor. She'd close her eyes and hit that floor hard, working out her anger and frustration until she felt everything was gonna be okay. Then you could almost see the smile bubbling up from her feet. It was a happy sound. She taught us that you can use the arts not just for fun, but for healing and transformation as well."

One night while watching Donnie and Marie Osmond on *Johnny Carson*, it dawned on him that what he really wanted to be when he grew up was the next Sammy Davis Jr.

"I wanted to be a singer, actor, and dancer," he said. "I also wanted to use my talents to help people not to give up on life, but to prosper and be better."

He enrolled at University of Southern California and earned a BFA in drama. While auditioning for TV, movies, and commercials, he quickly learned that racism was very much alive in the Hollywood of 1973.

"There were no leading roles for blacks in those days," he said. "My white friends would get eight to ten auditions. My black friends were getting one or two. Most of the work for blacks was in singing and dancing."

Which was, interestingly enough, what he ended up doing in Hollywood. He danced at Disneyland. He danced in the Blues Brothers movie. He danced with a touring Christian rock festival.

"Four months into that tour," he recalled, "we were in Topeka, and this girl came up and said she saw the *Light* in me. She was talking about the Light of Christ."

Something about the encounter led him to question his choice of vocation.

"Was I just there to entertain people, or was my role to help them?" he wondered. "If my job was to help them, then I didn't have a clue how to go about it."

He quit the tour and enrolled at San Francisco Theological Seminary.

"I was called to be a minister at twenty-six," he said. "I wasn't sure I wanted to be a preacher, but if I was, I knew I didn't want to be a boring one."

He began exploring ways to put his skills as an entertainer to work in the service of his ministry. That's when he figured out that he could tap dance his sermons.

"I'm fifty-four years old and still growing," he said. "I'm still a powerful instrument for alternative forms of ministry. Spirituality is not confined to set modes and patterns. I see tap dancing as a form of prayer. I use it to teach people about life and to make peace with the uniqueness that they are."

Meredith and David Vaughn take laughter seriously

As it was for a lot of boomers, 1967 was a watershed year in the life of Meredith Vaughn. That year, thousands of kids descended upon San Francisco's Haight-Ashbury District for what would come to be known as the Summer of Love. Two books topped everybody's reading list in 1967. One was *Siddhartha* by Hermann Hesse, the other, *Autobiography of a Yogi* by Yogananda.

"One of my professors turned me on to Hesse," said Vaughn, who was studying romance languages at CU Boulder at the time. "*Siddhartha* was Hesse's version of the Buddha's life. Born of wealth, he experimented 'til he found his way. The book touched me deeply."

As for *Autobiography of a Yogi*, "It freed me from the cultural prison I'd been confined to in American society," Vaughn said. "I was never the same after that. Christianity just didn't do it for me. I saw there were other options."

She's been exploring and teaching those "other options"—among them hatha yoga and transcendental meditation—ever since. (Note: It was at Vaughn's instigation that Kaiser Permanente began offering classes in yoga and qigong to its Denver clients in 1992).

In February of 2006, one of Vaughn's yoga students showed her an article about the "laughter yoga movement" in India. Laughter yoga, the article said, was the brainchild of a Mumbai physician named Madan Kataria, who examined studies on the health benefits of laughter and determined that not only is a good chuckle a great stress buster, it also strengthens the immune system, retards aging, stimulates blood circulation, improves muscle tone, increases endorphin levels, helps control high blood pressure, improves sleep, reduces depression, alleviates bronchitis and asthma, and promotes world peace. What's not to like?

Kataria invited a group of friends to meet in a Mumbai park, where he encouraged them to tell jokes and tickle one another's funny bones.

"But the jokes got old," explained Meredith's architect husband, David Vaughn, who is himself a laughter practitioner. "They were sexist, deprecating, and the women stopped coming."

Kataria went back to his research and found that even fake laughter will bring about the same physiological benefits since, on a cellular level, the body doesn't know the difference. He invented exercises that engage the laughter muscles, threw in some yogic breathing, and before long, laughter yoga clubs began sprouting up all over the world. Today there are an estimated five thousand of them in forty countries, operating under the slogan "World Peace through laughter, one laugh at a time."

When she learned that Dr. Kataria would be offering a teacher training seminar in Pasadena, Meredith decided to attend.

"I knew immediately that this was what I wanted to do," she said. "It clicked with me. Old age was looking rather daunting. I decided I wanted to go out laughing."

"I'm going with you," said husband, David, who has assisted his wife in her yoga and qigong classes over the nearly forty years of their marriage.

"At first, I was skeptical," he admitted. "I wasn't much of a laugher. I'm a serious architect, and I was laughter challenged. But gradually, we were able to ad-lib, roll with it, and have some fun, and I found myself genuinely laughing."

After seven days of intensive training, the couple came home and started the Denver Laughter Club, which meets every Monday noon at Denver's Cheeseman Park Pavilion in summer, and at First Unitarian Church, Fourteenth and Lafayette ("Laffy-ette") after Labor Day.

"Laughter yoga adjusts your set point for happiness upward," David said. "When you feel down, initiate the "ho ho ha ha ha" exercise.* It opens the body up, pumps oxygen into your system, and gets you out of a downward spiral of depression."

"The communities we've formed from the laughter yoga groups are a meaningful connection for us as we age," Meredith said. "I call my class the Sane Asylum. Laughter erases all rational thought and opens your heart. I've travelled all over the world, doing trainings and studying yoga, and what it really comes down to is opening your heart and learning to love."

Chant "ho ho ha ha ha" while clapping in rhythm to the words. This repeated movement activates acupressure points in the hands and becomes a positive trigger for laughter.

Michael McGrath: "uplifted" by Christ

Children's book illustrator Michael McGrath describes himself as a "Prophetic Christian."

"We used to be called seers," he said. "We act as a kind of mouthpiece for God. Some of us hear his voice. Others see him in dreams and visions. Such experiences are not uncommon in the spiritual community I belong to."

McGrath is a teacher and community leader in something called the House Church Network, a loosely organized group of believers who meet in one another's homes for worship and spiritual companionship.

"It's comprised of people who feel that the organized church no longer works for them," he said, "people who are tired of the hierarchy and who want a more intimate experience of Christianity."

Home Church adherents are not fundamentalists, nor do they proselytize. "I don't beat people over the head with the Bible," McGrath said. "I'm an experiential Christian. I have to experience the teachings for myself in order to believe in them. And the experience has to be transformative."

McGrath had just such an experience on September 11, 2003. Early that morning, he awoke to a voice calling his name. The voice said, "Wake up, Michael. We have work to do."

McGrath climbed out of bed, walked into the living room, closed the door, and lay facedown on the floor. "That's how I pray," he said, "lying facedown."

He heard a rustling noise, looked up, and saw Christ—or a vision of Christ—standing above him. "He picked me up off the floor, and suddenly, the room dropped away, and Christ grew into this towering figure, maybe seventy-five feet tall. I'm hovering in front of his face. His eyes are brown, his skin is dark, his hair is black and curly. I can feel his breath on my face. I can smell his body. He said, 'Michael, I have loved you since before time began. You are mine. You belong to me.' Then he held up his hand, a huge hand with a scar on it so big that I could fit into it."

McGrath was so overwhelmed by the experience he burst into tears. "I just lost it," he said. "I sobbed and sobbed. It was the first time in my life that I felt seen, understood, and loved unconditionally."

The experience, McGrath maintains, completely transformed his way of looking at himself.

"I was the child of an abusive mother and an indifferent, emotionally distant father. If you've read *A Child Called It*, you'll know what I was up against. She used to call me a worthless piece of shit. She even tried to kill me one time."

Naturally, McGrath grew up hating himself. "I was consumed with self-loathing," he said. "I'd look in the mirror and hate what I saw."

As an adult, he began seeing a psychiatrist who put him on antidepressants. The vision changed all that. "Inside of me, everything seemed to click into place. I started liking what I saw in the mirror. I couldn't stop appreciating how beautiful everything was. I felt a sense of unrestrained joy, and I didn't know whether to laugh or cry."

Prophetic visions? Voices in the night? Sudden drastic mood swings? A history of childhood abuse? Has something genuinely transformative occurred in the life of Michael McGrath, or is he suffering from an extreme case of bipolar disorder? McGrath said he's talked it over with his psychiatrist.

"He's totally cool with it. He doesn't think I'm bipolar or mentally ill. His position is if a vision changes your life for the better, then it's good for his patient."

McGrath has also discussed it with his wife. "People are going to think I'm nuts," he told her.

She took him by the shoulders and turned him to face her directly. "Don't ever say that in this house again," she said. "I've got a new husband, and I don't want the old one back."

Steve Roth: witness to a miracle

In an age where there's a rational explanation for just about everything, nobody believes in miracles anymore. Unless, of course, you happened to have been there for one. Steve Roth, a longtime practitioner of Tibetan Buddhism, was lucky enough to have witnessed just such an event. Thirty-seven years on, he's still scratching his head over it.

In October 1974, Roth was asked by his teacher, the late Chogyam Trungpa Rinpoche, to serve as personal chauffeur to a visiting dignitary, the sixteenth Gyalwa Karmapa, who at the time was head of the Karma Kagyu Sect, one of the four great lineages of Tibetan Buddhism.

During his visit, the Karmapa expressed a desire to meet with the Hopi Indians in Arizona. His American hosts, Roth among them, immediately set about making the necessary arrangements.

"We even rented a brand-new gold-colored Cadillac to serve as his official vehicle," Roth remembered. "We left for Arizona trailed by a caravan containing a translator, a retinue of Tibetan monks, and a couple dozen American Buddhist practitioners from Boulder."

The following afternoon, the party arrived at Second Mesa, a high plateau on the Hopi reservation that looked to Roth like an old chocolate cake. "A man who looked to be about eighty years old, wearing a plaid shirt, jeans, and tennis shoes, came up and introduced himself," Roth said. "His name was Chief Ned, and I remember that there was a sweet, gentle, very loving air about him. Through the translator, His Holiness asked him how his people were faring."

"Not too good," replied Chief Ned. "We haven't had rain in seventy-three days." The temperature was well over one hundred degrees.

"Maybe I can do something for you," replied His Holiness.

The entourage got back into their cars and headed down a dusty road to the Hopi Cultural Center and Motel, where they were scheduled to spend the night.

"As we drove, His Holiness, who was sitting next to me in the passenger seat, began chanting and making sacred gestures with his hands," Roth remembered. "I looked out at the sky and noticed a tiny, sheeplike, fleecy little ball of a cloud, all by itself way out there on the horizon. I didn't give it much thought."

The Karmapa kept on chanting, and ten or fifteen minutes went by before Roth glanced up again. He was astonished to see little puffballs of cloud now polka dotting the sky from horizon to horizon.

"The third time I looked, the clouds had congealed into a solid gray mass," he said. "This was getting interesting. By the time we reached the motel, the sky had darkened to an ominous black. Not just black, but a classic Cecil-B-DeMille-Moses-and-the-Ten-Commandments black!"

They rolled into the motel parking lot, and one of the attendants jumped out to open the door for His Holiness. He got out and walked to his motel room where another attendant stood ready to open the door.

"I watched his back as he disappeared into the motel," Roth said. "At the very instant that the door clicked shut behind him, there was an eruption of thunder and lightning like I've never seen in my life. Crash! Boom! The most dramatic display you could imagine! And then the rain started coming down hard. Buckets of it. Sheets and torrents of it. It went on and on like that, splashing down on the roof of the Cadillac like a waterfall."

Word got out to all the surrounding villages that an Indian king had made rain, and by that evening, a crowd had gathered around the motel.

"In every face, there was a look of awe and wonder toward His Holiness," Roth said. "He and his attendants were conducting a ceremony for them. We Western practitioners felt very much like outsiders. The amazing facial resemblance between the Tibetans and the Hopi suggested an ancient bond between the two peoples. To me, it felt like a reunion."

Pastor Jim Rogers: heal the sick, raise the dead

A few years ago, Pastor Jim Rogers was in Fort Collins conducting a class for faith healers. "We were praying for a guy who had two metal rods along his spine held in place by screws," Rogers remembered. "After the service, he was able to bend over and touch his toes."

The next day, the man caught a flight home and found, to his surprise, that he could walk through the metal detectors at DIA without setting them off. Back in Baltimore, he went to see the neurosurgeon who'd done the original implants.

He took a new set of X-rays, examined them quizzically, and said, "Okay, who took the metal out of your back?" When his patient explained about the meeting in Fort Collins, the doctor replied, "Well, I guess it has to be a miracle, then."

Not an easy admission for a man of science, but all in a day's work for a faith healer who's seen, or claims to have seen, his share of miracles. Like the time in West Africa when he was visiting a group of pastors, and there was a knock at the door. In the doorway stood a man holding his dead daughter in his arms. She was eight years old and he'd been carrying her for four days. He set her down on a table, and Rogers and his cohorts gathered round and started praying.

"Actually, we were speaking in tongues," he recalled. "She was not a pretty thing. She'd already started to decay. But after twenty minutes, her eyelids fluttered, and she sat up. Her skin was totally normal. There was no brain damage. The room just erupted. It was nuts. Total chaos!"

Jim Rogers has been an associate pastor at Denver's Bridgeway Church for the past nine years. He also runs his own healing ministry—Experiencing His Presence—which has taken him on missions to 47 countries worldwide. Last year, he logged 225,000 air miles, not only to heal the sick himself, but to teach others to do so as well.

"I'm in the Charismatic stream of the church," he said. "We believe that miracles can and should happen all the time."

He was raised a Lutheran ("The Frozen Chosen") but became interested in faith healing after experiencing it firsthand. In 1990, he'd sustained a head injury that had led to seven years of fainting episodes. "I'd feel pain, and I'd conk out for fifteen minutes," he said. "As a result, I had two accidents in my truck and another one where my car caught on fire and some highway workers had to pull me out."

Rogers joined the Vineyard, a Charismatic church where faith healings are a regular part of the Sunday services. "In 1997, I went up for the prayer and felt movement in the back of my head," he said. "The blackouts stopped instantaneously. I've been fine ever since."

His interest piqued; he began seeking out healers all over the US who might be able to impart to him the capacity to heal. "As I started travelling and praying for more and more people," he said, "the gift grew. I started seeing results: deaf ears opening, blind people actually starting to see."

These days, Rogers goes overseas six to eight times a year. He said his success rate is much higher in foreign countries than in the US and admits that he's at a loss to explain why. He insists that it's not necessary to be a Christian for healing to work.

"We have open-air meetings all over the world where nonbelievers get healed," he said. "They come out of desperation, not out of faith. First, they get healed, and then they become Christians. I don't claim any special ability, by the way. It's not me doing the healing. It's the power of God moving through me. When I go into Africa, I'm not going alone. *He* goes with me."

Professor David Eller seeks a new image
for atheism in America

Professor David Eller, who teaches anthropology of religions at Community College of Denver, believes it's time to rehabilitate the image of atheists in America.

"We're not just a bunch of angry guys in their basements shaking their fists," he said. "We're trying to be constructive and contribute positively to society."

To that end, he argues in favor of non-theistic alternatives to priests and ministers as officiants at weddings and funerals. He'd also like to see an atheist holiday at the end of the year instead of Christmas. And how about "Rational Recovery" vs. Alcoholics Anonymous, and maybe a National Day of Reason to counter the National Day of Prayer?

"We've started placing signs on the sides of buses to send the message that religion can't monopolize the public space," he said. "We sponsor atheist blood drives, and we're publicly out there doing good things like cleaning up the highways. We also have a booth at the People's Fair and other events."

Atheism as a public stance began gaining traction, both nationally and here in Colorado, with the inauguration of George W. Bush in the year 2000.

"With the faith-based initiative and their attacks on science, they were starting to tear down the wall between church and state," Eller said. "They were trying to push their religion on the rest of us. Some of us felt the need to push back."

That year, Eller founded Atheists and Free Thinkers of Denver, an organization dedicated to promoting discussion, and to building bridges to like-minded groups in the area: Humanists of Colorado, the Freedom from Religion Foundation, and Denver Atheists and Free Thinkers (DAFT).

"Mainly we're about consciousness raising," he said. "I think of myself more as a teacher than an activist."

As a kid growing up, Eller went to church and Sunday school. His grandmother had pictures of Jesus on her walls and even played the accordion at Evangelical tent revivals. "Christianity was in our background," he said, "but it was not an explicit force in our lives. I never believed any of it, but I didn't think of myself as an atheist. I was more of a cultural Christian."

As fate would have it, his college academic advisor turned out to be a professor of religious studies. Eller became fascinated by the subject and went on to create his own undergraduate degree in what he called "Patterns of Human Experience," focusing on religion, philosophy, and psychology. But the more immersed in the subject of religion he became, the less he believed in it.

"It never made any sense to me," he said. "If you have a hundred religions, how can you say that ninety-nine of them are false? It seemed arrogant to me. The best argument against religion is all the other religions. If you let them argue with one another, they will implode under their own weight."

In 2004, Eller published his first book on the subject. Entitled *Natural Atheism*, it argued that "Atheism is the default position." In other words, we're born atheists and "catch" religion.

"Most people catch religion before they know anything about it," he said. "That's why they try to indoctrinate kids when they're really young. But Reason is like a vaccine against religion. Once inoculated against it, you can't catch it."

So why study religion if you don't believe in it?

"Religions are an important part of the way people behave in the world," Eller explained. "So if you're going to understand people, you have to understand what motivates them. Religion is one of those elements. It's a little bit like language. To understand people, you have to speak their language, but it's not necessary to adopt it as your own."

And atheism's effect on how Eller lives his life?

"It's reaffirmed my basic humanity," he said. "It's freed me from other people's dogmas and two-thousand-year-old beliefs that don't really help in the modern world. Atheism helps me to appreciate the world and my fellow creatures because in the end that's all we've got. Make this life meaningful. It's the only one you've got."

Steven Kramer tunes in to vibrations of the universe

Steven Kramer, a.k.a. Sada Anand Singh, is a master of the Tibetan singing bowl, which he uses to bring about both spiritual and physical healing in his clients.

"It's like a nontoxic chemotherapy," Kramer said. "Tibetan doctors use singing bowls to cure ailments from muscle spasms to cancer. When I work with a person, I have them lie down, and I surround them with the bowls. I have them breathe deep to relax. Then I ask them, 'Is there anything that you want or need in your life? Is there anything that's hurting? Is there any part of your body that needs relief?' After that, I put the bowls right on the body. Our bodies are made up mostly of liquids. You surrender to the sound of the bowl, and the vibration takes the liquids of the body and brings them into harmony with the vibrations of the universe."

Though only recently introduced to the West, sound healing has been a feature of both Oriental medicine and Asian spiritual practice for thousands of years. So how did a nice Jewish boy from Miami come to be a master of this ancient modality?

"I grew up Reformed Jewish, but knew nothing of my own religion," Kramer said. "After high school, I started reading *The Tibetan Book of the Dead* and also books on Zen by Alan Watts."

So infatuated was he with Asian spirituality that he taught himself how to meditate. "It was like natural Prozac," he said.

The Vietnam War and the Civil Rights Movement were in full cry at the time. For anyone interested in alternative spirituality, California was the place to be. Kramer had a thousand bucks burning a hole in his pocket, so he jumped on a Greyhound Bus and joined the migration to the Coast. At LA City College, he studied Oriental philosophy, eventually transferring to the University of Hawaii to earn his undergraduate degree.

After college, he returned to Miami, did construction work, got married, and moved to Paris to go to cooking school, which ultimately led to the establishment of his own Miami-based catering business. By then, he and his wife had seven kids to feed. Despite his hectic schedule, Kramer's interest in Asian spirituality remained keen. Somehow he always found the time to meditate.

Somewhere along the line, he hooked up with a guy named Mitch Nur, an American master of the Tibetan singing bowls. Something about the bowls, well, resonated with Kramer, and he started taking classes with Nur.

"I'd go into a darkroom to play them, and I'd feel calm, almost euphoric," he said. "Bowls are an adjunct to meditation. The vibrations bring you into an alpha state rather quickly. You can't help but surrender to the sound."

When the last of his seven kids went off to college, Kramer, now divorced, started thinking about retirement. "The East Coast was never a good fit for me," he said. "I'm a hippy at heart, and Miami was all about the money." For a mediator into skiing and triathlons,

Colorado seemed like the logical next step. There was, of course, the added inducement of the state's burgeoning meditation scene.

Since his retirement, Kramer has devoted himself exclusively to teaching meditation and healing through the use of the Tibetan singing bowl. "It's not a science," he said. "There are no set rules. Most important is the intention of the practitioner. You do it with love and with an open heart and wish your patients abundance, happiness, and equanimity."

Kramer said he loves his new life in Colorado and the work he's doing here as a teacher and healer. "I couldn't ask for more," he said. "I have a lot of friends who are doctors and attorneys, and they're all so miserable. My greatest fear is that in my next incarnation, I'll come back as an attorney."

Rev. Jerry Herships holds church in a bar

It's Monday night at the Irish Snug, a popular watering hole on East Colfax Avenue in Denver. On the table in front of you sits an ice-cold beer, and your waitress is laying down an order of corned beef sliders. You take a hefty swig of your brewski and are just about to reach for a slider when the church service begins.

Church service? Welcome to Church in a Bar, the brainchild of Methodist minister and "Chief Love Monger" Jerry Herships.

"We call it Happy Hour," he said. "It's like church but without the parts that suck."

Actually, it's very much like church, the iconoclastic setting to the contrary notwithstanding. The twice-monthly gatherings (there's another service second Mondays at the Blake Street Tavern) contain pretty much all the elements of a traditional service but with a twist. There's an opening prayer ("Heavenly Father, once again you've found a way to blow us all away"), followed by a very public "sharing of joys and concerns," after which the congregation takes a break to make peanut butter and jelly sandwiches for the homeless.

"I'm always stunned by the level of transparency, even among first-timers," he said. "The bar environment breaks down pretence, and people seem more open and willing to share their joys and concerns. Church should be a hospital for sinners, not a museum for saints."

There's no choir, but there *is* music (usually '60s soul, Chicago blues, or alternative rock from Herships's iPod). Herships delivers a short sermon and serves Communion. About 80 percent of the people partake. Herships's worship differs from traditional church in one other significant detail: people tend to stick around after the service.

"In regular church, all you see are elbows as everybody tries to get away," Herships said. "Here they've got friends and a beer. People crave community, a place to connect with others. I think Facebook proves that."

Methodist Minister was not at the apex of Jerry Herships's list of career options. Before he got the calling, he did stand-up comedy for twenty-eight years in Orlando and Los Angeles, writing jokes on the side for the likes of Jay Leno.

"I always had a spiritual if not a religious inclination," he said. "I was raised Catholic and remained so through college. But when I went to LA, I stopped going to church and stayed away for ten years."

It was his wife who brought him back.

"She got me going to St. Luke's United Methodist in Orlando," he said. By then he was simultaneously managing a local night club, travelling around the country doing stand-up, and making big bucks emceeing corporate game shows.

"I was not, however, getting famous," he said, "and I was starting to feel a little restless."

The Rev. Bill Barnes, who was pastor at St. Luke's, sensed his restlessness and suggested he become a minister.

"Bill," responded Herships, "I like brown liquor. I curse like a sailor. I look at pretty girls. I'm the last person that should be a pastor."

"Maybe that's *why* you should be," Barnes responded. "Maybe we need more real people in the pulpit willing to share their struggles with the congregation."

Herships went for it.

After his ordination in 2009, he was assigned to St. Andrew's United Methodist Church in Highlands Ranch, where he got the idea of doing a service for people not comfortable with formal religious structures.

"A lot of people struggle with the rigidity of organized religion," he said. "They struggle with creeds and dogma. The good news for the church is that one hundred million Americans go to church every Sunday. The bad news is that two hundred million don't. Our mission is to ask the question, 'Why don't they?' and to provide a connection to God for the two hundred million. I compare what we're doing to Boutique Hotels and microbrews for people not comfortable with Budweiser. We're the chocolate oatmeal stout of Church."

David Stevens, Psychic Accountant

Depending on your point of view, David Stevens is either a psychic with his head in the clouds or an accountant with his feet on the ground.

Actually, he's both. To keep food on the table, he does the books for area eateries such as Swing Thai and Watercourse Foods. To feed his soul, he runs Yoga of the Mind, a school for intuitives and energy healers located just upstairs from the Hornet Restaurant at First and Broadway. If you're so inclined, Stevens will give you a free aura reading any Tuesday from 5:30 p.m. to 7:00 p.m.

"I've done a couple thousand readings in the last ten years," he said. "Most people come because they're in transition or crisis. I try to get a snapshot of what they're working on as a spirit in this chapter of their lives."

The "snapshot" often comes in the form of a mental image, the meaning of which—like art—is subject to interpretation.

"Readings are not an intellectual process," he said. "They're more about receptivity."

The conventional view of auras is that they're a kind of halo, a visible emanation of color and light that surrounds the body. Stevens said he doesn't actually see physical colors in the objective world. Rather, he senses them mentally or feels them tactilely, and yes, they do surround the body in layers—seven, to be exact—each of which governs an aspect of our being: health, sexuality, work, love, communication, intuition, and divine inspiration. One's personal vibrational field can be influenced for good or ill by the vibes of others, even in casual encounters or over the Internet. The job of an energy healer is to help you become aware of those unwanted negative energies and to supplant them with positive ones.

Stevens, who was born and raised in Pueblo, said psychic ability runs in his family.

"My mother used to say things like, 'You can tell what kind of people live in a house by how you feel when you walk by it.' Mom was not a designated psychic, but she had a native ability."

As a child, Stevens wanted to "know everything." At nine, he began reading the encyclopedia. At fourteen, he encountered Allen Watts's *The Book: On the Taboo against Knowing Who You Are.*

"Before I read Watts," he said, "I had a sense that life was a battle and a struggle, but now I knew there was a unity beneath all the conflict."

Six months later, he and a couple of friends began doing Transcendental Meditation. The practice ultimately led him to enroll at Maharishi University in Fairfield, Iowa, where he got an undergraduate degree in English. He would return nine years later to earn an MBA with an emphasis on accounting.

It was in that intervening nine years, working a lot of short-term jobs ("none of which worked out") that Stevens finally found his calling.

"A friend from Maharishi University, a guy named Robert Grey, was doing psychic readings over the phone at the time." Stevens said. "He did maybe thirty readings on me."

The readings led Stevens to an awareness of the unspoken "energy agreements" he—and by extension, all of us—have with the people in our lives. "I was fascinated by what Grey was doing. He showed me that I was on my path, even if it *was* a little rocky."

Once he had established his own accounting business, Stevens began devoting more and more time to his psychic studies, taking classes in clairvoyant reading and energy healing at Denver's Inner Connection Institute.

"My studies helped me to access my intuition at will," he said.

In 2004, he launched Yoga of the Mind, a school for people who want to "stretch, strengthen, and balance" their intuitive powers.

"We all have psychic ability, but it's either been repressed or ignored," he said. "Being around others who believe intuition is real is validating. When it's validated, the psychic world begins to open up."

Lou Florez is the wizard next door

He doesn't wear a long robe or wave a magic wand, but Lou Florez is a bona fide wizard nonetheless.

He lives in a tiny pueblo-style alley house in the neighborhood just west of DU. The dwelling sits in the cool shade of tall trees and is surrounded by what at first appear to be weeds but are actually medicinal herbs that Florez raises to treat his clients. He's a lineage holder in a number of spiritual traditions: an *Ifa* priest in the West African *Orisha* tradition, a voodoo priest in the *Bacongo* tradition, a high priest in the *Wicca* tradition, and a *curandero* or healer in the Mexican American folk tradition. He didn't go to Hogwarts. He went to Naropa, where he earned an interdisciplinary degree in psychology and religious studies.

Wizards are chosen. Florez first became aware of his destiny at the age of twelve, when his eldest sister became pregnant with her first child. For no apparent reason, young Lou got sick. Very sick.

"In traditional Latino communities," he explained, "there's a belief that the first pregnancy in a family is a time when all the previous ancestors who need healing or light or 'upliftment' come forward and cause disturbances in a household: car wrecks, illnesses, job losses. In my case, my guts started burning, and I was seeing shadows. My parents took me to doctors and psychiatrists, none of whom were able to help."

What *did* help was a vision he had the following spring in which a big African woman dressed in blue came to him and said, "You have work to do. You can hide from it, but you won't leave this life until it's done. Either heal yourself and fulfill your purpose or continue to be sick."

Over the next six years, he threw himself into a study of *curanderismo*, the ancient healing tradition of the Aztecs and Mexicas.

"*Curanderismo*," Florez explained, "is curing in both the spiritual and physical dimensions. We believe that when there's illness or trauma, the soul leaves the body. So we heal the body with herbs and bring the soul back with prescriptive rites."

For example, someone comes to him with a cough. Florez picks a bouquet of rue and horehound, mixes it with honey, and offers the patient a tea to relieve her symptoms. Simple.

Bringing the soul back, however, is a little more complicated. It begins with an interview in which he learns, say, that in addition to the cough, the patient has just lost his job, his marriage is on the rocks, and he's down in the dumps. To discover the appropriate prescriptive rite, Florez uses a method of cowry shell divination that he learned at Denver's Ile Ori Egum, an *Orisha* temple in the Nigerian Yoruba tradition, located somewhere in the heart of deepest, darkest Aurora.

Cowry shell divination is called *Dillogun*, which is Yoruba for "sixteen" and refers to the sixteen shells that are flung out on a table to be read by the diviner.

"The spirits speak through patterns in the shells," Florez explained. "Reading them, we can see what blessings are trying to come in and what's obstructing them and how to remove them from your life."

He then assigns the patient a practice that can involve candles, baths, scents, oils, powders, prayer, meditation, introspection, or behavior modification.

A curandero has to eat and pay the rent, so Florez charges for his readings. "That's part of it," he said. "You have to be able to give and make some sacrifices."

He earns between $1,500 and $2,000 a month doing readings, healings, and consultations, and augments his income by offering classes and workshops at venues such as Denver Free University and Isis Bookstore. Florez said he sees himself as a spiritual consultant.

"I try to offer my clients practical ways of working through obstacles and difficulties," he said. "It's not about me saving the world. It's about making connections, engaging people one on one and helping them with the tools that I have."

Part 8

Expats, Sailors, and Mongolian Sheep Counters

Devon Parson walks the Colorado Trail

Walking the 480-mile Colorado Trail from Watertown Canyon to Durango was a rite of passage for river guide Devon Parson.

"I went to high school in Wheat Ridge and studied philosophy at Fort Lewis," he said. "In college, I found myself drawn to the kids who were into the outdoors. For me, the trail represented a transition from city life to the mountain mentality."

During the summer of 2006, Parson (then twenty-two) and his friend Bill Whitacre quit their jobs and spent a couple of weeks studying trail maps, packing gear, and sending food parcels to post offices in towns along the route. On the eve of their departure, they weighed their packs.

"Seventy pounds," Parson said, "half my body weight. I could hardly stand up."

Three days in, they found themselves setting up camp in an area blackened by forest fires.

"By then we'd only covered twenty miles, and I had this huge blister on my foot," Parson said. "Our morale was really down, and we were trying to decide whether we wanted to go on."

He called his father, who drove down from Denver to pick them up.

"By the time he got there, we were feeling a little more hopeful," Parson said. "We decided to continue." They took the opportunity to lighten their packs. "I handed my dad this big hardback anthology of poetry," he said. "I knew I could live without it."

After that first grueling week, they were able to take the daily obstacles and challenges in stride.

"Like one time when our canteens ran dry, we found some pretty nasty-looking water in a tire rut. There were cow pies all over the place. We didn't care. We just purified it with iodine and drank it down. This was on day 23, and by then, stuff like that was no big deal."

The low point came late one afternoon when they were hiking above the tree line at thirteen thousand feet. Storm clouds were gathering, and they had to decide whether to set up camp and take their chances with the lightning or risk walking downhill on a muddy trail in the dark. They decided to camp.

"We had one tarp between us, and it had a metal pole," Parson said. "There was a hole in it, and water dripped through all night long. It was cold. Our bags were soaked. But we were so tired we slept right through it. You learn to abide by the rules of the weather when you're on the trail. If it rains, you find shelter, roll a cigarette, and wait it out."

The high point? Elk Ridge near Silverton.

"It was a foggy morning," Parson said, "and all I could see was Bill's silhouette up ahead as we climbed to the top of the ridge." At the summit, the clouds parted, revealing a valley carpeted with Columbines, Mountain Blue Bells, and Yellow Arnicas. "That 20-second window of beauty made the whole 480 miles of blisters and pain worth doing."

Parson and Whitacre spent 35 days on the Colorado Trail, "mainly thinking about cheeseburgers and women," Parson said. "By the time we got to Durango, our knees were shot, and I was down to 119 pounds. Never did get the woman, but I did get a cheeseburger."

He also got a raging case of culture shock.

"Everything felt fast and superficial. I couldn't sleep that first night."

Lessons learned?

"The hardest to see is what's right in front of you, and you won't see it if you don't slow down. There's so much more to experience when you take it easy and pay attention. For me, the trail became a metaphor for how I plan to lead my life. I may not know where I'm heading, but I do know I'll keep on going."

Tibet journey teaches Andrew Holecek
"the curse of convenience"

When dentist Andrew Holecek decided to go on sabbatical in 1996, he made two phone calls. The first was to his Buddhist teacher, Ponlop Rinpoche, who suggested he visit Tibet and pay respects to His Holiness the Karmapa at Tsurphu Monastery. "The monastery sits at fourteen feet in the middle of nowhere," Holecek said. "The Karmapa is head of the Karma Kagyu sect, one of the four great lineages of Tibetan Buddhism."

The second phone call was to the renowned medical service organization Doctors Without Borders. Would it be possible, Holecek wanted to know, for him to do dental work on the Tsurphu monks under the aegis of DWB? The answer they gave him was unequivocal: "If you go into Tibet, you go on your own."

Holecek and his then-wife, Laurie Matthews, decided to risk it.

"We had to figure out a way to smuggle dental supplies and equipment into Tibet under the nose of the Chinese," Holecek said. "We decided the best way in would be by car from Katmandu to Lhasa as part of a tour with a dozen other travelers."

They spent twelve to fourteen hours a day packed into a Land Rover, bumping along a road that was unpaved, tortuous, and steep. Sheer drops of two and three thousand feet were not uncommon, and there were no guardrails. Frequent landslides interrupted the journey, as did regular and interminable searches for contraband by the Chinese.

In addition, there was no time to get accustomed to the altitude. On the second day, a German woman came down with cerebral edema and almost died. An eighteen-thousand-foot pass lay ahead of them, and as a doctor, Holecek knew she would not survive it. At his insistence, they turned around and brought her and her travelling companion back to Nepal before resuming the journey.

From Lhasa, Holecek and Matthews took a bus to Tusrphu Monastery, where they set up a makeshift dental clinic and began offering palliative care to the monks. It wasn't long before word got out, and people from the surrounding villages began pouring in.

"We worked ourselves to the bone," Holecek said, "eating dried yak meat and heating ourselves on a yak dung stove. For me, being a lily-white, comfort-infected Westerner, this was like a bucket of cold water being thrown in my face. I witnessed for the first time how life is for most people in the world."

Five days later, Holecek and Matthews rejoined their group in Lhasa for the flight back to Katmandu. Surrounded and questioned by machine-gun-toting Chinese guards as to the whereabouts of the two missing German women, the group was only allowed onto the plane after forking over a hefty bribe.

"We did a fair amount of good in a short period of time," Holecek said, "but I realized it was too dangerous to keep doing it like that. Now we only go to places where there's a host sponsor."

For one month each year, Holecek goes to a village in Nepal called Bandiphur, where he personally treats up to seven hundred kids a week. Global Dental Relief, an organization he and Matthews founded in 2001, sponsors a team of volunteer dentists who treat some ten thousand children a year in India, Nepal, Guatemala, and Vietnam.

"The Tibet experience was the germ of the whole thing for me," Holecek said. "I never saw my world the same way again after that. For one thing, it changed my relationship to my profession. I realized I could use my skills to help others. For another, it made me realize how dangerous the level of comfort is that we enjoy in this country. You come to expect it, and it puts you to sleep, and you don't even know it. I call it the curse of convenience. I came back exhausted, dirty, and sick. But it was the best time I ever had in my life."

Lily Muldoon: coming of age in Kayafungo

"Think Arizona," said Lily Muldoon. "Dry desert. Cactus. It's a hundred degrees in the middle of the night. There's no water. No electricity. No sanitation. No infrastructure. A house is a mud hut. A bed is a straw mat. School is a tree. The kids do their sums in the dirt with a stick."

This is Kayafungo, Kenya, where Muldoon spent a portion of her junior year in college living with a local family.

"Every morning at six," she remembered, "the village women—even girls as young as four—would walk a mile to the dam to get water and carry it back on their heads. A twenty-liter plastic bucket weighed forty pounds."

One day, they invited Muldoon to join them.

"I was only able to manage half a bucket," she said, "and by the time we got back, my neck was sore and I was exhausted. The water was filthy. You could see bugs and worms floating around in it. There wasn't enough firewood to boil it and no money to buy chemicals to filter it either."

Muldoon contracted intestinal worms and spent a month vomiting and battling diarrhea. The experience was a turning point in her life.

"I was struck by the injustice of it," she said. "I resolved to do something about it."

Back at Pomona College, Muldoon started a campus chapter of Student Movement for Real Change (SMRC), an organization founded by an East High classmate named Saul Garlick.

"What we wanted to do," she said, "was bring the water closer to the people."

Together with a group of volunteers from Engineers Without Borders, they devised a scheme to pipe water from a spring to a centrally located holding tank. From there, the water could be piped to each of the twenty-five villages in the region.

SMRC formed a partnership with the Kenyan government in which the government agreed to build a 1.5-million-gallon holding tank and the supply line to it. For their part, SMRC would provide funding for the distribution pipelines from the tank to the surrounding villages. Muldoon's job was to raise the money for the distribution pipelines.

The water tank the Kenyans built was a magnificent edifice, two stories tall and "as big as a church," but today it stands empty, a monument to third-world graft and political corruption.

What went wrong?

"The piping they used was narrower than what was called for in the specs" said Muldoon with a trace of irritation in her voice. "Somebody somewhere pocketed the difference."

Her entreaties to the Kenyan government fell on deaf ears. If the Student Movement for Real Change wanted to raise another million to correct the problem, she was told, they were more than welcome to do so.

Muldoon decided to return to Kayafungo anyway. She had a $40,000 grant from Rotary International burning a hole in her pocket, and with it, SMRC was able to build two schools, fourteen concrete latrines, and several hand-washing stations. They trained 160 community health workers to promote sanitation in the region, and with an additional $4,000 from SMRC, they created a food-for-work program to build a dam.

"That first day, two hundred people showed up to work on it," Muldoon said. "It's a U-shaped wall, twenty feet tall, fifty feet wide. We directed the River Choga to flow to it during the rainy season. It's centrally located. They still have to hike, but it's not as far."

Now back in the States, Muldoon has taken a year off from medical school at UC San Francisco to work on a master's in public health at Harvard.

"It's beyond just treating individual patients," she said. "It's a matter of making large-scale policy changes that can save thousands."

World traveler Steve Bouey: "Go big or go home!"

One particularly difficult afternoon on their eighty-thousand-mile, round-the-world road trip, Steve Bouey and his travelling companion Steven Shoppman were pulled over by AK-47-wielding rebels at a checkpoint in the Republic of Congo. Fortunately, they were road savvy and travel hardened enough to know how to handle themselves.

"Our strategy was to break the ice, show no fear, be confident but not cocky, ask questions, and be engaged," Bouey said. "We handed out cigarettes and cash and took photographs. We told them we were tourists, not government officials. It took us fifteen minutes to explain what a tourist was. That was the place where I felt the farthest from home."

The trip was Shoppman's idea. Over a couple of beers, he talked Bouey into going with him; although, truth be told, it didn't take a whole lot of convincing. Bouey had just returned from three months of triathlon training in New Zealand, and the experience had kindled in him a thirst for adventure.

"Steven kind of caught me at a vulnerable moment," he said. "I'd worked for six years in the Colorado State Auditor's Office, and I was having a hard time going back to wearing a suit and tie."

That evening Shoppman, a graphic artist and freelance web designer, handed Bouey a book called *Who Needs a Road?* Back in 1965, the author, Harold Stephens, had driven around the world in a Toyota Land Cruiser. Stephens argued that the world was becoming so dangerous that his would most likely be the last round-the-world motor trip anyone would ever take.

"We took that as a challenge," Bouey said. "We decided it was 'go big or go home.'"

"Going big" would mean driving through eighty countries. And having a car would mean customs, permits, insurance, and Chinese driver's licenses.

Make that two cars.

"We knew that if it was just the two of us together in one car for three years, we'd be at each other's throats," said Bouey. "So we decided to take two vehicles and open the trip up to friends and family."

Thirty people took them up on it, among them a Thai Buddhist monk, a young South African woman, a guy from Argentina, and a government-mandated minder in China who turned out to be a twenty-one-year-old kid in jeans, T-shirt, and a New Zealand rugby hat.

To help defray the expedition's estimated $200,000 price tag, Bouey and Shoppmann put together a ten-page marketing proposal and shopped it around to all the major car dealers in the Denver metro area. Stevenson Toyota stepped up with what Bouey describes as a "soccer mom, grocery grabber Sequoia SUV" plus a Toyota Tundra with a camper shell in back for the gear.

On February 10, 2007, "with only 20 percent of the planning completed," the lads drove to LA and shipped the vehicles to Australia for the first leg of their thirty-month odyssey.

Favorite country?

"Mongolia, hands down," said Bouey. "It was like taking a step back in time."

They were fed and sheltered in yurts wherever they went. At a Mongolian wedding, three hundred kilometers from the nearest town, the father of the groom raised a toast to his "fellow nomads" and gave them money to help them on their way.

"Crossing the Gobi," Bouey said, "we spent three days without seeing another human being."

He said his travels have revealed to him more similarities than differences among the peoples of the world. "Everybody wants peace," he said. "Everybody wants to feed their families and to have prosperity and comfort."

The experience also led him to simplify his life and shift his priorities. "When I came back, I got rid of a lot of the material clutter," he said. "I can live a happier life by helping others."

In 2009, *National Geographic Magazine* named Steve Bouey and Steven Shoppman "Adventurers of the Year."

John Baumann's motorcycle odyssey to the end of the world

Sometimes the best thing that can happen to a guy is for everything to go to hell all at once. That's what happened to John Baumann, a Denver social worker with a jones for travel—big travel, as in Tierra del Fuego and back. And not on an airplane or a cruise ship either. For Baumann, it's always been about the bike.

"I was sitting on a Harley when I was nine," he said. "At age ten, I hopped on my big brother's Sportster, popped it into gear, and drove it through a cyclone fence."

In 2008, Baumann was offered a job at Denver County Human Services as supervisor of the child protection team. "I saw some horrific stuff," he said. "Kids who were malnourished, some with broken bones, two—and three-year-olds beaten to death. It was very, very stressful."

So stressful, in fact, that Baumann decided to quit the job and take a trip around the world with Mrs. Baumann. But then she started having second thoughts, not only about the trip, but also about their marriage. She asked for a divorce, and before he knew it, Baumann was on his own.

"I was not getting any younger," he said. "But I *was* in good health. So I decided the time was right to make the trip and realize my old dream of following animal migrations."

Animal migrations? Well, yeah, see, 'cause Baumann was not just planning some random pilgrimage, here. The guy had a plan . . . one that had been festering in his brain ever since the fifth grade.

"My social studies teacher, Mr. Gagliano, liked to spice up his lectures with stories about animal migrations," he said. "This put it in my head that someday I wanted to see all the great animal migrations: the grey whales in Baja, California; the monarch butterflies in Morelia, Mexico; the leatherback turtles in Guanacaste, Costa Rica. I was fascinated by their journeys."

So in May 2008, he bought himself a spankin' new Harley, ripped all the chrome off it, pointed it in the direction of the Baja, and booked. After a month of communing with the whales, he took the ferry to Mazatlan and rode to the Monarch Preserve in Morelia, which in turn fired him up to go to Costa Rica for the turtle migration. In Panama, he hoisted his Harley onto a dugout canoe and sailed with some Kuna tribals through the San Blas Islands to Cartagena, observing the swan and crane migrations as he went.

He rode through monsoon rains and 110-degree heat down the Pacific coast to Chile and up over the Andes into Bolivia, battling fierce winds that kept his bike tilted at a 45-degree angle.

"No matter how bad it got," he said, "whenever I'd be tempted to give up, something would come along to draw me on."

Like that time he found himself in the middle of the jungle and some locals came out, and they all danced together to the music of Michael Jackson.

Eight months and thirty thousand miles later, Baumann roared into Tierra del Fuego and had his picture taken in Ushuaia, the "City at the End of the World."

"Not once did I ever feel threatened," he said. "Never once got robbed. People embraced me and took me into their homes. Nobody even looked at me weird."

Which is interesting in light of what happened to him when he got back over the US border.

"I checked into a Motel 6, locked down the bike, and went to bed," he said. "Next day, I discovered my King Tour Pack had been stolen. I just had to laugh. Heading down, I was wound pretty tight. But the trip taught me to trust, to loosen up and go with it. I learned to live in the moment, and I miss that."

David Nichol's year of living dangerously

David Nichol was sitting a meditation retreat in 1983, when he heard Korean Zen master Seung San say, "If you meditate just for yourself, b-i-i-i-g problem. If you meditate for others, n-o-o-o problem."

"It was like somebody turned on a light in my head," Nichol said. "My whole worldview did a complete one eighty."

The son of a State Department diplomat, Nichol had been knocking around the planet for years. He'd gone to schools in Geneva and Liverpool, studied environmental biology at Colorado College, dropped out of school for a year to go travelling in India, Sri Lanka, and Central Asia, studied Zen at a monastery in Korea, and for five years had owned and operated a natural foods grocery store on the west side of Colorado Springs.

But lately, he was feeling at loose ends, which is probably why his Zen master's words had struck him with such force. He needed, he realized, a sense of direction and purpose. As the retreat drew to a close, Nichol resolved to study medicine and dedicate his life to the welfare of others.

He enrolled at the University of Colorado Medical School, but almost from the beginning, he was at odds with his teachers. "I was a rebel," he said. "I asked a lot of questions. I was interested in alternative treatments and complementary medicine at a time when such ideas were not popular with the establishment."

At the end of his third year, he failed his internal medicine clinical rotation and was called before the Progressions Committee to discuss his future. The committee suggested that he take six months off to reevaluate his choice of career.

For most people, suspension from medical school might be a major setback, but Nichol saw it as a chance to explore other options. He began his sabbatical by attending a yoga teacher training course at Kripalu Institute in Lennox, Massachusetts.

"There were resident holistic doctors there," he said, "and I saw them as role models for a different approach to healing than the one I'd been getting at CU. They'd managed to synthesize the best of both Eastern and Western medicine, and I wanted to know more."

Meanwhile, half a world away, the Russians were invading Afghanistan; and in a very understated way, the US was providing logistical support to the resistance. "I'd been in Afghanistan on my trip to Asia in the '70s, and I really liked the people there," he said. "So when the Russians invaded, I naturally wanted to help."

He went for an interview with an organization called Freedom Medicine in New York and was hired on the spot.

Assigned to an adobe fortress on the Pakistani side of the border, Nichol spent the next five months teaching first aid and practical medicine to young Afghani medics. ("It was not uncommon," he said, "to hear gunfire in the distance.") Soon he was assisting in surgery, working the emergency room, going on rounds with the Afghani doctors, and treating wounded Mujahedeen fighters and injured civilians.

At one point, he taught what would turn out to be a groundbreaking three-day seminar in psycho-pharmacology. "This was particularly interesting to the Afghanis because so many of them were suffering from depression and post-traumatic stress disorder," he said. "The notion that you could find relief in a pill was astounding to them."

But the seminar marked a turning point in David Nichol's career as well, because it was here that he finally understood what he was meant to do with his life. "Everything—my personal struggles with depression, all those years of yoga and meditation—had led me to the unavoidable conclusion that what I really wanted to be was a psychiatrist."

In January of 1989, he returned to medical school and passed the clinical rotation. He graduated in 1990 and went on to the Menninger Clinic in Topeka, Kansas, for his psychiatric residency. The final irony in this tale is that Dr. David Nichol is now a teacher of psychiatric medicine at the University of Colorado Medical School.

Rich Reading: counting sheep in Outer Mongolia

For Dr. Rich Reading, director of Conservation Biology at the Denver Zoo, the love affair with Mongolia began in Montana while he was up there working on a grassland conservation project in the early '90s. A co-worker who had spent some time in Mongolia kept telling him about how the country looked like Montana before the white man showed up: no fences, no paved roads, nomadic people living in yurts and tepees.

"That piqued my interest," Reading said. "So in 1994, I went over for three months and ended up staying two and a half years, working as an ecological consultant for the UN and other NGOs."

While there, Reading had the good fortune to meet a local ecologist named Amgalanbaatar, (Mongolian for "calm hero"). "Amgaa was absolutely passionate about preserving the Argali," Reading said.

Argali are Mongolia's answer to our own Rocky Mountain Bighorn Sheep, although these bad boys are about twice the size of their Colorado cousins. "They're the biggest sheep in the world," Reading said. "Males can grow to over 440 pounds, and their horns curl twice or more around."

Big? You betcha! Powerful? Absolutely! Invulnerable? Sadly, no.

"There are probably only twelve thousand to fifty thousand of them left," Reading said as he ticked off the dangers they face. "Big game hunters will pay up to $50,000 to shoot one. Poachers track them for meat. Their habitats are being taken over by mining interests. They're forced to compete with domestic livestock for grazing land."

The only thing standing in the way of their complete extinction, or so it seemed at the time, was Reading's newfound friend, Amgalanbaatar.

"Amgaa was Mr. Argali," Reading said. "He regularly stuck his neck out to save them. He's had his life threatened by corrupt politicians who want a percentage of the trophy money while he fights to make sure at least some of it gets back to preservation."

Inspired by Amgaa's passion, Reading started working with him in an effort to save the iconic Argali. In 1996, Reading was hired by the Denver Zoo to establish a conservation department.

"I wanted to keep working in Mongolia," he said. "At the time, the country was undergoing a transition from Communism to a free-market economy, so we started the Mongolian Biodiversity Project to help the government there expand existing protected areas before competing land uses like mining got in. In order to enlist local support, we tagged our efforts to the charismatic Argali. We started looking at areas where there were good Argali populations and eventually established a conservation project in Ikh Nart Nature Reserve. Just by our presence there, we've been able to stop the poaching and illegal mining that was threatening their habitat."

To help bring money into the community, the Denver Zoo set up a tourist camp at Ikh Nart and established a women's co-op called "Ikh Nart is Our Future" to make handicrafts to sell there. In addition, they hired park rangers from among the local population, thereby giving them the option of making a living protecting the park.

The effort has paid off.

"In our protected area, the Argali population has tripled, and the animals are now starting to disperse and establish satellite populations," Reading said. "The UN Development Program ranked our park the best in the world. It's now used as a model for other protected areas. Kirghizstan and Tajikistan are asking us to establish similar programs. Today we have ninety projects in twenty-two countries."

Reading's friend Amgalanbaatar now works for the Denver Zoo in Mongolia as a conservation biologist. He also runs his own nonprofit, the Argali Wildlife Research Center, and is writing a doctoral dissertation on Argali preservation.

"Mongolia is one of those transformational places," Reading reflected. "It's a place you go to and come away different. To have helped my colleagues to do this work and to see them blossom as professionals has heartened me. It's made me realize we *can* make a difference."

Pinki goes to Hollywood

Venita "Pinki" Wood remembers her late husband as "a man who knew no stranger. Woody loved everyone," she said, "and everyone loved him back."

Woody died of liver cancer in April 2003.

"It was pretty quick," Pinki said. "Just four months from the time he got the diagnosis. He was in a lot of pain."

After he passed, she'd walk out to the garage and look at Woody's motorcycle and think to herself, *What the heck am I supposed to do with this thing?*

Woody's passion for motorcycles dated back to 1974, when he joined Denver's El Jebel Shrine Temple and started riding with the Noble Cycles. Eighteen members strong, each astride a 1,500 cc, two-tone turquoise Goldwing Honda, you'd see them out there—loud and proud—at the St. Patrick's Day Parade every year. The Nobles used to take their wives on road trips to Shrine conventions all over the USA and Canada, where they'd compete with other biker groups for prizes.

"We won a lot of trophies," Pinki said.

Now Woody was gone, and Pinki kept thinking that he'd taken the good times with him. But then it occurred to her that "he wouldn't want me to just hang around the house. He'd want me to get out there and live my life as though he was still around. He'd want me to learn how to ride that bike myself."

The problem was that it was just way too much machine for a 5-foot, 130-pound, 69-year-old grandmother to handle.

Then one day, her son-in-law, Patrick Clancy O'Grady, was down in Colorado Springs where he stumbled across a place called Apex Sports. Apex, he learned, specialized in converting bikes into trikes. A three-wheeler might just be the solution to Pinki's problem, although the price tag—a cool sixteen grand—was a little steep.

"I went ahead and bought it anyway," Pinki said, "and it was worth every penny. I've had so much fun on it."

Her son, Donald, had to teach her how to ride it.

"He took me down to the Englewood Park-and-Ride and said, 'You can do it, Mom.' I practiced and practiced. Shifting gears was my biggest challenge. It required a lot of hand and foot coordination. But after you learn how, it just comes natural."

After several solo trips into the mountains, Pinki got to where she was feeling pretty confident. So confident, in fact, that she decided it'd be a dandy idea just to ride on out to San Luis Obispo to visit her sister Grace Lane.

"'Course, my kids weren't too crazy about the idea," she said, "but they didn't hear about it 'til I got back."

On April 18, 2005, Pinki Wood headed west on I-70. When she hit snow in the mountains of Utah, she pulled into an Arby's to thaw out. "My hands were freezing. I got lots of looks, let me tell you. People couldn't believe I'd come all that way by myself."

It took her two and a half days to get to Southern California. From there, she and Grace continued up the coast on Highway 1 to Napa Valley.

"It's beautiful out there," Pinki said, "especially on a bike. We saw sea lions giving birth near Hearst Castle. Whenever we'd get tired, we'd check into a small-town motel and spend the night."

She covered nearly three thousand miles on that jaunt and wouldn't mind doing it again. Since then she's taken two or three trips every year around Colorado and Wyoming. "Usually," she said, "I don't tell the kids until I get where I'm going."

Advice to other women?

"Just go for it," she said. "For so many years, I rode on the back. Now I'm in the driver's seat, and I wouldn't have it any other way."

Colin Flahive: "China is the new Wild West"

On the morning the bomb went off at Salvador's Café in Kunming, China—December 24, 2008—Denver native Colin Flahive was standing outside on the sidewalk. Thick black smoke poured from the doorway, and his employees, all young women from the surrounding countryside, were screaming. When he ran in to shut down the electricity and gas and lead his workers and customers to safety, he saw Chinese currency scattered everywhere.

The perpetrator, an electrician on his way to pay his crew with a satchel full of cash, had stopped off for a mocha and waffle. He stepped into the bathroom and was assembling the device, apparently intending to use it elsewhere, when it went off by accident. He was still alive when the cops arrived, though his body had been severed at the waist. "A pile of mush" is how Flahive describes it. Before he died, the electrician confessed to the bombings of two buses in Kunming earlier that year.

Fortunately, no one else was injured, but the restaurant was a shambles, and Flahive himself was badly shaken. "I didn't want to reopen," he said. "Our girls are like family, and I didn't want to expose them again."

Despite his misgivings, he and his partners spent the next six weeks repairing the damage, and Salvador's reopened in February of 2009. Business boomed after that, but for the next year, Flahive suffered from a severe case of post-traumatic stress disorder.

The bombing sparked some soul-searching and reevaluation in the young entrepreneur. He thought a lot about his twenty employees, all hardworking young women from the same village in South Yunnan Province.

"I began wondering if in addition to employment, we could offer them a better future as well. The logical next step was a two-week road trip where we met the families of all twenty of our girls. We did interviews focusing on education, health care, poverty."

What they discovered was that with the country's burgeoning economy, rural people were abandoning their farms and villages and moving to the cities to seek employment, better health care, and a higher standard of living.

"We wanted to see if we could create more opportunities in the villages themselves to kind of stem the tide," Flahive said. "Our motto is 'What can we do to help?'"

The fact-finding mission led to the founding of Village Progress, a 501(c)(3) registered in Colorado. Among their many projects, the charity is sponsoring a team of cardiologists who teach village doctors about the diagnosis and treatment of high blood pressure.

Colin Flahive has lived and worked in China for ten years, but he's been going there in one capacity or another since 1998. A graduate of Denver's East High School and CU Boulder, he went initially as a backpack tourist between his sophomore and junior years. His initial reaction was not favorable.

"Travelling in China is a lot of work," he said. "When I got back, I threw away my Chinese-English dictionary. I was sure I'd never return. But when I thought about it, I realized how much I'd grown to love it, especially rural China, where the lifestyle hasn't changed in a thousand years. It felt like I'd only gotten a taste, and I wanted more."

He went back a second time to do research for his senior thesis on the forced urbanization of rural people as a result of Three Gorges Dam. He went back a third time to study martial arts at a Shaolin temple, and by then he was hooked. He started looking around for a way to stay there. He and a couple of guys opened Salvador's in Kunming in 2005, and he's been there ever since.

"I've got a gazillion ideas for business and nonprofit," Flahive said. "China is like the Wild West. There are huge opportunities to do business there and a kind of freedom we no longer have in the US. China is the land of opportunity in the world right now."

Luke Eberl: chilling out in Inuvik

In May of 2009, Boulder filmmaker Luke Eberl found himself at a red carpet book release party on Rodeo Drive in Beverly Hills. The book in question was the autobiography of a guy named Sam Childers. Childers, a.k.a. the Machine Gun Preacher, had made a career of rescuing boy soldiers in the Sudan. He'd been setting up orphanages to house them for fifteen years.

"I was struck by the contrast between the glitz of the event and the substance of Childers's work," Eberl said. "It was exactly the same as an opening of a new Miley Cyrus movie: stylish people in gowns and tuxedos, there to be photographed. It was an interesting and funny experience. It was all about the money and glamour."

After the party, Eberl heard from friends who were doing volunteer work overseas, and he was inspired to run an online search for possible volunteer opportunities for himself. He came across a Web site for the Frontiers Foundation, offering a chance to work with native kids at a high school near Inuvik, in Canada's Northwest Territories. The site described a challenging environment with minus-seventy-degree temps and a long dark winter. Unlike some of the other volunteer positions, this one offered a stipend and simple accommodation. Eberl wrote offering to teach basic filmmaking skills and to provide cameras and equipment.

"Two weeks later, I got an e-mail back from them saying, 'Come on up.'"

He went in August and was completely surprised at how cosmopolitan it was. "There were people there from all over the world; the US, Europe, Africa. There were also a lot of Canadian government people, a transient population of folks who had come up there to work."

Eberl taught filmmaking skills at Samuel Hearne Secondary School to Quichin and Inuit tribals in their late teens, many of whom were considered "Code Red," which is Canadian school "administratese" for "at risk." As part of his duties, he was invited to go along on field trips as a videographer, filming in minus-forty-degree weather, sleeping in tents, cabins, and rudimentary igloos and battling frostbite and cold-damaged equipment.

The field trips, guided by tribal elders, were a means of reacquainting native kids with tribal ways and traditional survival skills. "The younger generation," Eberl said, "could play Farmville on their laptops but no longer knew how to live off the land."

As a participant observer, Eberl learned how to trap muskrats, marten, and ptarmigan. "I was a vegetarian before I went up there," he said. "But now I have no problem with hunting. The elders were passionate about preserving their ancient skills. I could see that they really cared about the land. To them it was a living, sentient element in their lives. Many of the troubled kids in school turned out to be real stars in the wilderness."

Back in LA, Eberl said he missed the silence and simplicity of his life in Inuvik. "The experience reinvigorated me as a creative person," he said. "I'm excited about making movies again. I came away with a sense of myself that is not tied to how much I'm approved by the Hollywood caste system. Up there I was away from the hype and corruption of the creative process in Hollywood. All I want to do now is make films from the heart."

Kris Stenzel: Aurora Jungle Woman

At least once each year, Kristine Stenzel takes a four-day boat trip up the Amazon to the town of San Gabriel. From there she boards a twenty-four-foot-long canoe for another five days of travel deep into the Amazonian jungle, sleeping in shelters in villages along the way and eating the simple fare—manioc, insects, and hot pepper stew—provided by her hosts. There are several times during the five-hundred-kilometer journey when the canoe has to be lifted out of the water and portaged around rapids that are as swift as they are dangerous. At other times, the water level on the river might be so low that not even a canoe can get through, and the journey has to be cancelled altogether.

"It's always an adventure," Stenzel said. "I never know for sure if I'm going to get there."

"There" is the village of Caruru Cachoeira, population 120. What sets this village apart and makes it attractive to someone like Kris

Stenzel, is the fact that it contains a school that was built and staffed entirely by the natives themselves.

Stenzel is a linguist trying to help the Wonono/Kotiria people recover and preserve their native language and traditional culture.

"This group has been in contact with European civilization for a long time," she said. "As recently as the 1960s, Catholic missionaries were burning down their traditional longhouses and sending the children out to Catholic schools where they were forbidden to speak their native tongue."

When Stenzel first went there ten years ago, the group had no formal system of writing.

"They wanted me to help them put together a written form of the language so they could create textbooks for their school. That was the first phase of my work there."

The second phase is language documentation, creating an audiovisual archive of the language.

A graduate of Aurora's Smokey Hill High, Stenzel went to Brazil in 1979 to learn Portuguese and study social sciences at the Federal University in Rio. To support herself, she taught English and sang in a Brazilian pop group called Garganta Profundo (Deep Throat). It was in Garganta that she met her future husband, Jorge Simoes de Sa Martins, a musician and high school physics teacher. In 1998, the couple, along with their son, Julian, moved to Boulder to earn advanced degrees. Stenzel opted for a master's in linguistics.

"Intellectually, I'd found my niche," Stenzel said. "Also I was really good at it."

One day, it dawned on her that there were literally hundreds of indigenous languages in South America that had never been described and were in danger of going extinct. For her dissertation, she decided to describe once such language and began looking around for a group to work with. The obstacles were formidable.

"I couldn't just traipse off into the jungle in search of a lost tribe," she said. "I had a family to raise."

As luck would have it, somebody put her in touch with a Wanono/Kotiria Indian named Mateus Cabral, who just happened to be living in, of all places, Fort Lupton, Colorado.

"He'd been here five or six years and was working in a tomato greenhouse when I met him," Stenzel said. "It was like winning the linguistics lottery."

Through Cabral, Stenzel began documenting a language that might have as few as 1,500 native speakers. While working on her dissertation, she traveled to Brazil and made her first face-to-face contact with the tribe in its native habitat.

"I have to admit," Stenzel said, "I was scared shitless the first time I went there. But after that, I knew what the unknown looked like, and it was okay. I feel incredibly privileged to have been allowed into this culture. I believe that human diversity needs to be preserved as much as does the diversity of animals and plants. I believe that preserving language is a way to preserve the diversity of our species."

Davy Davis: a birthday at the Holocaust

In 2005, Davy Davis, who teaches stage design in the theatre department at Denver University, took a trip around the world with the idea of seeing as much local theatre as possible. In Kenya, he helped write a play. In India, he watched traditional dance drama. In Japan, he saw Kabuki, Noh, and a rock version of Hamlet with a happy ending and an all-female cast. But it was in Krakow, Poland, that his travels began taking on a different twist.

"It was my birthday, February 2, Groundhog Day," he said, "and I realized I couldn't do my usual birthday routine, which is to pick a bar somewhere in Denver and invite all my friends to join me for a drink."

He decided, instead, to go to Krakow's premier world heritage site: the prison camp at Auschwitz.

"I was blown away by the scale of it," he said. "It's huge. The barracks the German's built have all been torn down. There's a mile-long walk from the main gate to the Memorial through this endless expanse of chimneys, chimneys as far as you can see. It brought up a very emotional response in me. I felt sorrow and anger, and I resolved that at least *I* would never forget."

Flash forward five years to another birthday, this time at ground zero in Hiroshima, Japan.

"I went there deliberately to be there on my birthday," Davis said. "I wanted to spend the entire day at Peace Park, which is located at the epicenter of the blast. Somehow, I thought it would be similar to Auschwitz, but it turned out to be very, very different."

For one thing, Hiroshima was full of people: school kids on field trips, tourists snapping pictures, women handing out paper cranes sent by children from every corner of the country. Auschwitz, on the other hand, was deserted.

"I was there for four hours and only saw three people," Davis recalled, "all of them tourists. There was a sense of shame hanging over the place. You got the impression that the Poles wanted to ignore what had happened there. And the Germans were in complete denial."

Something else about the museum at Hiroshima also impressed him.

"It was one of the most honest historical museums I'd ever been to," he said. "It doesn't just blame the US. It gives equal blame to the militarism of the Japanese people of the time. To me this represented an unusual acceptance of responsibility on their part."

Much of the museum was devoted to the radiation sickness that afflicted those who survived. Davis said he saw nothing at Auschwitz about the effect it had had on the Jews, gays, and gypsies who walked away from Hitler's death chambers.

"For that matter, there are no monuments to the genocide of the Incas, Aztecs, or Native Americans on this continent, either," Davis pointed out. "On the other hand, promoting peace is almost institutionalized in Japan. Practically every city I went to had some sort of peace park. Only by going there will you really understand. Physical presence is necessary in order not to forget what happened. My takeaway? It's possible to both accept responsibility for yourself and your nation and to move past it. Acceptance is part of the process."

Sierra Brashear takes passion for trash to Zanzibar

Sierra Barshear has a passion for trash.

She's vitally interested in the amount and content of the crap we as a species manage to generate each year. (In case you're wondering, the EPA reports that the USA alone produces enough garbage annually to bury the state of Texas twice).

Brashear has been fighting for the environment since grade school. As a kid growing up in Conifer, she was so appalled by plans to develop Elk Meadow that she took it upon herself, at the age of eight, to write a letter to the editor expressing her concern.

"The developer," she said, "wrote back saying, 'If you're so worried about it, buy it yourself.'"

Later, as a student working on a degree in international environmental policy and development at Colorado University, she volunteered at the student run CU Environmental Center, sorting and recycling campus waste.

"I was fascinated by the content and amount of the waste we generated on campus," she said. "We'd fill up a thirty-foot roll off twice a week."

In 2006, Brashear went to Zanzibar to do a study on costal ecology as part of her course work. Zanzibar, an island off the coast of Tanzania, has in recent years become a destination for sun-seeking Europeans. It's an island of stunning natural beauty, ringed with white-sand beaches, crystal-clear waters—and trash as far as the eye can see.

"Plastic bags, bottles, cans, batteries, chip bags," she said. "The landscape was covered with it."

In her conversations with local teachers, government officials, hotel owners, and ordinary citizens, Brashear came to a stunning realization. In pitching their trash out on the beach, the people of Zanzibar were not engaged in some form of aberrant behavior. Nor were they being callous or indifferent to their surroundings. They were practicing an ancient form of recycling that up until now had worked just fine for them. In traditional Zanzibari culture, a shopping bag, for example, might be woven of grass, an organic material that could be discarded with the certain expectation that the earth would soon reclaim it. Not so with modern materials such as plastic bags, which take forever to decompose.

Having brought capitalism to the island, and with it modern materials such as plastics, we have, Brashear insists, "a responsibility to help the people of Zanzibar figure out how to dispose of it."

Back in Boulder, she spent a year thinking about the problem. Then one day, her mother offered a simple suggestion. "The solution," she said, "lies in education."

Mother, Brashear realized, was onto something.

She applied for and received a grant from the CU Undergraduate Research Opportunity Fund to design a curriculum to educate Zanzibaris on how to deal with their trash. While it emphasized reduction of consumption, Brashear's program also contained some novel suggestions for recycling. Plastic bags, for example, could be cut into strips and crocheted into reusable purses and market bags.

An Italian environmental group active in Zanzibar, the Association of Rural Cooperation in Africa and Latin America (ACRA), was so impressed with her ideas that they funded a program to teach them to local school kids. They're also pushing to have her suggestions included in the national school curriculum.

"To be honest," she said," I still feel disheartened by the amount of trash we generate. I look at people's grocery carts and see how much packaging it takes to produce just one meal . . . all that plastic and cardboard. There's definitely a link to food production. So much of the trash in Zanzibar was food related . . . juice containers instead of juice from locally grown fruits, for example. I think the solution to the world's trash problem lies in the localization of food production and in the individual empowerment of people to control their own food sources."

PJ Parmar: 3 years, 50,000 miles, 101 countries

Something about his chosen career didn't sit right with PJ Parmar, but it would take him three years and fifty thousand miles of hard-assed travel to finally figure out what it was.

Back in the year 2000, Parmar was working as an environmental engineer for a company called Parsons Engineering Science in Denver.

"I was young and restless and very impatient," he said. "Like a lot of Americans, I only knew this country. So there was this big gap in my knowledge, and I needed to fill it in. I wanted to get out and see the world."

He talked it over with his employers and was pleasantly surprised when they told him, "Go ahead and travel, son. The job will be here when you get back."

"This was a dream come true for a single guy in his mid-'20s," he said. "It meant I'd have reliable off-and-on employment to pay for my travels."

Over the next three years, he trekked to Europe, Asia, Africa, and South and Central America. Each odyssey lasted between two and six months, a length of time that Parmar said is ideal for personal growth and transformation.

"It takes time to get to where you actually grow from your travels," he said. "Too short and you learn nothing. Too long and you get travel fatigue. So for me, three to six months was the sweet spot."

Before setting off, he established some ground rules, the first of which was not to get too comfortable in any one country.

"My personality is to keep moving," he said. "That way it's more exciting, more of an adventure."

Rule 2 was to avoid air travel wherever possible. So on his first trip, he and a buddy got a car and spent a month driving around Europe from Norway to the South of Spain. They took buses across Turkey, Syria, Lebanon, and Jordan but were forced to fly from Cairo to Karachi when Iran refused to grant them visas. From Karachi, they continued overland through Pakistan, India, Nepal, Southeast Asia, and China, before heading back to Europe on the Trans-Siberian Railway.

By 2003, Parmar had set foot in 101 countries, and now back in the States and once again working full-time at Parsons, he took a good long look at his profession from the larger perspective of what he'd experienced overseas.

"One of Parsons's specialties was UXO (Unexploded Ordnance)," he explained. "They got contracts to clear former bombing ranges in places like the Badlands of South Dakota. So we were spending millions each year to prevent one cow from getting blown up, while in Cambodia, kids were losing limbs every day from stepping on mines. We were doing very little to help them. It seemed asymmetrical to me. That realization led me to a change in direction. I wanted to help people, especially the underserved."

The following year, Parmar enrolled at CU Medical School.

"I chose not to specialize," he said, "but to do family medicine for the broad training it would give me to help as many people as possible."

In his third and final year of residency, Parmar volunteered one day a week at CAHEP (Colorado Asian Health Education and Promotion), an organization dedicated to serving the medical needs of Denver's immigrant and refugee populations.

"I don't have to go to the world anymore," he said. "Now the world comes to me. Eritreans, Bhutanese, Burmese, Afghans, Rwandans: we see everything from tuberculosis to hepatitis, war wounds, and female genital mutilation."

Reflecting on his vocational transition, PJ Parmar said, "Engineering wasn't a great fit for me. I wanted to work with people. I wanted more responsibility, and I wanted to see the results of what I was doing. I thought my talents could be put to better use elsewhere."

Doug Eliot: home is the sailor

The last time I saw Doug Eliot, he and his wife Diane were living aboard *Salacia*, a thirty-eight-foot sloop they'd bought in Houston and sailed to Key West for a refit. The date was September 11, 2001, and we sat together in the cabin, watching the horrific news on TV.

Eliot was in town last month on the homeward leg of a 2,800-mile motorcycle odyssey. The cycle adventure was emblematic. He's been on the move for ten years.

In the '90s, he and Diane were living in Albuquerque, where he bought a local employment agency that he managed to grow into a major head-hunting concern with a national focus. But it wasn't long before he began to have misgivings about the ethical conduct of the corporations he was dealing with.

"These were Fortune 500 companies," he said, "and nobody in any of them was focused on long-term growth. Only short-term gain for themselves. Most of them couldn't spell *morals* if you gave them six letters."

Eliot faced a dilemma. "The cash flow was great, but I felt myself disintegrating. I was neglecting my spiritual center, and it was clear that I needed to make a change."

At this point, he did what any self-respecting businessman and entrepreneur would do under the circumstances. He talked to his wife.

"I told her I'd been thinking of taking early retirement, buying a boat, and going to sea. Bear in mind that if she agreed to it, she would be giving up a promising career as a psychologist with the New Mexico Department of Corrections. But all she said was, 'Hey, let's go!' She's one plucky lady."

They bought *Salacia*, leased the house, got rid of the cars, turned the business over to a manager to run until they could find a buyer, and sailed off into the sunset where they lived happily ever after.

Not!

"We had this romantic notion of cruising," Eliot admits. "You know. Pristine beaches, palm trees, margaritas. The reality was more like the toilet breaks, and you have to deal with the stinky consequences. Not tomorrow. Right now. Bow to stern, keel to mast, everything required attention. All the time. And it was not like there was just one thing to deal with. Usually, it was more like five."

Despite the hardships, the Eliots were enjoying their time at sea until something happened that led them to sell the boat and go ashore. In October of last year, some friends were sailing near Isla Borracha off the Venezuelan coast when some locals approached in a fishing boat, asking for water and cigarettes. Without provocation, one of them pulled out a gun and shot the boat's owner through the heart twice. The story quickly spread through the boating community.

"After ten years on the water," Eliot said, "we were already thinking of getting out. But his was a pretty clear indication that Venezuela was no longer safe for gringo sailors."

Was it worth it, the hardship, the danger?

"Yeah. Definitely. Before I went to sea, I was kind of abstract and intellectual. But I came to distrust secondary thinking and to rely on that first flash of intuition. A lot of gringos were raided in Venezuelan waters, but in all our time there, we were never once attacked by pirates. If the place had a bad feel, we'd leave. We learned to trust each other's intuition, and we came through it okay."

Dennis Quinn heeds the call of the open road

Dennis Quinn was running a successful property management business in Boulder when the downturn hit. Not this downturn. The last one, back in 1987, when oil shale went bust. As a consequence, Storage Tech laid off nineteen thousand employees.

"Everyone in Boulder felt the aftershocks of that move," Quinn said. "As for me, I had to sell my rental properties. I also lost the management business."

Far from feeling devastated, Quinn saw the evaporation of his personal net worth as a unique opportunity to turn his life around.

"It came to me at the closing table that although I was losing my property, I was gaining something so much more important. I was getting my freedom back. Freedom," he said, "is not well thought of here in the land of the free and the home of the brave. I decided never to give up my freedom again."

He walked away with eight-hundred bucks and a plan in his head to ride his bike across the country. A friend who worked for the airlines gave him a buddy pass, and he and his bike flew to LA, where he began his long trek to the East Coast.

"That first week was really painful," he said. "I kept wondering what I'd got myself into. But the first week of any trip is where you get into shape." He averaged sixty-five miles a day and rode two out of every three days, resting and sightseeing on the third. "It took four months to get across, and it cost me six hundred dollars. But it was on that trip that I learned how to travel."

Long distance cycling has become a way of life for the fifty-eight-year-old former landlord and property manager. In the past twenty years, he's cycled from Denver to Vancouver and down the

West Coast several times. He's also bicycled around Europe on three separate occasions and has spent six months traversing Australia and New Zealand. Last year, he rode from Denver to Anchorage and back.

"The hardest part was getting out of Colorado," he said. "Alaska's kind of a boring ride. Long distances between stops, and there's not much to look at."

Does it get lonesome out there?

"I never get lonely," he said. "Sometimes I'll see couples travelling together on bikes. The guy's generally pissed off, and she's in tears. That usually cures me of any desire to travel with a partner. As for boredom, let's just say I've solved all the problems of the world out there on my bicycle."

Does he miss his days as a businessman?

"Naw," he said. "'Real life' means nothing to me anymore. Everything I do these days is geared toward my next trip."

The son of a US Army chaplain, Don Morreale spent much of his childhood on military bases in Japan, Germany and Taiwan before settling in Colorado at the age of 14. He holds a bachelor's degree in comparative religions from the University of Denver, and a master's in creative writing from Denver University College. The author of two books on Buddhism in America, he teaches meditation both at home and worldwide aboard the ships of Royal Caribbean Cruise Lines. He also writes a popular column about interesting local characters that appears weekly in the Denver Post YourHub, and on-line at Examiner.com. *Cowboys, Yogis, and One-Legged Ski Bums* is a compilation of some of his favorites.